Sept. 03

To Hank
one of th
authors —
Hal Miller

D0341784

Publishing

A Leap from Mind to Mind

Publishing

A Leap from Mind to Mind

Harold T. Miller
President and Chairman
Houghton Mifflin Company

Fulcrum Publishing
Golden, Colorado

Copyright © 2003 Harold T. Miller

Library of Congress Cataloging-in-Publication Data

Miller, Harold T.
  Publishing : a leap from mind to mind / Harold T. Miller.
    p. cm.
Includes bibliographical references and index.
  ISBN 1-55591-407-1 (alk. paper)
  1. Houghton Mifflin Company—History. 2. Houghton Mifflin
Company—Interviews. 3. Publishers and
publishing—Massachusetts—Boston—History—20th century. 4.
Educational publishing—United States—History—20th century. I. Title.

Z473.H83M55 2003
070.5'09744'61—dc21

2003006478

Jacket design: Anne Clark
Jacket front cover photograph: copyright © Chad Baker/Getty Images.
Interior design: Patty Maher

Printed in Canada
0 9 8 7 6 5 4 3 2 1

Fulcrum Publishing
16100 Table Mountain Parkway, Suite 300
Golden, Colorado 80403
(800) 992-2908 • (303) 277-1623
www.fulcrum-books.com

Contents

Preface

On Reading

I've been thinking about the book and even before the book in codex form, when there were scrolls and other ways of writing on other materials. In other words, reading. We've always read through our eyes. We have had to hold what we read in our hands. The conditions of reading are pretty well set by the physical limitations of the human condition. So reading today is no different from reading 200 or 2,000 years ago. All the way back, reading has been reading and nothing has changed; the elements and methods are basically the same.

There are certain conditions that make reading easier or more difficult. In the age of print, the optimum is governed by the rules of typography that have evolved over 500 years. That's the business of publishers and printers to make conditions right for reading—or active, purposeful reading. I like Mr. Houghton's definition of the book. He was talking about a book to be loved, cherished, and carried nearest to the heart. When he described the typography he said, "Print was to be tight, clear, and round." In other words, the type should be easy to read.

He was very particular about the paper for his books: "thin, but opaque." This is difficult to achieve but important, as it carries the words to the reader relationship. As a publisher, you know the importance of just the right paper. When he talked about binding, he said it should be "as plain, as simple, as the dress of a Quaker maiden." Absolutely right, then and today and forever.

There are some things that never change, but certainly the techniques of getting into print are changing very rapidly. Books are still books, and the nature of reading is consistent and always will be.

—Rocky Stinehour
Founder, Stinehour Press
Lunenburg, Vermont

Introduction

Publishing: A Leap from Mind to Mind is the story of Houghton
Mifflin Company from World War II through 1990, as told by the
people who made it happen. This book uses excerpts drawn from
many of the nearly 100 recorded interviews about book publishing
I've conducted over the past ten years. This approach enables you, the
reader, to learn from authors, editors, and others their thoughts and
observations about publishing. The complete collection of interviews
(in both print and electronic format) is housed in the library of the
American Antiquarian Society in Worcester, Massachusetts. The selection
of individuals contacted and the questions asked were based on the
experience and knowledge acquired over my forty-year publishing
career—a career that includes the positions of textbook sales representative, editor of norm-referenced tests, general manager of the
Midwest region, head of the educational textbook division, and for the
seventeen years before my retirement in 1990, the company's president and
chairman.

The interviewees include authors, editors, printers, sales representatives, consultants, financial officers, lawyers, and other participants.
They capture the day-by-day excitement, expectations, and, yes,
dreams, as they relate in their own words their Houghton Mifflin
experiences. Others interviewed were the users of our publications,
including teachers, school superintendents, the owner and founder of

an outstanding independent bookstore, competitors, and a lawyer and an investment banker whose guidance aided in our continuing corporate independence. I am unaware of any other collection of interviews about book publishing of equal comprehensiveness.

The people selected formed a representative sample drawn from those who from World War II through 1990 forged Houghton into an ever-expanding contributor to the nation's culture. Major publications—such as Rachel Carson's *Silent Spring,* Churchill's memoirs of World War II, David Macaulay's *The Way Things Work,* Paul McKee's Reading for Meaning Series, and Kenneth Galbraith's *The Great Crash*—are but a few of the works on our long publications list.

These discerning individuals were committed to creating the most central and material core of the company's published intellectual properties. Many of the participants were shaped by the Great Depression of the 1930s, World War II, the Marshall Plan, MacArthur's reconstruction of Japan, the Cold War, and an educational experience that only began to prepare them for the technology explosion. Their academic degrees were in the liberal arts, and many of them could claim military experience with its emphasis on discipline, leadership, and loyalty to one's unit and its people. They held to a sense of corporate memory reaching back to Henry Oscar Houghton's special interest in the authors his company published, a concern that overarched mere commercial considerations. Out of this commitment came an esprit de corps and sensitivity dedicated to the publication of books of value along with their pursuit of the innovative. They published books influenced more by a strong belief in the value of the book's content than its financials—the bottom line. But the practice of their strong beliefs and their culture ensured financial solvency, as proven by the one and one-half centuries of the company's independence.

The physical limitations of this book preclude using all of the recorded interviews. To those interviewees not included, I offer my sincere request for forgiveness. What a great and giving group of individuals—I'm proud that I could know each and every one of you. Each interview, whether used in part for this book or not, contains insightful information about Houghton Mifflin Company, book publishing, and education. And it is in the broad sense that, taken together, they constitute information that should serve publishing scholars, researchers, biographers, and others for years and centuries to come.

The entire interview collection will provide future generations with access to the Houghton Mifflin culture, how it came about, and how it functioned through the words of those who lived in it and contributed to it. Chapter 1, "Houghton's Culture," and Chapter 2, "Betting the House of Houghton on Manuel Fenollosa," provide the reader with an introductory appreciation for that culture.

Another reason for writing this book is my concern for public school education today. The public schools are charged with taking on all comers in our diverse nation and equipping them to function in our society. To that end, they must ensure the success of the central supporting element in schooling: the teaching/learning process based on dedicated curriculum, intelligently and skillfully constructed for the nation's elementary schools. Yes, I said elementary schools, and that specification applies to private as well as public schools. However, given the crucial need to educate all of our population, if we are to make our constitution work, it is the public schools where the crisis exists.

Many of today's proposed solutions to improved education miss the core point. The same weary political diatribes harping on getting back to the "basics" (never defined) with proposed solutions of smaller class size, increased spending, and mandated tests are not specific enough. Alternative solutions set forth by "do-wellers," as some proven successful educators refer to various well-meaning volunteers, border on making matters worse.

Successful elementary school education depends on teachers' having the knowledge, skill, and experience to carry the teaching/learning process to a successful conclusion: to educate kids. Perhaps the term *teaching/learning process* has you asking what I mean, since no one ever seems to talk about it. It is the specific system needed for children to learn to read, do math, or write, presented in an organized, sequential way so that learning is ensured. See Chapter 3,

"Preaching the Gospel: The Houghton Mifflin Teaching/Learning Approach to Reading," for an example of what I mean. Teachers, just as skilled artisans, require proper tools to perform their work and are judged by the quality of what they produce. In education, that means a curriculum centered on the fundamental skills taught in an established sequential context—textbooks—accompanied by tests designed to identify the school systems' and pupils' weaknesses so that timely remedial action can be taken. Failure to execute that responsibility foretells difficulty for a student's future years in school and in the workplace. There is an old saying I first heard in Pennsylvania: "If you have to eat a toad, there is no sense sitting and looking at it." The toad confronted in far too many classrooms is unruly pupil behavior. Parents and society must stop sitting and looking at that toad. Teachers and textbooks need their cooperation to create classroom behavior conducive to successful schooling.

As I show in Chapters 5, 7, and 10, Houghton Mifflin's textbooks were developed by proven, reputable author/educators relying on years of scholarship and research. Their works were then the beneficiaries of Houghton's extensive resources, including editorial, sales, and consulting services. Textbooks from reputable publishers of long standing, such as Harcourt Brace Jovanovich, McGraw-Hill, and Houghton Mifflin, were proven successful teaching tools. Their publications carried the "hash marks" of use in the classroom trenches. They were honed by revisions, using information garnered from that use. Those textbooks were the tools that ensured productive pursuit of the content in a sound curriculum.

Textbooks and tests—elementary school through college—are the beneficiaries of their publishers' unequalled knowledge and information base. Publishers see firsthand what is working, where it is working, and where it is not. Given this singular asset, publishers, such as the three just named, combined their base knowledge of intellectual properties, from children's literature to adult books sold to the parents in bookstores. In education, publishers' involvement in a number of instructional areas, such as reading, mathematics, and, importantly, norm-referenced tests, provided them with an information base that went beyond what was known by others in education and the "do-wellers." This book cites the proof of that claim. Credence must be given to the comprehensiveness of their textbook and norm-refer-enced test publications, recognizing the reality and influence of national curriculum trends. No state or local school system operating in academic isolation can provide all—yes, all, including the excep-tionally able students—their due.

In the concluding chapter, details of the ongoing efforts of the company to prevent a hostile takeover or loss of its independence are told. Those of us into whose hands came Houghton Mifflin never fully subscribed to the synergistic business model, the conglomeration claim that big is better, nor the self-adoration thought to come from rubbing shoulders with writers. We were concerned about selling the publications of our textbooks to foreign companies. Our business was to find, develop, and manage intellectual properties in the Henry Oscar Houghton model. We were Boston and independent publish-ing. That's what the entire project and this book seek to make known.

All but the last few interviews were conducted prior to the mys-terious sale of Houghton Mifflin Company to a foreign conglomerate. It adds to the interviewees' credibility that they were not influenced by this recent loss of Houghton's independence. Sold to Vivendi Universal in 2001 for reasons never publicly reported, and, in turn, placed on the auction block in 2002 by Vivendi, Houghton is, as of this writing, in the hands of a Boston-based consortium of equity investors who reportedly intend to keep Houghton Mifflin in Boston. It is my hope, one shared by many others, that this new twenty-first century ownership will look to the many rich and prolific elements that grew the nineteenth- and twentieth-century Houghton culture.

Abbreviation Key to Interviewees

*(A complete list of interviewees and roles
are listed on page 309)*

Initials	Person	First Quoted
ACP	Andrew Craig Phillips	.44
AH	Albert (Al) Hieronymus	.163
AS	Anita Silvey	.16
BH	Betty Hansen	.53
BN	Belverd E. (Bel) Needles	.237
BP	Robert (Bob) Pirie	.270
CC	Carol Case	.80
CE	Cynthia Essex	.179
CVA	Chris Van Allsburg	.107
DB	Donald (Don) Beggs	.165
DB	David Barton	.247
DL	David Levine	.221
DM	David Macaulay	.114
DS	Dale Scannell	.167
ED	Edward (Ed) Drahozal	.194
EK	Edward N. (Ed) Kelly	.227
FL	Francis (Lauf) Laufenberg	.64

Initials	Person	First Quoted
FL	Faye Lowe 215
HF	Harry Foster 10
HTM	Harold T. (Hal) Miller 8
JM	Eugenia (Jean) Muller 63
JR	John Ridley 78
JT	Jerry Theise 66
JW	Jack Williamson 260
LC	Lee Capps 129
LF	Leonard (Len) Feldt 184
LG	Louis (Lou) Goodman 274
LLH	Lynn Long Hoffman 265
MM	Mark Mahan 229
MS	Michael (Mike) Shaw 56
MT	Marlow Teig 224
NS	Nancy Sargent 74
RC	Richard Clowes 214
RH	Ruth Hapgood 11
RBG	Richard (Dick) Gladstone 14
RSC	R. Sidney (Sid) Cooper 43
TB	Morton H. (Terry) Baker 9
TM	Thomas (Tom) McDermott 253
WD	William (Bill) Durr 74
WHB	William (Bill) Berman 230
WL	Wanda Lister 51
WL	Walter Lorraine 110

Publishing

A Leap from Mind to Mind

CHAPTER 1

Houghton's Culture

How It Evolved

When referring to the house of Houghton, University of Iowa test author Albert Hieronymus uses the word *family,* as does Harvard's economic guru, Kenneth Galbraith. Neither of these highly successful authors stands alone in using the word to describe the valued relationship that existed over many years with Houghton Mifflin, which earned the company a reputation as an author-centered house.

Taken at face value, the claim that a book publishing house is author centered belabors the obvious. Publishing houses publish authors' works because that is their business. Candidly, a publishers' statement overemphasizing that phrase can ring hollow. It is what the house brings to that author-centered undertaking that matters and that defines the differences between publishing companies.

Galbraith and Hieronymus, given their insightful language, so often in evidence among leading authors of intellectual properties, applied the word *family* to the company. Why? Because over their many years working with Houghton, they had come to know and appreciate its special culture. That culture is the subject of this book.

The complex web of that culture was formed and perpetuated over nearly a century and a half by creative, individualistic, entrepreneurial

1

people (authors and publishers alike, beginning with Henry Oscar Houghton). It was a publishing style that evolved and was peculiar to the individuals in the company who lived and breathed it.

The attributes of being both civilized and cultured, for example, counted and were much in evidence. Pompous-sounding it may be, but meritocracy prevailed at the expense of bureaucracy. Title ranking and hierarchy were secondary to one's record of publishing success— a successful publications list, for example. Authors, editors, artists, and all others who brought meaningful information to their published works functioned best in such an unfettered environment. Lest this description sound misty-eyed, as if the family farm had just been taken over by the bank, be assured that not everyone who entered this culture remained. It was demanding by its very nature.

The authors and editors appearing on the following pages were the makers of the company's culture. Senior management provided suitable conditions in which that culture could flourish or, for that matter, bring about its demise. The culture that authors Hieronymus and Galbraith knew came into being over many decades through the combined efforts of many people. Some wag once observed that the CEO's job at Houghton must be similar to that of herding a bunch of cats. Perhaps so, at times, but if you understood and believed in that culture, then working in it was as good as it gets.

One may rightfully inquire how this culture came about. The answer is to be found in the company's history. For a complete account to the early 1900s, Ellen B. Ballou's *The Building of the House* is recommended. It was heavily relied upon for this book. Editor Paul Brooks's *Two Park Street: A Publishing Memoir* has no equal in describing with feeling the author/editor relationship that was so much a part of the culture. *Yesterdays with Authors* by James T. Fields, including accounts about such greats as Thackeray and Hawthorne, gets to the very roots of the culture that evolved at Houghton Mifflin. *American Literary Publishing in the Mid-Nineteenth Century: The Business of Ticknor & Fields* by Michael Winship also merits attention. Henry Oscar Houghton and William D. Ticknor knew each other well, including each other's publishing values and the business climate in which each operated. One cannot overly stress the importance of Ticknor and his publications as Houghton expanded his role into the world of publishing.

> One of Houghton's most gratifying printing associations was with William D. Ticknor and the various firms which from 1832 had always borne his name, Allen & Ticknor and Company (1832–1834), William D. Ticknor and Company (1843–1849), Ticknor, Reed and Fields (1849–1854), and Ticknor & Fields, which came into being in 1854. Ever since his Bolles & Houghton days (1849), Houghton had done work for Ticknor. By 1863, most of Ticknor & Fields' printing was executed either by Houghton or his nearest rival, Welch, Bigelow's University Press. (Ballou, p. 45)

The culture of Ticknor & Fields was so influential in the formulation of my own personal publishing culture that I brought it back into being in 1979 and appointed Chester Kerr, long-term director of Yale University Press, as its president.

Henry Oscar Houghton: A Biographical Outline by Horace E. Scudder is another fine source. For the purpose of this work, a few selections from the past serve to identify the foundation upon which the corporation's author-centered culture rested.

In today's often memoryless corporate environment, to credit Henry Houghton with influencing the company's management during the post–World War II years may appear to be a reach. Yet the man possessed a value system, a work ethic, and a strength of character that were felt by his successors. His legacy influenced all of us who followed him. It became embedded in us and remained there into the 1980s.

Horace Scudder, literary advisor and editor-in-chief for general publications from 1864 to 1902 and editor of the *Atlantic* from April 1890 to July 1898 (then owned by Houghton), worked with Henry Houghton for years. In *Henry Oscar Houghton: A Biographical Outline*, he describes Houghton's influence:

> As I have mentioned, the secret of Mr. Houghton's power in business lay in the relation which he bore to his work: he was

not thinking of himself and his own aggrandizement—he was thinking of the institution he was creating, and by a paradox, though he threw himself heart and soul into the enterprise, he effaced himself to a remarkable degree. It was impossible that so positive, so vigorous a personality should not be conspicuous in the business, and yet he shaped his industry with distinct reference to the growth of an organism. (pp. 92–93)

The core ingredient in Henry Oscar Houghton's publishing legacy—and we all came to know it extremely well—was "The Powwow." Its very existence, traditions, challenges, and publishing discipline meaningfully influenced everyone, including the president, financial officer, editors at all levels, production, and directly or indirectly, the authors too. It was the glue that kept us all on mission. As Scudder describes it:

> It was in keeping with the largeness of his ideals in business and his far-sightedness that he did not require the demonstration of immediate success. If an enterprise commended itself to him as sound, he was willing to wait for returns. There was, indeed, something very attractive to him in projects which were based on broad, fundamental principles, and would take time for their execution, and those projects were all the more acceptable if they took the shape of modest beginnings. He felt his way with experiments, but he was constantly seeing the probable development. He had the courage which comes from a large business imagination. At the same time no one could be more resolute in a demand for the cold facts in the history of undertakings. He perfected a system of records by which he could ascertain the exact history of every one of his ventures, and carried about in his pocket for frequent reference what he called his Bankrupt List—a merciless showing of the books that were not paying. Great was the satisfaction when one book or another would slowly emerge from the list and take its place among those which had paid for themselves.
>
> Perhaps the most significant illustration of Mr. Houghton's treatment of his business as an institution is to be found in a step which he took not long after the formation of the firm of Houghton, Mifflin & Company. He established a weekly council, to which he gave the name, half in jest, half to conceal its

importance, of "The Powwow." To it he invited his partners, and those persons who were heads of departments in the business, or charged with special functions. He made out a formal order of business and appointed a secretary, who kept the records, which were read at each session. At the meetings the various enterprises of the house were discussed, especially the new books which were recommended for publication, and action taken which was held to constitute the policy of the house. Such councils are no doubt common enough in large firms and corporations; but I think it is an unusual course for a house to invite subordinates, who have no direct pecuniary interest in the concern, into an equal share in deliberations and votes which definitely affect the conduct of the business. Naturally this recognition of the interest of subordinates in the welfare of the house led to a caution on their part in asserting themselves. There was a mutual concession without any loss of independence; and though friction might now and then arise, the weekly conference, year after year, of the same men, engaged in the same general work, effected just what Mr. Houghton designed—a solidarity of mind. He saw that each member of "The Powwow" was likely to look at every project not only from his personal point of view, but with the consideration suggested by the function he performed in the business, so that there would be diversity of judgment, and every plan would be subjected to a variety of tests. He saw also that the discussion would inform all the members of what was going on, and lead to greater union of action, a matter of great importance when the tendency of each was to become engrossed in his own part of the business. In the early years of "The Powwow," he not infrequently expressed to me his doubt whether on the whole it was worthwhile; he was more than once piqued by our criticism of measures, or rendered impatient by the expenditure of time over plans when he knew what was wanted and only wished to get it done. But, as time wore on, these expressions of doubt grew less frequent, and he threw more weight into the decisions of "The Powwow." As in other cases, he struck out in a course, upon which he had deliberated, with decision but with moderation, feeling his way, and perhaps only partly aware of how much the step meant. But it is clear enough now that he builded (sic) well, and that the power of organization which he showed at the beginning of his career, when he was captain and a large part of the crew, always looked toward the creation of an institution so perfected in its parts, and so self-perpetuating, that his final withdrawal in the fullness of time should not appear to disturb a normal action. (pp. 119–122)

Every Houghton Mifflin book, including those covered by this work, bears the seal of the company's Powwow system. In later years, the multiplication of works published modified the mechanics of execution. Financial levels were set for a Powwow review and approval. Up to a predetermined financial commitment, each publishing division's management committee was authorized to act. For the largest investments, the board of directors needed to approve. All Powwows crossed corporate management desks.

This stratification, while necessary, did not always maintain the quality of publishing integrity before such stratification. When I was head of the Educational Division, I had to present each of my Powwows before the president, chief financial officer, and other in-house members of the board. I can attest to the clarity of purpose that such an experience brought.

The Education Department was established in 1882. Henry Oscar Houghton foresaw educational publishing as an area of promise, and so it proved to be. Shortly after the turn of the nineteenth century, book publishing patterns began to change. By World War I, educational sales exceeded those of trade. This occurred in a house known for its general publications, especially literature; yet, throughout the remaining years of the twentieth century there persisted within and outside the company the perception that the educational wing of the company was of recent vintage relative to books sold to the general public—trade publishing.

Public school enrollment in 1882 stood at about ten million, and by 1920 the figure more than doubled. It was during these years that a defining change was effected that brought Houghton into the real world of textbook publishing. The defining change was the company's progression from schoolbooks that drew their content from trade. The Riverside Literature Series, still sold to this day, is a prime example of textbooks specifically written from trade books.

In 1905, two impressive-appearing young men, Stephen B. Davol and James Duncan Phillips, came to share the administration of the Education Department. Neither was an editor or educator, but each had a vision for the future, and accordingly in 1907 they recruited an experienced educator, Franklin Sherman Hoyt, assistant superintendent of schools in Indianapolis, Indiana, who was known for his educational experiments and innovation.

Schoolbook publishing requires research, market evaluation, monitoring of changing patterns of pedagogy, defined author recruitment, and numerous additional editorial and operational practices. The *author/publisher* relationship had come to the house of Houghton in addition to the established *author/editor* relationship.

From that time forward, there existed a kind of bifurcated environment within the house, given the diverse publishing fundamentals of the two enterprises. *Bifurcated* may seem to be too strong a word, so clarification is in order.

The literary-based histories of book publishing are replete with accounts of highly productive and mutually beneficial author/editor team efforts and friendships. Understandably, these creative relationships deserve to be much admired and written about. But this chapter also discusses the author/publisher relationship. Both can exist in an *author-centered* publishing house.

A trade author today can be, and often is, heavily dependent on his or her editor. By performing within normal editorial responsibilities, the editor can have the unintended effect of keeping the author at arm's length from the broad span of functions and people within the publishing house. This editorial role evolved over time and was by no means part of the publishing scene in the beginning days. In her history of Houghton Mifflin, *The Building of the House,* Ellen Ballou, writing about the mid-1870s, observes:

> Though honored as a profession of gentlemen, publishing had always been a business. In the nineteenth century, authorship also entered the market place. In the beginning, the publisher was but a middleman, a distributor, operating between the printer, the author, and available markets. As the possibility of distribution

outlets multiplied, a multiplication inherent in population growth, the publisher's value to the author increased; so did the publisher's speculative investment. (p. 141)

Immediately following World War II, and for several decades thereafter, two leaders held sway. William Spaulding, head of the Educational Division and later president, and Lovell Thompson, head of the Trade Division, were each dedicated to publishing books that greatly mattered, but with sharply differing beliefs as to how to accomplish that objective. Fresh from the victories of World War II and emerging from the depression of the prewar years, the nation's population had a thirst for education at all levels, and the GI Bill brought unprecedented numbers of veterans to college classrooms. Concurrently, the events of the war years provided fodder and inspiration for many successful adult trade books, such as Churchill's volumes on the history of World War II and *Mr. Roberts*.

Understandably, there was intense competition for corporate leadership between the trade and the textbook publishing groups. Whose priorities would prevail? Terry Baker, head of production for the Trade Division, and I spent many hours discussing the two differing philosophies.

HTM: I remember an experience at the University of Iowa, where I went frequently as test editor and also later from time to time as president. I would meet with the test authors: E. F. Lindquist, Leonard Feldt, Hieronymus, and others. Jack Leggett, who had once worked at Houghton and later wrote the best-seller titled *Ross and Tom*, was then the head of the highly respected University of Iowa Writer's Workshop. Lindquist and the others, all of whom were perfect hosts, knew that Jack had worked at Houghton, so when we would get together for dinner, they would sometimes invite Jack.

One night I was seated beside him and I remarked, "Jack, I'm glad you're speaking to me now." He gave me a quizzical stare, and I continued, "Well, do you recall in *Ross and Tom* when you were describing your early days in Houghton's Trade Division and mentioned that there were also these people around Two Park

Street from the Educational Division who were really producing more money for the company than trade, but as part of the Trade Division you never spoke to them? Well, I was one of those people you never spoke to," And Jack said, "God, I knew that line would come back to haunt me." And we both laughed about it. But that inharmonious atmosphere existed in the company, which Steve Grant, when he became president, tried to abolish, as did I.

TB: Bill Spaulding and Lovell Thompson were two ambitious men. They each wanted to be president of the company, and each had a vision for the company that was very different. They were diametrically opposed. Spaulding made teaching tools, and Thompson made books for readers. Spaulding planned his textbooks, and Thompson knew that you can't overplan a trade book. It just happens.

Spaulding's textbook-based approach was to develop textbooks, often multigrade text series, with accompanying manuals and ancillaries and to see to their revision every few years. This required extensive planning and the active involvement of the author team working with numerous of the company's employees. Because of the textbook revision process, that broad, close-working relationship could extend over decades.

The author/publisher relationship, involving the authors working directly with a team of individuals within the publishing house, most frequently, but not exclusively, exists in the elementary/secondary textbook and standardized test areas. Carol Case, for many years director of the school advertising department, noted that authors, such as elementary math textbook creator Lee Capps, record working with many different people in the company without singling out just one particular editor. Carol's observation about Lee holds for a number of textbook authors.

Thompson's focus was not normally series based, although properties such as the Peterson Field Guides shared some similarities to the textbooks. Still, Terry's few words say it all for Thompson.

My neighbor of some thirty years, Joseph Warren Gardella, M.D., former dean of Harvard Medical School, one-time captain of the university's football team, and always his own person, has been described by colleagues (medical and nonmedical) as "a 1,000–sided work of art." Spaulding and Thompson, the two men central to this discussion, can also be so described.

There is no question that each man was a fine book publisher. Each of them had his own publishing philosophy and implementation approach. Their individual publishing histories from post–World War II to the 1970s attest to that.

Unquestionably the differing convictions of the two strong-minded publishers influenced the corporation's external and internal relationships. Logically so, because each headed up a different book publishing process, but both published books of import. On that point they were as one in the company's culture.

Editor Harry Foster worked on both college textbooks and trade books. He functioned successfully in both the Spaulding and the Thompson publishing environments. He brings to the discussion an overarching perspective deserving of careful thought.

HF: One thing that I liked about college publishing, at least at the time that I was able to be an editor there, I had the feeling that quality would be rewarded, that we knew what kind of book we wanted to do.

At the time that I was working on the biology text, we had research material from everybody who taught biology on what subjects they covered, how much emphasis they gave, what sequence they followed. We knew exactly what the competing books were. There was a feeling that, if we do this right, it will work.

Trade publishing is much more of a guessing game, and while you hope quality will be rewarded, it isn't always. You can do great books that just don't click for some reason. Occasionally you can do something that is not so great but becomes a huge success. In trade publishing, you have wonderful authors who work for years on a book and never get paid anything remotely worth the time that goes into it.

In college publishing there is much more of a coordinated, group effort all along the way between the publishing house and the author, and among people within the publishing house. You have more people doing fewer books, and you have to focus on making each textbook right.

Harry performed productively in each publishing environment. He always knew where he was and what must be done to function as an editor in that publishing area, and obviously his well-honed, broad editorial skills enabled him to be successful. His years of work with the Peterson Field Guides and a list of highly regarded nature books are but part of his valued record.

Harry's colleague, Ruth Hapgood, is the deservedly proud editor of an extensive list of trade books she chose to edit. She is the editor to whom I often turned when my office received an unsolicited manuscript appearing to have legs. I operated on the premise that if someone thought enough of Houghton to send me their work, it merited the respect of my placing it into the hands of a conscientious, qualified editor like Ruth. As the head of house, you come to rely on such people, for they speak straight from the shoulder and always ably follow through.

RH: I looked for a book that had a pump of a concerned audience that had to have that book.

Now we had a theory that you wouldn't talk to an author who came in off the street with a manuscript under arm, because it was just a waste of time. If you hadn't read the book, you couldn't say anything sensible. And we always required them to leave the book. If it was worth our time, we would talk later.

And I was sitting at my desk worrying about the fact that I had no doctor to help me with the aftereffects of my broken ankle, and what would I do, and how would I manage, and would I perhaps get one of the Massachusetts General Hospital orthopedists? I was sitting there feeling pretty low. And the front desk downstairs called up, and they said, "We have an author here who has a manuscript that she wants to show you; it's an exercise book." And I thought, "Well, anything to change my mind-set." I said, "Send her up."

HTM: Who was that?

RH: That was Judy Alter. We published two, possibly three, of her books. The book that was under her arm was called *Surviving Exercise,* which we did extremely well with. So we talked about the book. Then I asked her, "Do you take private patients?" She said, "Well, I do, but right at the moment I'm writing a thesis for Tufts." And I said, "Please, will you take me on?" I used to go down to her house, and we'd sit on the rug. And she created for me a set of exercises to reclaim that ankle so that I could start my dancing again. As a result—I mean, talk about living your book!

HTM: What did this whole business of publishing really mean to you? It was a livelihood, yes, but it was far more than that.

RH: I was able often enough to be glad to have been alive to help an author make his or her book what was wanted. If I had strength as an editor, it was to empathize with the sources of that book within their hearts. The thing that kept them working five years to make that book, or whatever. The effort that goes into just creating the least little manuscript.

And to me that spark is what leaps to the reader and makes that book alive. It isn't really the technical stuff; it isn't the wordage, the wording, the polishing, the format, necessarily. It's that leap between mind and mind.

And so, it seems to me, I learned early on—goodness knows how I did it—to find what they were trying to do, and to make my advice and my insistences at times, be all directed toward making this more the book they envisioned when they started, so it would really do the thing that they wanted to do.

If that's where you are and they perceive that you're helping, they'll listen.

I remember one guy, one of our editors, who was very doctrinaire. And he told this author, "Do this, do this, do this," and this is a chap who had written a very innovative book.

So this doctrinaire editor leaves us and goes somewhere else, and I inherit this book. The author says he's going to come up from New York and see me, and I make a date and expect him. And reception calls up from downstairs and says, "These two gentlemen from New York are here to see you, and they're coming up in the elevator." And I said, "Two gentlemen? What's this?"

And they arrive. And he brought his lawyer from New York to protect him. And they sit down, sort of feeling ill at ease to begin with. I start in, and I say, "It's a very interesting book," and so on. I said, "Now, of course, I realize that it's your book, and if anything we're suggesting doesn't strike you as being an improvement to that book, then you won't do it. We recognize it's your book. I do have some suggestions, but you have to feel that they're helping the book."

Well, these two guys looked at each other—and the author is probably thinking, "I don't need you, do I?"

HTM: He was paying for the guy.

RH: But that was the clearest demonstration I probably ever had of the difference between these approaches.

What would trade publishing at Houghton have been without the Lovell Thompsons and the Ruth Hapgoods? Think again about Ruth's lines:"If I had a strength as an editor, it was to empathize with the sources for that book within their hearts," and, "It's that leap between mind and mind."

Richard Gladstone, a Houghton executive for a long time involved with the company's reading program, describes in detail and with conviction how the author/publisher relationship can function to the benefit of authors, publishers, and most of all, our children. Dick worked closely with

Paul McKee and Bill Spaulding, and was in fact a fully committed disciple, as his words so clearly demonstrate. Spaulding was not the founder of the company's author/publisher modus operandi. Its beginnings preceded him, but without question he gave it definition and meaning.

RBG: The publisher took the initiative in cahoots with the author. It was the publisher who actually had to produce the vehicle that eventually went into the schools, of course. It had embodied in it the author's ideas and methods.

Paul McKee, as you may recall, sat in a little cottage in Greeley, Colorado, with a breadboard on his lap, and in the marginal times when he wasn't teaching at Greeley State Teacher's College, which is now the University of Northern Colorado, wrote a manuscript for a professional text. It was a huge tome that was a kind of forerunner of the day when people would talk about "integrated language arts," because McKee's opus dealt with both the teaching of language and the teaching of reading.

When it came in, all ten or fifteen pounds of it, Spaulding took a look. He was impressed, but realized that he couldn't publish it as a single volume for courses in education, so he talked McKee into splitting the work into two books. One evolved into *Language in the Elementary School* and the other, *The Teaching of Reading.*

Then he persuaded McKee, who wanted to publish an elementary reading program, to develop a language series first, which, if I remember correctly, was published in 1940. Rather than going out and talking to people in the schools and asking what they wanted by way of a language course and then publishing according to their specifications, they analyzed the communication process and decided how teachers could do a better job in training children to communicate orally and in writing. Thus, Language for Meaning was published, a dramatic departure from anything that had been published in the language field previously.

The typical elementary English book at the time was provided in a small format. There was no logical organization to it.

For instance, there would be a unit on a grammatical concept followed by a unit on writing, with no apparent connection between the two. McKee, however, organized the book for each grade level into so-called language jobs and taught the mechanics of language in terms of the language jobs into which they were integrated and applied.

Spaulding understood the nation's educational needs. His creative mind, working in combination with educator McKee's, rendered the complex simple; hence, they published two programs: one in the language arts, one in reading.

RBG: Then, having published the language series, Bill and Paul turned their attention to the reading program. George Nardin was a key man in that development, working with editors Mary Canty and Arthur Clark, and authors Annie McCowen, Lucile Harrison, and Elizabeth Lehr, who were on the faculty at the State Teachers College of Education, Greeley, Colorado.

In the years from 1945 or so through 1949, Reading for Meaning was developed, and in February of 1949 it was launched and continued through revisions into the 1980s.

Spaulding and Thompson knew they could not place all their editors, at least those worth their salt, into a common mold, nor did they demand such conformity of them. Putting aside their personalities, their two different publishing styles carried them to the same outcome: they published successful books.

The Educational Division's McKee Reading Series, as described by Gladstone, was developed with Bill Spaulding's central involvement and direct participation. Lovell Thompson's approach was very different, but every bit as key to a trade author's success as Spaulding's to a textbook author.

Anita Silvey, editor emerita of *The Horn Book Magazine* and more recently head of Houghton Mifflin's juvenile trade books department, illustrates the differences beautifully.

AS: Virginia Lee Burton came in with a manuscript to Houghton called *The Trials and Trails of Jennifer Lint.* And Lovell Thompson looked at her, and he said, "You have a lot of talent as an artist; with that, there's no problem." But he said, "You need to sit with children and see what children read now." He asked, "Do you have any children?" She said, "I have two sons." He said, "Go read this to them and then go read other books to them."

And the next book she came back with was *Choo-Choo,* and the one after that was *Mike Mulligan.* It's not that you sit and tell the author, "Well, you just don't have the semicolons in the right place." You give the author a profound piece of insight into themselves or their own work—in this case, in Lovell's case, saying, "You're a wonderful artist; you have terrific artistic sensibility, but you haven't thought about who this book is for. Go think about who this book is for, and then bring me your next book."

HTM: That's the trade editor's role.

AS: That is exactly what a great editor does. Houghton always used the example of Scott O'Dell, because Scott O'Dell was an adult novelist. And then, in his sixties, he wrote this brief historical work, which he passed on to Hardwick Mosely, who was a sales rep for the California territory where Scott was living. And Scott said, "I don't have a clue what this manuscript is, but will you take it to your 'adult' publisher?"

Hardwick read it on the train, and he went to talk to the adult publisher. But they handed it over to the juvenile department, who read it and thought it was a children's book. Of course, Scott won the Newbery Award for *Island of the Blue Dolphins.* It established him as one of the foremost children's history writers in the United States.

And so the theory always was that not everybody great knows they want to write a children's book. So you therefore hunt for creative people who might have something to say to children. One of the editors had read a magazine story by Lois

Lowry, and the editor wrote to her and asked, "Have you ever thought of writing a children's book?"

Now Lois Lowry, certainly one of the greatest fiction writers for children of this century, had never thought about writing a children's book, but she was starving, penniless, and an editor was writing to her. And so she said, "Well, let's give it a try. There's somebody interested in my work." And she produced *A Summer to Die*, which won the International Reading Association Award for a first novel. She would go on to have a great career, because having done one book, she loved writing for children. She really did have something to say to children.

And so that was the kind of thing that went on all the time. You didn't just look at what came in, but you didn't do what some people now do in this market—is they try to make a book. They say, "Well, we want a book about airplanes, and we want to put together a marketing plan, and then we'll go tell somebody what to write."

That wasn't our theory. Our theory was that creative people can express themselves in a wide variety of ways. You put yourself where creative people are, and you may find great books for children.

Ann Rider found one of her best illustrators on top of a ski lift. Betsy Bowen was there and Ann said, "Oh, do you do art?" And she said yes, and Ann said, "I'll come over to your studio and see it." So you hunt for talent wherever it might be.

You have to come into your job every day thinking, "This is the day I find a great book. This is the day that I discover in those piles of manuscripts on my desk the book that's going to make a difference." You can never lose that enthusiasm, and so you're always hunting for it out in the world. But that's different from craftily determining the nature of the book.

There was Anne Barrett who acquired Tolkien, and now Tolkien is all over the TV and movie screens with never a word about Anne. Paul Brooks, who was once head of the Trade Division, in his book,

Two Park Street, quotes Anne's editorial report on *The Lord of the Rings:* "A rich book and a deadly serious one. I think it is wonderful, but it has its drawbacks. Who will read 423 pages, about an unfinished journey undertaken by mythical creatures with confusing names? Probably no one, but I still say it is wonderful—and with my heart in my mouth—*to publish.* October, 1953."

I repeat Anita Silvey's line: "You give the author a profound piece of insight into themselves or their own work." Or, in Lovell Thompson's case saying, "You are a wonderful artist; you have terrific artistic sensibility, but you haven't thought about who this book is for. Go think about who the book is for, and then bring me your next book." Lovell's editorial counseling here, as on numerous other occasions, was characterized by wisdom and a special kind of calm judgment acquired over a lifetime spent in publishing.

Houghton's CFO for many years, Franklin K. Hoyt, son of Franklin Sherman Hoyt, describes William Spaulding as Houghton Mifflin's most outstanding editor of all time. That assessment undoubtedly is based on the many authors and their successful publications as well as the revenues Spaulding brought to Houghton. His publications list includes college texts, standardized tests, and of course the elementary school language arts programs. His creative thinking and vision, consistently based on the fundamentals requisite to sound education and a carefully thought-out teaching/learning process, influenced all of the publishing operations throughout the company and the industry. It was his idea, presented to Theodore Geisel, that spawned *The Cat in the Hat.*

That culture drew the ablest of authors, editors, sales representatives, administrators, and others to Houghton Mifflin. Why? Because success draws people. But more important was the sheer quality of the publications. Authors, such as reading program creator Paul McKee, test developer E. F. Lindquist, and David Macaulay and Rachel Carson, who wrote trade books that broke through the status quo, launching new ideas that one could believe in, and they produced results. Those works had to be published and sold, and acceptance was not always easily achieved, but everyone at Houghton was dedicated to going forth and "preaching the gospel." We believed in what we were selling. Dale Johnson, the North and South Dakota elementary/secondary sales representative, upon losing a textbook adoption, was not averse to revisiting the school system and informing them that he had returned "to give the system one more chance to make the right decision and adopt his books for the sake of the kids."

Henry Houghton; William Ticknor; Horace Scudder; Bill Spaulding; Lovell Thompson; children's book editor Walter Lorraine; Manuel Fenollosa, the man who would later guide Houghton to its extraordinary educational success; and Norrie Hoyt, longtime editor of secondary texts—to name only a few of many—fostered a demanding culture of intellectual discipline and intense belief in the company's publications and values. Publishing in such an environment, you expected to be respected, and you were. That culture influenced authors and publishers alike, and from out of that a sense of family came into being.

In conclusion, do a fast-forward from the beginning of Houghton Mifflin Company. Over the decades, the universe of intellectual properties created by successive waves of individuals who were part of this book publishing undertaking is awe-inspiring. The impact and the influence that their contributions had on humankind (consider Rachel Carson's *Silent Spring*) are beyond calculation. There is good reason to understand a book publishing entity and its culture that had much to do with the life we currently live.

CHAPTER 2

Betting the House of Houghton on Manuel Fenollosa

How Houghton Mifflin's Educational Division Came into Its Own

In 1971, The Riverside Press, Houghton Mifflin's taproot, was closed out, and textbooks became the major engine for Houghton's growth. Manuel Fenollosa's leadership in managing the textbook division, beginning in the late 1950s, weighed heavily in that accomplishment.

No one can realistically contend that Manuel carried that challenge off single-handedly. Nor should anyone harbor the illusion that the company was without a solid base of intellectual properties, authors, and personnel, all existing within a corporate structure, which if properly led could be forged into a leading textbook publisher. However, the accountability for reaching that goal was placed squarely on Manuel's shoulders when he became a member of the Houghton board of directors in 1955 and, in 1957, the head of the education department, which included all of the company's textbooks and standardized tests.

I have settled on the 1955–1957 years when the responsibility for leading Houghton was placed on Manuel's shoulders. He needed to lead the company's entire textbook and test publishing activities to a level of national prominence in the industry. It came at the very time that The Riverside Press, founded by Henry Houghton, was in decline. Could Manuel use the corporation's resources—financial, human, and others—to develop a textbook publishing presence successful enough not only to offset the demise of The Press but also to generate the growth of Houghton to a position of leadership over future years? In that sense, as with many key business decisions, a stake had been placed.

The trade department was not in a position to take on that responsibility, given the basic economic limitations of trade publishing. Reinforcing that conclusion was the existence of a limited corporate vision for growth held by the department's management. All counter speculation aside, the hard and unvarnished fact is that the ball was in Manuel's court.

I've chosen sections of Manuel's reminiscences in an essay he wrote in order to give the reader some appreciation for the corporate environment in which he operated. It was most assuredly not yet the structured corporate surroundings of today's MBA world.

In the winter of 1955, I attended a College Department sales conference in Washington, D.C., at the invitation of Stephen W. Grant, the department head, to talk with the college fieldmen about the use of tests in colleges. Chairman Laughlin, one day after lunch, asked me to come to his room in the Statler Hotel, as he and Mr. Spaulding wished to talk to me. He told me that the Board of Directors intended to put my name in nomination for the Board at the Annual Meeting of the stockholders in the spring. I was, of course, very much pleased with this turn of events.

After I became a Board member, Mr. Spaulding, never one to put much stock in titles, suggested that I call myself Managing Editor of the Educational Department in addition to Test Department head, so I began delegating more Test Department responsibilities to others in the department. Two years later Mr. Spaulding became President of the company and Mr. Laughlin remained Chairman of the Board. My work as Managing Editor, which, in reality was Head of the Educational

Department, made it impossible for me to continue to direct the work of the Test Department. In August of that year (1957), Harold T. Miller was transferred from Pennsylvania to Boston to take over my Test Department work.

Capable leaders who were also good and respected friends were in charge of the various sections of the Department: Arthur Clark, constantly "helped" by interference from Mr. Spaulding in the field of reading, did a prodigious job of editing as well as writing at the elementary level; Norris H. Hoyt was producing one successful high school textbook after another; Stephen Grant had the College Department well in hand; and I had no complaints about the progress of the Test Department. George Davol, sometimes thought to become needlessly involved in the affairs of the branches (regional offices), did an excellent one-man job of keeping our inventory under control.

Some years later as the company's president, I labored to replace those who had retired, including Manuel, with equal talent. It was then that the full impact of the high caliber of that group Manuel had assembled hit me, and it hit me hard. Harry Truman is quoted as stating, "Leadership is the art of getting other people to run with your idea as if it were their own." The members of that group, all of whom were perfectly capable of coming up with their own ideas and did so, fully subscribed to Manuel's objectives and game plan and, through their own leadership, supported it.

Manuel started his Houghton career as a "trainee" at The Riverside Press in June 1934. The following sentences from his own account of his career, titled "Rambling Reminiscences," intrigue me by their "what if" implications.

> Twenty-five or more years later, at a Board of Directors luncheon, Mr. Laughlin told me that he had never known of my wish to work at The Riverside Press at the completion of the training course. He then paid me what I have assumed was meant to be a compliment by saying that had he known of my wish, the future of The Press might have been different. Surely, my future with the company would have been quite different.

Yes, Manuel, your future would have been very different had you remained with The Press, just as the future of many of us would have been different. Speculation leads me to suggest that the entire future of Houghton Mifflin would have been very different. Press leadership, tuned to the changing technology implemented by its competitors, could well have resulted in a very different balance of contributing divisions in the company. The question is: would the 1955–1957 commitment to educational textbook publishing have been made, given the presence of a successful press? And if so, who would have been available and qualified to lead it?

As good fortune would have it, Manuel did not remain at The Press. Rather he was assigned to the company's Midwest office in Chicago, where he traveled as an elementary/secondary textbook salesman until he entered the Army during World War II. After the war, he returned to the Chicago Office to continue his sales work. Those years in sales—working with such large cities as Detroit and Chicago as well as the rural areas of Michigan—equipped Manuel with a basic understanding of how textbooks are purchased and sold. Of equal importance, he learned firsthand about the total publishing skills and abilities, including design and printing, of our innovative and hard ball-playing textbook publishing competitors. These realities were driven home as Houghton's newer publications immediately following World War II, though pedagogically sound, compared poorly in presentation or format. Manuel addressed this weakness early on.

Out of this background and in the context of the time, the stage had been set. Now for the rest of Fenollosa's story.

> When William E. Spaulding became president of the company in 1957, I was designated as the representative of the Educational Department on the Executive Committee although my title was still Managing Editor. In addition to Mr. Spaulding and me, the other members were Franklin K. Hoyt, Treasurer; Lovell Thompson, Vice President and Head of the Trade Department; and Stanley G. French, Director of The Riverside Press. For the next seven years, as a member of the Executive Committee, I assumed the leadership of the Education Department.

In order to pull the control of the Department together I instituted weekly meetings with me of Messrs. Davol, Grant, and Freeman. At this time, Freeman, as General Sales Manager, and Grant as head of the College Department, were located in rented offices at 47 Winter Street, while Davol and I were at 2 and 3 Park Street.

At each weekly meeting I reported the actions and discussions of the weekly Executive Committee meeting, which were not confidential and which I felt were important for the others to know about. Each of the other three did the same with respect to areas of the Educational Department that were under their supervision. In this way, the four of us shared our knowledge of just about everything that was going on in the Department, and to some extent in the company. It helped to coordinate our work; it prevented each of us from taking off in a direction that might have been inimical to the others. It is my feeling, as I look back at that period, that if we had not held these [meetings], or something like them, the organization of the Educational Department could easily have fallen apart, and we could not have laid the foundation for the tremendous growth of the next decades. They were a great help to me personally, for, by knowing the thoughts of my colleagues, I gained confidence in expressing my ideas in Executive Committee discussions.

Stephen W. Grant became President of the company at the Annual Meeting in 1963, William E. Spaulding became Chairman of the Board, and Henry A. Laughlin retired from the Board. At Houghton Mifflin Company, the President was the Chief Executive Officer, not the Chairman.

As I now look back on this period, roughly 1964 to 1971, I think of it as the time in which giant leaps forward took place in Houghton Mifflin Company. The two major problems which could no longer be overlooked involved The Riverside Press and the Common Stock of the Company.

The Riverside Press has often been referred to as the "captive" printing plant of Houghton Mifflin Company. Actually, in earlier times the exact reverse was true: All printing and binding of the publishing department had to be done at The Riverside Press in Cambridge at Riverside's prices regardless of whether or not they were competitive with the prices of other book manufacturing establishments.

In the early 1960s, the Educational Department was authorized to establish its own production department. This new department was empowered to call for bids from all likely book manufacturing plants, including The Riverside Press, and to choose those that quoted the best, prices, quality, and service. Since Riverside could rarely meet the bids of the competition, it lost most of the work of the publishing departments.

Houghton, Mifflin & Company was a partnership until 1908 when it was incorporated as Houghton Mifflin Company. In 1967 the Board of Directors recommended to the stockholders that the present common stock be split by a sizeable multiple, some additional new stock issued, and that Houghton Mifflin Company common stock be publicly traded on the Over-the-Counter market. Four months later, having met the requirements for listing on the New York Stock Exchange, Houghton Mifflin Company was first traded on September 15, 1967, under the trading symbol "HTN."

In discussing the period of great growth of the Educational Division, mention must be made of the parts played by Norris H. Hoyt and Gordon R. Hjalmarson. As head of the High School Department, Norris Hoyt had determinedly followed a policy of publishing the very best and easiest-to-sell books in each field that he entered or not to publish at all. Limited to a small editorial staff, he was forced to publish only a few books over what seemed like an interminably long time. One of the editors he added was Gordon Hjalmarson, a high school mathematics and science teacher at the Huntington Beach High School in California. With the encouragement of Norris Hoyt, Gordon built a stable of authors who produced mathematics books, which in record time swept the country in sales and established Houghton Mifflin as the foremost ranking publisher of high school mathematics textbooks in the country.

Much credit for Mr. Hjalmarson's publishing success goes to Norris Hoyt who trained him in every step of editorial work and inculcated in him the desire to spare no effort to make his publications the best in the field. Once the high school mathematics textbooks had become well-established leaders, it followed that we should enter again the area of elementary mathematics. Mr. Hjalmarson got the authorization, which he so eagerly wanted, to build an elementary mathematics program under his successes at the secondary school level. Like his high school mathematics books, his elementary program was an immediate success, and within a few years from its publication date, Houghton Mifflin Company was the dominant publisher of mathematics textbooks from kindergarten through senior high school.

Chapter 7 contains an interview with coauthor Lee Capps of the elementary school textbook series. Chapter 5 contains a discussion among author Bill Durr and his editors in which they explain how they revised the company's reading series, achieving a major breakthrough in the elementary school during Manuel's administration. Back to Manuel:

> In the late 1950s and 1960s, I heard of overtures being made for the acquisition of the company by RCA, CBS, Hunt Foods, Learn, and Readers Digest, and I myself was involved, along with others, in exploratory talks with the principals of Litton, Raytheon, Westinghouse, and Singer. In all our talks we never got an answer that made any sense to our question about what advantage there would be to Houghton Mifflin if we became an independent part of their conglomerate. To their promise of "unlimited" money to expand our publishing efforts, we replied that we had never yet had to curtail for lack of funds a publishing program that we really wanted to undertake and that a promise of boundless credit would only encourage careless publishing. This seems to be exactly what has happened to some of the firms that have been taken over; their publishing became careless and then, of course, the funds were no longer "unlimited," and control from above shackled every publishing operation.
>
> Through Paine, Webber, Jackson, and Curtis I learned that a small computer company in New Hampshire was in need of cash and would be willing to sell up to twenty-five percent of its common stock to increase its working capital. Up to this time we had stayed on the sidelines as we watched the development of programmed books, computer instructional programs, TV and radio educational programs, none of which made much sense to us. Maybe this was an opportunity to learn from the inside the potential advantages and limitations

of the computer in instruction. A meeting was arranged with Richard Bueschel, president and founder of Time Share Corporation of Hanover, New Hampshire. Some of us inspected his offices and met his staff in Hanover, and on our recommendation, the Houghton Mifflin Board voted to buy stock with options to acquire more later if we so desired. Time Share Corporation and the Educational Department built programs of computer-assisted instruction and tests to accompany a few of our books; while the profitability did not increase dramatically, the joint venture project helped the sales of some Houghton Mifflin publications and enhanced the company's image in the marketplace. We bought more stock in the company, and in 1976, Time Share Corporation became a wholly owned subsidiary of Houghton Mifflin Company and greatly expanded its operations in the United States and Canada.

In the mid-1960s, the make-up of the Board of Directors of the future was much in the minds of all Board members. Our Board consisted of employees holding high positions in the Trade, Educational, Administrative, and Manufacturing Divisions. In a sense, to be invited to sit on the Board was a reward for doing a reasonably good job in one's division and for being socially acceptable.

But the growth of the company was making our kind of Board obsolete. Too many people held really responsible posts for all of them to be recognized by Board membership. Beneath it all ran a feeling on the part of both the Educational and Trade Divisions that each one should hold a controlling interest on the Board. The Trade Division, having once been dominant in company affairs, felt a responsibility for maintaining the prestige of the company. The Educational Division now accounted for a major portion of company sales and almost all of company profit. In 1965, because of some retiring Board members, the Trade Division proposed adding Austin Olney, a Trade editor, to the Board, thus giving Trade a majority of Board members. The Educational Division proposed Richard Gladstone, who was about as acceptable to the Trade as any Educational person could be. I felt that I could propose Harold T. Miller for the Board, as a long overdue recognition of the part the Geneva Office had played in the company's prosperity. With the support of the other Educational Board members and most of the Trade, Mr. Miller was nominated for a third position on the Houghton Mifflin

Board. I have never known whether or not Lovell Thompson was aware that by this action the Educational Division obtained a solid controlling position on the Board of Directors, and this eventually defeated his plans for his own future in the company. The stage was now set for the decisions that were to be made, which would determine the future, or at least the immediate future, of the company: becoming a publicly owned company, introducing outside Board members, making the Board a working Board supported by working committees composed of members holding responsible positions, ending the financial drain of The Riverside Press; in short, laying the foundation for Houghton Mifflin Company to seize the position of leadership it now holds in the industry. I consider the election of Harold T. Miller to the 1965 Board of Directors to be the single most important action in my 39 years of employment, and I am pleased to have taken part in that action.

In April of 1968, George Davol, Richard Gladstone, Harold Miller, and I held our first so-called "Long-Range Planning Conference." Its purpose was open and frank discussion about the future of educational publishing. Having agreed generally on what educational publishing would be like approximately ten years hence, we then moved onto the question of how the Educational Division could best prepare itself to serve the needs of education in the late 1970s.

In the next three years, we four and Norris Hoyt, whom we appointed Editorial Director for the Educational Division, continued to meet at irregular times, but not in the company offices. One such meeting in 1969 was devoted almost entirely to College Department problems, for college sales were showing a steady decline from year to year. A result of this meeting was a whirlwind trip that I took to each of our five regional sales offices where I held a confidential conference with the manager and his director of college sales. We had planned a number of topics for discussion, and I kept careful notes of the opinions of these two men in each office about the reasons for our declining sales and profits. Upon my return to Boston, the notes I had taken were transcribed and distributed to the four other members of our "Long-Range Planning Committee." The unanimous conclusion that we drew from my reports, and from our own observations, was that we would have to find a replacement for Henry F. Thoma, the College Department head, and that that person was not now in our employment. Mr. Thoma received the news with a feeling of relief, having already made up his mind to step down from his position in the near future; that he would like to be appointed to a position of Senior English Editor of the College Department, a position which we had all hoped he would wish to accept.

As the decade of the 1960s drew to a close, thanks to soul-searching discussions involving planning for the future of the Educational Division, and with the strong support of President Grant and Chief Financial Officer F. K. Hoyt, decisions were made with regard to the course that the company would take in the 1970s and the persons who would lead it in the early years of the new decade.

Mr. Grant expressed the wish to retire one year early at the Annual Meeting in 1973. Mr. Hoyt would retire at the 1972 Annual Meeting. My retirement date was 1976 and Mr. Davol's one year earlier. Of the three younger Educational men, Messrs. Gladstone, Miller, and Hjalmarson, we leaned in favor of Mr. Miller but did not commit ourselves as to who would succeed Mr. Grant as President. We brought Mr. Miller to Boston from the Geneva office in 1971, made him a Vice President, in charge of the Educational Division, and I was kicked upstairs to a newly created position of Senior Vice President.

At some time during this period, Mr. Grant and a number of directors asked me to take over as President on Mr. Grant's retirement the following year. At the most, this would give me a three-year term of office, and although I had never thought to retire as early as at age 62, I had planned on retirement a year or so before the required age of 65. I felt greatly honored by the thoughts of my associates, but declined to accept their offers of support for a number of reasons: for the good of the company, and I really believe that this was basic to my reasoning, I felt that a two- or three-year term of office was too short a time to accomplish anything more than to lay the preparation for the new administration which would follow mine. Because of our careful planning sessions, that kind of preparation had already been done; we had identified three younger men, any one of whom we felt could be ready to lead the company in a year's time. Still, it was a tough decision to turn down a position which, I guess, I, like so many others, had hoped someday to occupy.

When the time arrived to make the final decisions, the choice of Harold T. Miller was unanimous. I was again much pleased when Mr. Miller asked me to stay on in his administration as Chairman. Fortunately, I was wise enough to know that he was prepared in all respects to take over the helm without my lame-duck assistance and that whatever mistakes he might make initially would provide him with worthwhile experiences to meet other challenges. The great forward stride that the company has taken under Mr. Miller's leadership attested to the wisdom of our decisions.

A publishing career is not for notoriety seekers. For authors it is, although even the number of authors attaining notoriety is limited. Still an author's name appears on the book's cover, in the publisher's promotional material, and the fortunate among them may obtain a spot in various media settings.

The editors and many others whose skilled efforts make the author's work available in a book are rarely known outside the house or the publishing industry. It's an unusual occurrence when anyone in a lay group discussing the best-seller can name the publisher, let alone the book's editor.

Within the publishing house, a somewhat similar situation exists, but with a different focus. Here the editors and those about them are known, but those individuals behind the scenes who make the total operation work are much less so. Throughout the chapters in this book the relationship between the authors and their in-house publishers—editors, designers, sales, and advertising—comes to the forefront. Yet little is said about those who provide the leadership equal to ensuring that all of these creative, entrepreneurial people, authors included, function productively. From what source does the planning and direction come that melds the creative juices of those responsible for a publisher's intellectual properties with the business-based demands of a company?

That source must be someone who can lead in a way to be followed by those who create the intellectual properties of the house while concurrently meeting its unforgiving financial and government requirements. The culture of the involved parties is for the most part diverse, yet successful corporate publishing house governance requires a total balanced effort.

George Manuel Fenollosa (Manuel), who was at Houghton Mifflin from 1934 to 1973, was one of those leaders. His sage leadership inspired and guided all of us who reported to him from the late 1950s to his retirement in 1973. The publishing environment of his administration encouraged each of us and those who reported to us to take the initiative in our own areas of responsibility, yet do so in a way consistent with his insistence on publishing excellence.

This resulted in Houghton Mifflin's emergence as a major and much-respected educational textbook publisher. Extracts from his personal papers have provided a revealing description of life at Houghton's senior management levels.

I knew Manuel for fifty years and reported to him for a good number of those years until his retirement. Thereafter, until his death, I continued to see him throughout the seventeen years I served as the head of Houghton Mifflin Company and after, as we both enjoyed retirement. My years as the company's CEO, in addition to the information gleaned from the many interviews I've conducted with people who also worked with Manuel, amply qualify me to know and understand the extraordinary nature of his achievement. He took the charge he was assigned and accomplished it.

I know of no one who did more for the well-being of Houghton Mifflin Company than Manuel Fenollosa. It was a great honor and privilege to work for and with him. He was a first-class act and the bet paid off.

CHAPTER 3

Preaching the Gospel

The Houghton Mifflin Teaching/Learning
Approach to Reading

As readers, you have somehow learned word-attack skills or decoding. You can identify in print all the words in your spoken vocabulary, plus those you have picked up in all your reading and your personal and professional experiences. If you come across a word you're not quite sure of, usually the context will reveal its meaning, or you will go to the dictionary.

Because *Publishing: A Leap from Mind to Mind* is about publishing, the topic of reading and how it is taught and learned is a key ingredient to understanding the main thrust of the book. I intend to show that pupils will learn when their teachers are given a research-based, classroom-tested teaching/learning process that is consistently and sequentially presented. It is even more important to the Houghton Mifflin strand of the story, because the biggest, most successful series we ever published was Paul McKee's Reading for Meaning, which later became the Houghton Mifflin Reading Series. Note the title of the original. The word *meaning* should be emphasized, because that is what made the McKee series different from all the rest of the programs on the market. The simplicity of his word-attack approach gave pupils the ability to read with meaning early on.

Not that I would suggest that the other series should have been called "Reading for Misunderstanding"! Surely their developers, whether they were an in-house group or signed-on authors, thought they were teaching children to read for meaning. In fact, the teachers who used these series thought that too. But actually, they were simply giving pupils the tools to recognize words in isolation: the *sight method* or *look-see,* as it was variously called. See a word on a chalkboard, a chart, and a page often enough, and sooner or later you will remember what it stands for. Put enough words together, and you will seem to read.

Paul McKee thought that approach did not go far enough to give children a reliable way to decode words on their own. His goal was to teach them to use context together with letter-sound association to unlock words they would recognize if spoken. How was the Houghton Mifflin reading series unique? First, according to Hal Donelson, a Houghton sales rep from Nebraska:

> Paul McKee was the only author I have ever read on the teaching of reading who had thoroughly thought out the entire process a student had to go through to learn to read in relation to some very basic characteristics of the language process. These are some basic statements that he made that suggested or justified his approach to teaching reading:
>
> 1. You can read only your listening and speaking vocabulary.
> 2. This means that the only thing new to the child in learning to read is the printed symbol that stood for the word that he already knew when he heard it spoken.
> 3. Reading is a thought-getting process. Not a word-naming exercise.
> 4. Consonants are more important to the beginning reader than vowels. All the child needs is enough phonetic instruction, letter-sound association along with oral context to recognize a word in his mind that he already knows. (Here's a McKee statement that I always liked: "A consonant has no sound other than its name." At first, teachers don't believe it.)
> 5. The child needs to develop a reliable decoding technique that he can use independently.

The previous statements were the bases or guidelines to his approach to teaching reading through the use of letter-sound association and context, a technique that the student could use independently.

To accomplish this, McKee started teaching children to listen to and use the oral context to arrive at a conclusion. The next step was teaching basic letters and the sounds they stood for. The third step was to combine oral context with letter sounds to key [identify] a word in a sentence. "Tip is not a big dog. He is a l_ _ _ _ _ dog." You know the sound that l has at the beginning of a word. Who knows what the word is? How did you know it was "little?" It makes sense and begins with l.

The purpose of *Getting Ready to Read* [the first book in the series] was to teach the decoding technique on an oral basis. The next step, in the pre-primers, was to make the conversion from the use of oral context to reading. The instruction now became, read this to yourself, and think of a word you know that begins with the beginning letter. "It is dark in here. Will you turn on the l _ _ p?" The instruction: Will you read the sentence? How did you know the word wasn't "light?" "Light" doesn't end with p. How did you know it wasn't "little?" Doesn't make sense.

Now the techniques or skills have been developed for the program. The decoding skill is employed very strongly through the first and second grades, then more emphasis is placed on the work-study skills.

Howard Stokes was the New York sales representative. He was also a superb piano player. He worked much of Upstate New York and was well-known for both his salesmanship and his musical talent. It was part of Howard's experience each year to be confronted by a superintendent of schools with a large order in hand and a statement that read: "You get the order only if you play at gradation."

The *phony alphabet* he refers to was developed by Paul McKee for his professional book. It was also used in a booklet called *Primer for Parents*. Symbols were created for just the consonants used in a very short story; the vowels in the booklet were represented by dashes. Its purpose was to give adults the experience of being faced with unfamiliar printed symbols and being expected to read them. According to Howard:

But we had something unique, that no other reading series had, the McKee "Phony Alphabet." The story of "Sam," written in it, gave us an inroad to arouse a new interest in reading. It showed teachers, administrators, and parents how difficult it can be to learn how to read. It showed adults the very same problems that children have when they receive their first reading books.

As you well know, and I say it again, "Ham that I am, I really enjoyed doing the 'Sam' story." I would always start out with "Sam," his name. This I would belabor! I'd write it on the blackboard in the phony alphabet: ⊥ __ ? , then ask my first question, "What's his name?"

I would get, "Tom," "Ted," "Bob," etc.

Seriously, I don't recall ever getting "Sam."

My second question: Why isn't it "William," "Howard," "Theodore"? Answers from teachers, "It has only three letters."

In conjunction with his use of the *Primer for Parents* story, Howard developed what he called his "3-Way Gimmick" to give further insight into the McKee word-attack philosophy. He would illustrate the three ways people could provide reading readiness to prepare kids for learning word-attack skills.

Let me take you through a session with Howard. You are in a group of teachers assembled to listen to him present Reading for Meaning. When you arrive in the room, you see that Howard has drawn a series of boxes on the chalkboard.

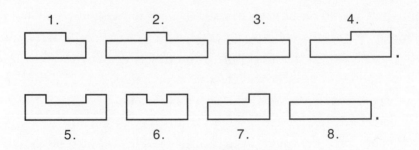

He would probably not have numbered them, but I have for reference purposes. First, he would point out that reading readiness that consists of word configurations alone is a waste of time, because many words have the same or similar shapes—3 and 8, for example, and 4 and 7.

Second, he would suggest that some reading series believe in using the vowel approach to readiness. Then he would divide the words into letter boxes and fill in the vowels for this sentence. Many teachers loved the vowel approach, but this exercise reveals its weakness. Can you make anything out of this?

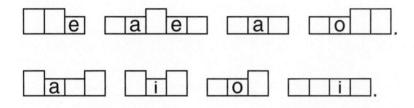

Third, Howard would erase the vowels and replace them with just the consonants in the sentence. Now the teachers could actually "read" the sentence, as can you. This was the McKee approach to word attack: use the consonants, to which the children will be introduced in *Getting Ready to Read,* the first book in the Reading for Meaning Series, along with the context, and you can usually figure out a sentence or a word that is in your spoken vocabulary. The teachers could see and relate to this concept, as I'm sure you can too.

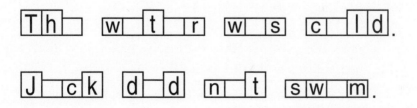

In discussing Hal's and Howard's comments about the McKee word-attack technique with Carol Case, I was reminded by her of the introduction to the advertising brochure announcing the fourth edition of Reading for Meaning. It succinctly sums up the McKee Reading for Meaning objectives.

> The Fourth Edition (1966) of Reading for Meaning aims directly at achieving these two important objectives: (1) helping the pupil develop the power to read independently, and (2) stimulating him to want to read a wide variety of worthwhile material.
>
> Through its revolutionary pre-reading program, *Getting Ready to Read,* Reading for Meaning gives the pupil a dramatic head start toward independent reading power before he opens his first preprimer! This highly acclaimed program for kindergarten or first grade teaches the child the basic understandings necessary for unlocking strange printed words. It teaches him to associate 18 consonants and four speech consonants with the sounds they represent in words, and to use oral context and the beginning letter sound to think of a word that makes sense with the rest of a sentence (after teaching him the meaning of the term *makes sense*).
>
> *Context plus letter-sound association*—this efficient and reliable procedure for unlocking strange printed words forms a strong foundation for all future development of the pupil's reading skills. And because he learns and practices this procedure early, he develops a self-confidence that carries over to *all* his reading, in or out of school.
>
> By taking full advantage of the understandings taught in *Getting Ready to Read,* the primary and middle-grade programs develop and refine the pupil's power to read independently. At the same time, the program nurtures his appreciation of good reading by providing him with enjoyable and stimulating content.

There is one other aspect of the McKee philosophy of teaching reading, and that has to do with vocabulary control. Paul McKee also focused on vocabulary control. As he wrote in his professional book, *The Teaching of Reading* (1948):

> The vocabulary of the reading selections used should be closely controlled. This control should be exercised on at least the three following points:

1. The number of strange words introduced in each selection should be relatively small. This provision enables the child to get some reading done, keeps him from looking upon reading as the act of identifying words, and prevents his learning task in word identification and word recognition from becoming unreasonably difficult.

2. Following its introduction in a given selection, each word that will be needed at later grade levels should be given a considerable amount of well distributed repetition in that selection and in subsequent selections. This provision makes it possible for the child to get the practice he needs with that word in order to learn to recognize it readily. It is understood, of course, that the need for repetition is no excuse for the senseless expressions, now found in many preprimers and primers, which make the talking of the characters in the selections unnatural to say the least.

3. The reading selections should include an ample number of words, which contain the phonetic elements to be taught in the first grade. This provision will supply the number of words needed for introducing and for providing practice in using each of those elements.

There you have it—the McKee teaching/learning philosophy of reading. Its importance cannot be overemphasized. All the dismay about how children are not learning to read today is probably because materials that adhere to sound teaching/learning concepts are not available to them. As one of our long-term top reading editors said recently, "We know how to teach reading. We just have to go out and do it." The same applies, of course, to other subjects, but reading is the subject we must master before we go on to the others.

CHAPTER 4

State Textbook Adoptions

How They Worked and How They Affected Publishing

A professor of biology, while addressing an audience about international politics, was interrupted by an attendee. The student inquired how it was that humans originated on the landmass called Africa instead of Europe. The professor replied that he didn't know and then asked why he had been asked a question so unrelated to the subject of his presentation. Whereupon the questioner responded that he wanted to give the professor an opportunity to speak about a topic he knew something about. (The message of this incident holds for the many individuals who have written and pontificated about state textbook adoptions.)

The Boston Latin School, founded in 1635, is generally credited with being the first town-supported public school, although there were schools in the colonies long before this date. In New Amsterdam, the first free school for children of communicants of the Dutch Reformed Church was established in 1633. Over the succeeding centuries, as wave after wave of immigrants have arrived at the nation's shores, the public schools were and remain the central contributor to equipping those millions to function, sustain themselves, prosper, and grow the nation. There are few other feats of equal contribution in our country's history.

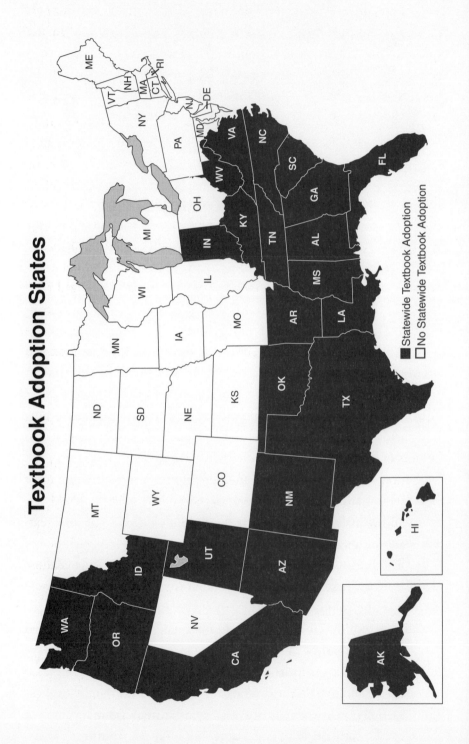

Textbook Adoption States

Statewide Textbook Adoption
No Statewide Textbook Adoption

The state textbook adoption movement was and is a major part of that accomplishment. It has served a necessary purpose in the spread of public school education. In the process, it has heavily influenced the nation's elementary/high school curricula and textbook publishers. Twenty-four states have statewide textbook adoptions: West Virginia, Virginia, North Carolina, South Carolina, Georgia, Florida, Mississippi, Kentucky, Tennessee, Alabama, Louisiana, Arkansas, Indiana, Idaho, Utah, Texas, Oklahoma, New Mexico, Arizona, California, Washington, Oregon, Hawaii and Alaska. They form a broad swath across the nation extending from the Southeast into the Southwest, and from there into California and the Northwest. One can rightfully wonder how the system came about and its aggregate influence on America's educational undertaking.

R. Sidney Cooper, now retired from publishing, managed textbook sales offices in Atlanta and Dallas, and also corporate offices in Boston. The movement started in the Southeast and then spread westward as the population migrated in that direction and statehood was granted to populated areas.

RSC: A major factor that brought on state adoption states was the economic condition of the states, primarily in the Southeast and Southwest. Laws were passed back in those days with the intention of providing free textbooks to all the students going to school simply because most of the people, frankly, could not afford to buy textbooks for their children. Providing free textbooks, and having a central purchasing power, gave each one of the states a little more purchasing power. In fact, back in those days, and not too many years ago at that, the states would only adopt a single textbook for a single course. We called that a single basal adoption, and North Carolina was one of the last states to get away from the single basal adoption, and that was in the late sixties—I believe 1968—when North Carolina adopted our literature program 9–12 along with McGraw-Hill's. That seemed to be a landmark decision in North Carolina.

The much-respected educator, Andrew Craig Phillips, North Carolina superintendent of schools for twenty years, recently told me: "I don't know how you guys feel about multiples…. The law already provided for multiple adoption, if the state board wanted to do it."

HTM: Single or multiple statewide textbook adoptions were always a big question for textbook publishers.

ACP: Yes. Of course, there were both sides of it. I never could understand why responsible book people—and when I say responsible, I was a believer in the big four or five publishers. I always respected the ones on the edges, but I could not understand why it wasn't in the best interests of the good folks to have a crack at that multiple, rather than single, because, you know, the single adoption for years and years, made somebody big and fat.

HTM: I don't have one specific answer. Largely we deferred to your call. Our business was to sell books, so we went after each opportunity, be it multiple or single adoption.

Over time, authors and editors (and I include myself in the group) in textbook publishing houses realized that you cannot build into one series—let's take a math series—all of the demands of a good teaching/learning program to meet all the needs confronting schools if all pupils are considered. There were, for example, some math series that were tougher, others that were simpler. We realized that, and we avoided a lot of grief, if a state had multiple choices and could select within the state books that were compatible with the varying needs of kids in and within different school districts. When states adopted one series for use all the way across the state, problems arose.

ACP: That's why we changed. Yes. And the citizens—parents—their concept of it was surely we ought to have access to more than just one textbook in geography and so forth.

HTM: You, as the state superintendent of schools, and I, as the president of a textbook publishing house, formulated our policies and actions on the best of available research and experience known to educate the kids, and I firmly believe you and I and many of our colleagues were of like mind.

Craig Phillips informed me that the first North Carolina state superintendent, Calvin H. Wiley, who traveled on horseback across the state to do his job, was in office from 1852 to 1855. He decided that he should "bring order to the confusion regarding textbooks by eliminating bad books, preventing frequent changes, and securing use of uniform series." He had no power to make counties accept his idea, but he was able to persuade local authorities to follow his recommendations. His first list, consisting of seven textbooks, seems quite appropriate even for today.

> *Webster's Spelling Book*
> *The North Carolina Reader*
> *Davies Arithmetics*
> *Mitchell's Intermediate Geography*
> *Bulliu's Grammar*
> *Worcester's Comprehensive Dictionary*
> *Common School Catechism* (contains questions and answers about North Carolina history, resources, education, and government)

In 1901 a Textbook Commission was appointed, with the state superintendent as secretary. A subcommittee was appointed by the governor to examine the merits of textbooks and report to the Textbook Commission. Over the ensuing years, the Textbook Commission made changes responding to the development and demands of passing time. Yet it held fast to its "primary goal for evaluating textbooks to ensure that textbooks are compatible with the North Carolina Course of Study; error-free textbooks are equally important to the North Carolina Textbooks." Their adoption process, one of the best but common to other states, has evolved into the following system.

North Carolina Textbook Adoption Process

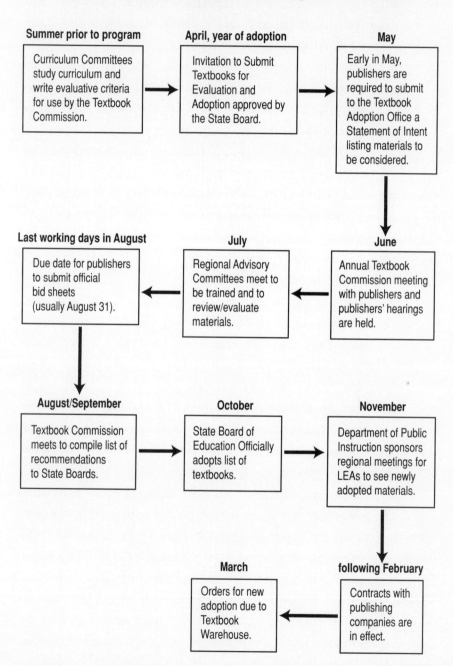

Summer prior to program

Curriculum Committees study curriculum and write evaluative criteria for use by the Textbook Commission.

April, year of adoption

Invitation to Submit Textbooks for Evaluation and Adoption approved by the State Board.

May

Early in May, publishers are required to submit to the Textbook Adoption Office a Statement of Intent listing materials to be considered.

Last working days in August

Due date for publishers to submit official bid sheets (usually August 31).

July

Regional Advisory Committees meet to be trained and to review/evaluate materials.

June

Annual Textbook Commission meeting with publishers and publishers' hearings are held.

August/September

Textbook Commission meets to compile list of recommendations to State Boards.

October

State Board of Education Officially adopts list of textbooks.

November

Department of Public Instruction sponsors regional meetings for LEAs to see newly adopted materials.

March

Orders for new adoption due to Textbook Warehouse.

following February

Contracts with publishing companies are in effect.

Now back to Sid Cooper:

RSC: Let me also deal with the depository question. The requirement started back probably in the early 1900s because transportation was a major problem. In those days, most of the textbooks were manufactured in the Northeast, largely Boston, and in many cases, schools in the South, Southwest, and Far West were always late getting their textbooks for the opening of schools in September of each year.

The states were making major purchases of textbooks for each of the grade levels in each of the school systems, and they wanted to make certain that the books were warehoused on location and distributed within the state, and on time. Therefore, an additional statute was passed related to state adoption procedure. It was the depository requirement. For instance, the Florida School Book Depository was established in 1917, and it is the only depository operating in the state of Florida. Of course, the depository requirement, as far as the state is concerned, only requires that the adopted textbook be warehoused and distributed from within the state. Supplemental material not adopted really did not need to be distributed through the depository, but normally is, as a service to the customers and the convenience of getting the textbooks plus workbooks, teachers' editions, and other items shipped to the school at the same time. Most of the publishers, including Houghton, of course, shipped everything through the depositories.

The state adoptions were big business for textbook publishers. With the population growth, it became increasingly important to textbook companies that they participate in their textbook adoptions.

RSC: I have had the opportunity to be the manager of both the Atlanta Office and the Dallas Office, and I would say that the separate offices are highly desirable. While I was in the Dallas Office, I spent much of my time in Austin working with the Texas Education Agency and the State Board of Education meetings. Texas is so important to that office that it is extremely critical the manager pay close attention to what is happening in Austin. Whereas in the Atlanta Office, we had ten states and some of those states were very critical, such as Florida, North Carolina, and Virginia, not to overlook the others, Alabama and Tennessee, but the workload was spread out over more than one state. But primarily the reason that I assume Houghton established separate offices back many years ago was a marketing decision. The competition required that we pay close attention to the state adoption states in the various offices rather than having one office with fifteen state adoption requirements and all of the paperwork and details necessary to keep track of deadlines. I don't know who the first company was that started the separate office in Dallas and one in Atlanta, but certainly all major publishers have the two offices, Southwest and Southeast. If we did not, then I think we would have been making a mistake.

Most adoption states, whether single or multiple basal, operate on a five- to six-year adoption cycle in each subject area. Textbook evaluation and selection of the publishers' texts submitted for adoption, especially within the geographic and demographic environment of the early years, fostered the need for a central agency. Logically, committees were appointed to serve that purpose.

With the passing of time, the power and reach of the selection forces expanded. Subcommittees and alternate committees, such as the California Curriculum Committee, came into being. The physical construction of texts, including paper and binding standards, copyright (texts two years old or more were rarely considered), prices for the term of the adoption, and, of course, curriculum content were all to be considered. Meeting the calls of the various states each year evolved as a way of life for the publishers. As more and more publishers went public, the financial community following the publishing industry monitored the larger state textbook adoptions and insisted on learning what areas were up for adoption each year. Elementary reading and mathematics adoptions were closely followed, since the combined textbook expenditure for these two areas represented roughly two-thirds of the elementary school textbook budget. Analysts wanted to know how the state "calls" correlated to a company's publications list and who got or did not get adopted, once the decisions were announced. We were asked these questions even in Europe—Scotland and Switzerland in particular—as we made our financial rounds.

This pressure on corporate headquarters generated intense pressure on sales management to "work" the state adoption bureaucracies, and in turn those state officials learned that they could work the publishers. Needless to say, such demands found their way to a company's editors and authors, often much to the distress of the open-territory sales managers, who could rarely cite marketplace demands of equal definitive detail and revenue potential. In their states, the selection of textbooks is a matter of local option—the state does not determine an approved list of textbooks from which schools must choose to qualify for state reimbursement. The open-territory states are Maine, New Hampshire, Vermont, Massachusetts, Connecticut, Rhode Island, New York, New Jersey, Pennsylvania, Ohio, Michigan, Illinois, Missouri, Wisconsin, Minnesota, Iowa, North Dakota, South Dakota, Kansas, Colorado, Montana, Wyoming, Nebraska, Idaho, Utah, and Nevada.

In a sense, the law of unintended consequences began to operate as the educators in the offices of the state adoption states advanced their interests to the publishers, and the publishers were influenced by this feedback, but not, at least early on, to the extent of compromising their authors' beliefs. Not until late in the period under discussion did the publishers and their authors lose their position of leadership to state Curriculum Commissions in certain large states such as California and Texas.

Many publishers, including me, viewed the state adoption process favorably. Why? For starters, because the states purchased a lot of textbooks as they ordered new or revised texts as part of their five- to six-year adoption cycle. Obviously, these large orders were good for the publishers' revenues and the bottom line. Business aside, however, a major benefit resulting from the introduction of new textbooks every five or six years was that it brought change to the teaching/learning activities in those states' classrooms. Texts were introduced that reflected the latest in research and lessons to be gleaned, collected little by little from use in hundreds and often thousands of classrooms nationwide. This process encouraged an unrelenting author/publisher search for the unique factor in their texts as teaching/learning procedures were refined and enhanced. A close working relationship evolved, therefore, between adoption states and textbook publishers.

By no means were all of the adoption states a pure play without a downside. Adoption cycles were changed, sometimes after publishers incurred large expenses in time and money seeking approval, or the listed texts were never purchased because of inadequate funding. Then, too, when a company failed to get a given text or series listed, there would be no purchase of those titles in the state over the next six years. In fairness it can be said that many school districts in the non-adoption states (the open-territory states) practiced system-wide textbook adoptions and updated their texts routinely, but they were not organized and less likely heard from.

Newly adopted texts encouraged the teachers using them to become acquainted with their accompanying manuals in addition to the contents of the pupils' books. Some critics contend that the state textbook listing committees made unwise decisions, and no doubt they did on various occasions; yet given that most states increasingly listed multiple publishers' books, usually about five different texts for each slot, the opportunity presented itself for school systems within the state to select from the choices available to them texts that would be the most likely to meet their needs and preferences.

There is another positive aspect of state adoptions. Elementary school mathematics author Lee Capps, reading author William Durr, and longtime proven elementary school editors like Nancy Sargent, in their interviews with me, emphasize the necessity for teaching skill-based subjects, like math and reading, in an organized and logically ascending sequence. Any basal series worth its salt must focus on a sequential step-by-step introduction of each skill that in turn supports introducing the next skill. The benefits derived from adhering to this commonsense teaching/learning system are self-evident. Pupil mastery of the ability to identify new words and read with comprehension (meaning) is more likely to be realized through this approach than if sequential continuity is bypassed or, equally bad, a single-issue curriculum is used, like whole language. Unstructured presentation of these crucial fundamentals, as often occurs in schools located in open-territory states where each classroom teacher selects his/her texts cafeteria-style without series continuity, is less productive. Even granting that no one textbook series can provide all the help each pupil needs, skill-based subjects such as reading and math depend on skills. It is readily apparent that the state adoption procedure favors the structured approach through its listing and funding for the purchase of approved textbook series. Teacher training institutions counterproductively often advocate the use of a variety of instructional materials in each classroom. This is fine if the fundamentals are covered, but all too often that doesn't happen. Private schools, given their special environment and pupil selection procedures, may be able to depart from a structured program, but public schools take on all comers. Reading supervisor, Wanda Lister, from Fresno, California, makes my point.

WL: I started teaching in 1953 and always taught pretty much primary grades. I was always very involved in teaching children to read. My first years of teaching, the first five years, I taught in lower socioeconomic areas, where we had many children who struggled with reading. And of course, during that time, we were given basal readers that the state printed with the plates from the publishers. I remember following that teacher's manual as a new teacher, because I had finished up at Fresno State, and at that time they required no reading courses. First, we had literature, and then we had a separate course for written language. So I had to follow the teacher's manual quite a bit.

Wanda's comment reminds me of an experience early in the 1980s. I was invited to attend a series of seminars in company with a number of other CEOs and university presidents for the purpose of discussing ways to improve public education. During one meeting, a college president turned to a colleague and commented that maybe the two of them should go down into the schools personally and show the teachers how to teach. Unable to restrain myself, I stated that I hoped they would not do that, for the teachers being criticized obtained their training and education in colleges such as their own. The visiting speaker, then head of the nation's private school association sought me out after the meeting and said that he was impressed that I had been willing to get to the heart of the problem and invited me to meet with him on my next trip to Washington, D.C. Just how long, I ask, must we keep ducking around the barn in our discussions about the major causes of problems in education?

Successful instruction in each learning situation, publishers must admit, consists of much more than a slavish commitment to a single basal textbook series, important as that is. For just plain horse sense, consider the following very direct observations made by Helen Shaffer, a one-of-a-kind reading and language arts Houghton consultant with whom I worked in Pennsylvania over half a century ago. Helen frequently spoke to teachers, assembled from several elementary schools, about teaching reading, and of course with the purpose of persuading those teachers to use our publications. Upon being introduced, she would look at the teachers for a few moments, and then in a manner bespeaking a shared confidence, which only they knew, say, "Teachers, you and I know after our many years in the classroom that with some kids you could put them in a telephone booth with the yellow pages and a dead cat, and they would come out reading. Those are not the ones you've got to worry about.

"What you've got to worry about are the ones who can't seem to learn to read, for they are the ones who will grow up and be on your school board." (At this point, you could imagine the teachers' heads bobbing in agreement.) Then Helen would tell them how the skills program embedded in our series, along with fine literature, could help solve their problem. Helen sold a lot of books, and she was invited back again because the series, when used, produced pupils who could read.

In addition to basal readers, with their crucial sequential skills development, notwithstanding, there is another obviously essential element in the educational—especially beginning school—experience that is a near absolute. That component is good, solid, worthwhile children's literature that generates enjoyment and a sense of enthusiasm for reading. No one describes that element better than educator Betty Hansen, also from Fresno, California.

BH: I'm going to go back to when I was a child consumer of materials prepared and published by noted publishers, because I'm a fourth-generation native of Visalia, California. We were the only black family in Visalia, and I was a fourth-generation native of that place, so I didn't have a typical black experience. When I talk about diversity and its effect on me, as I look at books and materials and the like, I'm not bringing exactly the typical experience to bear on that.

However, I remember my mother used to take us to the library every single week to supplement what we were doing in school. I'd bring my book home and read it, and she would say, "Okay, that's what you read today. What are you going to read tomorrow?" That inspired a love of reading that I carried into my first teaching experience and later into administration, and even after my retirement as the assistant superintendent in charge of curriculum and instruction in Fresno Unified.

Well said, Betty. All parents, and in turn their children, could profit by following in your mother's footsteps. Teachers face a formidable task as they teach the fundamentals young people must master to function successfully in today's society. They deserve all the help they can get, and parents are a prime source of that help.

It would be money well spent were President Bush to divert much of the increase in his education budget to finance programs: first to cultivate within the ranks of the nation's parents an appreciation for the value of a good education and the requisite schooling, in the instructional sense, required to obtain it; and second, a program designed to assist those parents with methods to go about instilling in their offspring a desire for learning, through preparation, such as Betty's mother did, and to go about performing their part as pupils in the teaching/learning process when in school. Public libraries are still open, just as they were for Betty and her mother. An untapped resource to assist with such parental programs is the business workplace, where initial exploratory efforts have shown promise. The incessant political/media litany calling for more money, smaller classrooms and national and state tests as the answer to improved education is glaringly bereft of fundamentals to improve the teaching/learning process discussed throughout this book.

Why are people opposed to teaching fundamental skills in subject areas such as reading and mathematics? One can only hope that it's for a better reason than many of us can give for our failure to read and use the assembly directions accompanying new purchases, such as a child's bicycle. In the case of many teachers, it's a function of inadequate training and questionable state certification standards. Then, when teachers are confronted with the realities of the classroom, some of them look to an established textbook program for help, but unfortunately others do not, and we hear and read about the consequences almost daily. So long as the publishers do their job well, the textbook is invaluable; but what happens when they don't do their job well? Reading supervisor Wanda Lister gets to the point.

WL: Moving into the sixties, we had basal readers. In the mid-eighties we switched to strictly whole language—the strong emphasis was in literature. I think the trade book publishing people kind of took over the reading. But prior to that time, it was the basal with the directions to the teachers.

Skipping over the structured approach made it simple to ignore that. And that really is troubling to me. And I think that we've lost a whole generation of readers.

Let me speak to what we have been using since the mid-eighties in California when we went strictly to literature and skills took a backseat. Teachers don't know what all the pieces that go into teaching reading are. It is a very complicated mental process that we do. We gave them the beautiful literature, and we all know that there are certain children that will almost learn to read by themselves. You probably learned to read by yourself. I know I did pretty much, because we were taught the look-see-say method of reading, and yet we somehow figured out a process of decoding words. We didn't know what we were doing. We weren't taught the phonics, so called. But we internalized it and were able to figure it out. But going back to the fifties probably, when we first started, or I first started teaching, we had the teachers' manuals. I was pretty conscientious and I followed the manual. But I know I had colleagues that just had the kids read the story.

Following that switch to literature- or whole language-based reading, the California reading scores dropped sharply. A long-held positive regard for the state adoption practice has suffered in recent years as a few such states have set off on a course of their own choosing, ignoring what research and experience have proven, therefore ending up with unwanted results. Here we see a state adoption state's call for whole language at the expense of skills and some publishers' willingness to deliver that as a prime example of such action. Then, in light of the falling test scores, there followed a reactionary public hue and cry for a phonics-centered program.

Tragically, various publishers turned their backs on their existing proven basal programs in pursuit of that California business. It doesn't require perceptive analysis to recognize what was happening to the existing leadership role in the publisher/state adoption relationship as authorities in a single state determined what they wanted, and the publishers diluted the fundamentals of earlier proven programs to meet the state's whole language specifications. Only a few years later, in the face of near-lowest-in-the-nation reading achievement scores, the state rejected the whole language approach and released new state specifications diametrically opposed to those of whole language. My view of the value of state adoptions has been challenged in recent years by such actions. Now we are seeing the emergence of questionable adoption state influence on the textbook publishing industry, and education for that matter. The age of commodity-based publishing seemingly is upon us. It appears as of this writing that it will remain with us into the future.

Former Dallas Office manager, Mike Shaw, describes another change, which, it should be noted, goes far beyond the traditional teaching/learning component of courses in reading and mathematics. Matters of race, national origin, scientific theory, and many other interests are also part of the adoption process and, in turn, textbook publishing.

HTM: Mike, you were very much on the hot seat here in Texas, given the size of the Texas market and, of course, adoption procedures.

MS: Yes. But only Texas managed to get on television, given the tendency for certain individuals to get themselves onto prime-time national TV.

HTM: You're referring to the Gablers, of course, that husband-and-wife team who were very vocal about their view of what should and should not be in Texas textbooks. They got lots of TV exposure.

MS: Yes. I really think that the Gablers, given the way they affected education, are way down the list in terms of the people who eventually took advantage of that stage and became part of this whole Texas textbook adoption process as it evolved into the eighties. And because of that, it will never again be what it was in the eighties. Because then it was an ironclad open-shut case of you either met Texas standards and you got on the list or, if you did not, you got kicked off. The Gablers took advantage of the adoption process, but others also took advantage of it. And, you know, Hal, they probably helped publishers in the long term. You will recall that I made that very point to you before, that the minority groups eventually found their way to that stage and said, "Look, we need to be better represented." I think Houghton Mifflin led the way in terms of listening to the minorities. And the women, in particular, found their way.

You see, the Gablers got all that sensational TV exposure. Then the others found their way onto that stage, and they made their points. But then they found out that, as opposed to the Gablers, they could work through the process with publishers.

It should be made clear that when Mike says minority groups demanded they should be better represented, we are no longer discussing basic reading and arithmetic skills. Prime-time television news, seeking the sensational without burdening itself with the rest of the story, played up the Gabler protests about evolution and other sensitive topics. In turn, their national audience formed opinions, even a mind-set, about Texas education and textbooks, largely without knowing which textbooks were adopted or what was in them. The sanctimoniousness that surfaced obscured the real task before Texas educators and the publishers alike.

MS: Now the real difference in Texas that made it the state adoption magnet is the $6 billion Permanent School Fund that was set up back in the forties with oil. Because of Texas's unique position, the land the state owned and the oil that was on that land meant that the oil monies went into what was called the Permanent School Fund.

And with the interest from that fund, they're able to dedicate monies to the textbook program. As a result of having that money, Texas came in and said, "Well, instead of sending money to the schools, let's just make sure that there's a chicken in every pot."

Texas made the decision to say, "We are going to be the customer, so if we're going to have a reading adoption, we'll have a list of five programs that we approve, and then we'll send that list out there to the schools. They will let us know which one they want; we'll buy a book for every kid." So that was the real difference.

HTM: A real difference is correct. And it made Texas a magnet, as you point out. It also meant that their Curriculum Committees could influence publishers to publish things their way.

MS: Right.

HTM: I don't think many people in the U.S. are aware of this fund. Does it exist to this day?

MS: Yes, it exists to this day. It was the Hale-Aiken Law, enacted back in the 1940s, and it was considered a visionary kind of law that was set up at the time, because we had some legislators who thought of the future. And you know, they could have easily sat back and missed that money. But they set it up so that they dedicated the oil revenues coming from Texas-owned land that they won as a result of the war with Mexico. They dedicated the funds to come out of this asset to the schools, both K–12 and higher education. And out of this fund, to this day, they're paying the base salaries for teachers in public schools and colleges in Texas. And one slice of the Permanent School Fund is what they call the "Textbook Fund." And that's basically operating off of the interest from that Permanent School Fund, which is now about $6 billion.

HTM: And the interest is used to buy books or …

MS: To buy books and …

HTM: Get the best teachers.

MS: Yes. To buy books and to pay the base salaries of teachers. Texas is able to say, "If we need 30,000 textbooks per grade, we'll buy 'em. Then we'll distribute them to the schools." And that ability was great. I mean it has made sure that every kid gets a book, rather than depending on some superintendent who would prefer to buy footballs in a particular year. It really made sure the kids got textbooks.

But the other part of this story is that suddenly, in the mid-seventies, this arrangement got twisted around and started down the path we were talking about earlier. They changed; they made a revision. It was in 1972, and there was one little innocuous sentence in the education bill that went through, Hal, that said (which is what all of us would want): "If we're going to have a Permanent School Fund and we're going to provide materials, we want to make sure that all of the schools maintain a defined curriculum." You and I would agree with that in a heartbeat.

HTM: Sure.

MS: I mean everything sounds fine, but from that innocuous sentence has grown a pile of curriculum guides. The bureaucrats said, "Well now, if you're going to ask us to have a defined curriculum, then we have to set up the rules." So it went from that innocuous sentence, where schools could have a choice of picking a unique program from Houghton Mifflin or a unique program from another publisher. Formerly, if it's math, let's say, they could decide, "Look, I don't want to teach fractions until the fifth grade," where another school says, "Heck, no! We want them teaching fractions in the third grade." A school system could do what works for them. But now that is gone. The bureaucrats said, "If we're going to have to manage this thing, we need curriculum guides." Starting in about '72, the state did start developing curriculum guides.

   The state purchases for all of the curriculum areas—and that was the genesis where it all started downhill. Then if the publishers didn't meet those curriculum guides, well, you can see easily what happened. Then the protesters grabbed onto that process. And they said, "Ah! So you're writing curriculum guides," and they got involved in that. And they'd beat publishers over the head if they didn't dot every "i" and meet every little minor item. Now, where do you introduce division, how do you teach the vowel sounds became priority business. You have educators worried about minute things rather than overseeing the system, so that when the pupils exit sixth grade they have the skills they need to go on.

HTM: It hampered innovation from the author/publisher quarters. The question now became: could publishers meet all of the Texas demands and concurrently not merely retain, but include, what ongoing research and use proved useful in the teaching/learning process?

MS: That's it exactly. Rather than pulling giants in the field of teaching reading together, like Paul McKee and other respected authors of similar stature, they decided instead they'd have some second and third grade teachers sitting down writing curriculum. In the next year or two they'd be having publishers publish to that.

HTM: In the California interviews this development comes up repeatedly. The California educators I interviewed speak of the days when the publishers' authors and editors developed the elementary school programs. The publishers used leading academics who were teaching and conducting research in the universities, colleges, and, yes, in the schools. Authors worked with skilled editors over a number of years, seeking always to improve their publications. They would test their programs, revise, test. These author groups were dedicated to developing the best; it was a major part of their professional careers.

MS: Oh, absolutely, yes.

HTM: Now it's quite the other way around, in that a state will call in some people for a year from various classrooms to write the curriculum. The publishers then publish for that curriculum, and then six or seven years later, the publisher finds out at the time of the next adoption that a new group threw out the old curriculum and wrote a new one.

MS: That's right.

HTM: And that's a major change from what I experienced on the only occasion I met with a Texas adoption committee, when I was a test editor in the 1950s. The members of that committee were all of high caliber. I presented our tests, and they asked informed questions. They were professional people who had been trained in testing.

Permit me to stray a bit. Fay Brown was then the manager of the Dallas office. He had requested that I come to Austin and present the Iowa Tests of Basic Skills and the Lorge-Thorndike Intelligence Tests. At the appointed hour, Fay and I went before the adoption committee and I presented the two tests. We left the meeting but, as was the practice, stood by in case the committee had any follow-up questions, and sure enough they did. Fay and I went back before the committee a second time. They asked more questions about the Lorge-Thorndike Test, the authorship, which was well-known and respected, but the tests were recently published and therefore not well-known. In due course, the committee head asked me where in Texas the tests were already used. This was a fair question, for Texas had never before held statewide test adoptions. I responded that I was in Austin from Boston test editorial, so I would turn to Mr. Brown for an answer to the question. The chairman then said, "Well, Fay (everybody in Texas either knew Fay or of him), where are the Lorge-Thorndike Tests used?" And Fay answered, "All over the place." To which the chairman responded, "Name one." Fay, in his best Southern style, exclaimed, "By God, you've got me there!"

The committee members roared with laughter. The tests were adopted on their merits. Now, only Fay could pull that exchange off. Fay knew the tests enjoyed no Texas adoptions and the committee members knew it too. The episode was representative of the professional tenor of the times, with its mix of the participants knowing what they were about as they evaluated and selected publications for adoptions, but doing it with a mix of humor and class. The committee was in fact a class act, but based on what you're telling me now, Mike, there is a marked change afoot, and one not necessarily for the best.

The rise of the tailor-made state-based curriculum generated forces of change that penetrated to the core of the prevailing norm under which textbooks were published for a nationwide school market. Meeting the Texas specifications for teaching such subjects as reading and mathematics changed the relationship between the Texas public school educators' and the publishers' author/editor-developed text-books. Textbooks solely for Texas specs are not likely to meet those developed in California and, almost certainly, not elsewhere in the nation's schools. Yet in actuality, what the open-territory schools get has long been much influenced by what a Texas or California demands.

The publishers' shift to a commodity-based culture represents a serious challenge to the integrity and quality of textbooks published by the major houses that choose to go that route, and fortunately not all publishers have done so. The silver lining here may well be that state calls for customized textbooks will open the way for the emergence of new start-up niche publishers, capable of finding unique, productive ways of enhancing the teaching/learning process while meeting the restrictive specifications of states, eventually large city school systems, and others, for that matter.

This creeping erosion in the former relationship between the states and textbook publishers has been accompanied by the conglomerization of the publishing industry. At a time when states like California and Texas are demanding customized textbooks, thereby diluting the publisher's one-text-for-all-states practice, the conglomerates are seeking homogenized operations through focus groups and marketing ploys, including extensive give-aways, workforce economies through outsourcing, and author royalty reduction through in-house development. These measures fall short of an innovative leadership role capable of producing new textbook programs deserving to be sought after by educators. Pursuing the costly and time-consuming procedure of finding authors capable of rendering the complex simple, conducting research, and creating works based on their own genius and experience is fundamental to textbook publishing leadership. Recently, the David and Lucile Packard Foundation financed a review of middle school physical science texts and found them full of errors and without the contribution of authoritative authors. Publishing inferior, error-laden textbooks, is an unconscionable act. Houghton language arts consultant, Jean Muller, and California educator, Betty Hansen, address the result as seen from the trenches.

JM: Hal, I wonder if I might just introduce another topic. I'd be interested in hearing what Betty has to say about it. You're here in a very large district (Fresno, California). You do state adoptions. You spend a lot of money on the adoptions that you make. How do you feel about a publisher developing a program just for your state, based on your framework?

BH: Well, I realize the publishers have to look at the bottom line too, and when you figure that California is about twelve percent of the nation's school enrollment, and by the time you get a text in California, you've got a pretty good foothold. It seems to me that it would be foolish for a publisher to totally disregard a state like California and ignore us if they're hoping to make some money.

JM: How do you feel about a publisher developing a program strictly for California, based on your framework?

BH: I suppose that is the epitome of looking at the bucks, you know. Well, if that's what's so important, I understand why they're doing it, but it seems to me the publishers are sacrificing something in terms of their integrity, their beliefs, and what they know about how it ought to be. Because if you pander to—and I'm going to use that term rather than cater—this state that wants to do this particular thing this year in this adoption, then you can be way out there in other places. So on the one hand, it could be financially productive for one time maybe. But you've sold your soul, so to speak, insofar as the other forty-nine states. I can't look at it from the publishers' point of view or from the person who is sort of in the middle of it. I think it's a very difficult decision that a publishing company has to make. And I can understand those who would make that decision, but I would hope that they wouldn't, that they would look to a higher purpose.

California state textbook adoptions are one of a kind. Dr. Francis Laufenberg, formerly superintendent of schools in Long

Beach, California, and president of the California State Board of Education, graciously agreed to be interviewed. I have always admired the openness of California.

Lauf, now retired, is a superb educator. He and I have known each other for a number of years, and being well informed about my project, he came prepared to discuss the history of textbooks in California. The following interview reveals the importance the state had accorded textbooks, why and how it is a major force in determining textbook content, and how complex state adoptions can be. Space does not allow for the full history, but a few high points are in order.

FL: First of all, California was founded as a state in 1849 because of the Gold Rush, and the first constitution they adopted in 1849 provided for a system of common schools. This is one of the key things. A school was to be kept up and supported in every district at least three months in every year.

And secondly, the constitution provided for a superintendent of public instruction to be elected by the people.

But another thing it did was to set forth textbook responsibilities as well as provisions for teacher certification at both the county and local levels. And it provided that textbooks must be used for at least four years.

Moving the clock forward some 120 years, the story continues:

FL: In June of 1970, the constitution was amended once more to remove the requirement that state-adopted textbooks for elementary schools be in a uniform series. And it removed the provisions charging counties with the responsibility for the examination and certification of teachers, thus leaving it up to control by state law. That was taking away local powers and moving them to Sacramento.

It specifically provided that the State Board of Education shall adopt textbooks for use in grades 1 through 8 throughout the state, to be furnished without cost as provided by statute.

I will tell you about the Curriculum Commission, briefly, because the commission was so important to the textbooks.

Not only did we have this separate, so-called Department of Education, which consisted of all of the employees in that huge bureaucracy, but then we of course had the state superintendent himself. Then we had the State Board. But another big factor—and this is an important one to publishers—was the Curriculum Commission. It was kind of an entity of its own.

The charge of the Curriculum Commission was to study problems of the course of study in schools of the state and, upon request of the State Board of Education, recommend to the State Board the adoption of minimum standards for the course of study in the preschool, kindergarten, elementary, and secondary schools. Courses of study in the public schools were to conform to the minimum standards when adopted. And that's where they came up with the frameworks, so-called, that the publishers had to write to, or if they didn't write to them, then they are out of luck.

HTM: Right. Here we see not just control of the texts used in California, but also the implications of that action upon texts used on a national basis. That's when life gets difficult for textbook publishers.

FL: They also developed criteria for evaluating instruction and materials submitted for adoption, so that the materials adopted would adequately cover the subjects in the indicated grade or grades, and comply with the provisions of Article 3 and Chapter 1 of the Education Code. Such criteria were to be public information and be provided in written or printed form to any person requesting such information. And those were the criteria that the little subcommittees of real teachers used in evaluating everything.

The Curriculum Commission was to study and evaluate the instruction and materials submitted and recommend to the State Board instructional materials that it approved for adoption.

I asked Jerry Theise, manager of the Houghton Mifflin Palo Alto Office, how he functioned so successfully in the environment just described.

JT: My approach was to establish a list of about 200 key people whom I could see would very probably have a strong hand in whatever textbook programs were selected there. I had some excellent help, particularly from Glen Britton and Dick Glass, two of our representatives.

HTM: You know, when you tell about working with all of these people in California for one textbook series adoption, it probably is confusing to the outsider. You're talking about the commission, but you're also talking about all those others who voted.

JT: That's why I talked to roughly 200 key people.

HTM: You were contacting those people over the next couple of years, which starts to become quite a task. I know you were rarely home. Added to that, I suppose outsiders would be curious whether you'd walk in to see the educators with a whole book bag full of books. How did you get your message across to each of these people so that (a) they would know what you were selling; (b) why it was good; and (c) why they ought to vote for you and then keep them in line? That took a kind of salesmanship that goes far beyond the usual sales norm. Maybe you could tell a bit about how you really made your point and converted them to your cause.

JT: Well, there's a structure. You had the Curriculum Commission; you had to control the votes of the approximately fifteen members. But of course, each one is like the trunk of the tree, and the roots go down from there. You've got State Board members among the trunks' 200 or so key people. I would work them and their higher-ups. I always tried to have two people, one key sales representative and I, in contact with all the most important people.

These people could easily contact one of us if they needed something. The sales reps were assigned people lower down the hierarchy. We had had very good training courses on the content of the material and on the sales approaches. We were working a hell of a lot more than just 200 people, because we had a good field staff of reps and consultants out there. We covered the works.

For example, one of the real keys in getting the math adoption—with modern math coming in—it was obvious there would be some additional training needed for teachers. I promised the state that I would do a series of color films. I would do a manual; I would provide it free, do a number of sets of these films, and rotate them through the schools. Ernie Duncan, the author on the math program, did them and occasionally with somebody else.

That was a very important factor in gaining the adoption. Those films worked very well. But we promised the state a lot of things. They didn't cost us a lot of money, but they provided a service. I hired two top math supervisors, county math supervisors in the state, to write the manual for the films. Ellis Blevins, who later joined the Palo Alto Office, was one of them. We put this whole thing together at no great cost, and nobody else even tried to compete with that.

HTM: What you have told me was merely the first part of the adoption. You won the adoption, but now you've got to come through on everything from having adequate inventory, shipping capabilities, and consulting services for the teachers in the schools after they start using the program. You just opened Pandora's box when you got the adoption.

JT: Well, you had different layers of responsibility, the warehouse and the supporting staff of the warehouse. We had correspondents who, by that time, all had their own desktop computers. We had given up on the major computers as our contact to the outside. That layer could really deal pretty well with stock, stock delivery. We had another layer of service, our consultants.

I set myself up to maintain my contacts with those key people, the most key of whom were the same ones I had worked with on that first math adoption. There was some turnover on Curriculum Commissions and on the State Board, but the contacts often got passed along through established friendships to the new ones coming on.

I was always impressed by the amount of attention California superintendents gave to textbook publishers. I recall to this day when Glen Britton, a California sales supervisor, called my office in Boston and said, "Hal, I really wish you would come out and talk with the school superintendents in the Los Angeles area. Would you do that?" And he set up a morning meeting followed by lunch. As I recall, about twelve superintendents from the Los Angeles area were in attendance. I sat with them all morning discussing what they wanted and what we publishers were trying to do. School people like Betty Hansen, Wanda Lister, Francis Laufenberg, and those superintendents are dedicated educators, and I respected each and every one of them.

Only a few years ago, over lunch in Boston, while discussing public school education with the president of a leading teachers' training college and several prestigious authors of books about education, each of whom I respect and admire, I suggested that the Northeast public schools constitute a somewhat isolated educational enclave.

As I spoke, I had in mind the adoption states and their aggressive activities, about which so much has just been written. I was, in essence, comparing the Northeast's influence with that of North Carolina, Texas, California, and the other state adoption states on the formulation of education standards, curriculum, tests, and importantly, textbooks. I soon realized that those around the table were in agreement with my statement, but apparently having assumed I was praising the enclave's activities, which in fact I was not.

I have since thought about that incident numerous times. The 1635 objectives of the Boston Latin School, located relatively near our luncheon spot, and the nineteenth-century objective of the adoption states were one and the same: to educate the nation's young people through public education. Implementation of that objective, over time, followed differing routes. The established reputation for educational excellence of today's Boston Latin School, though not fully representative of all the enclave's schools, reflects the Northeast's long-held intellectual independence. Textbooks, for example, are not adopted statewide and often not even school system-wide. I recall, back in my sales days, visiting each algebra teacher in a large high school where each teacher used a different book. Elementary school teachers were prone to use different math and reading texts from classroom to classroom or even within their own classroom. Such practices stand in sharp contrast to those found in the adoption states.

Stated bluntly, the adoption states were organized, as illustrated early in this chapter. Those states set the direction of public school education. Curriculum fragmentation across the nation is one outcome of that movement. The question then arises as to the qualifications of those appointed to the committees charged with creating courses of study and then measuring the outcome. It is too early in this period of change to determine the outcome. That said, it is worthwhile knowing more about the players.

A culture of mutual respect existed between many leaders in education and publishing. I've long since lost count of the senior educators, as represented by Laufenberg and Phillips, I've met and dealt with, but it is a substantial number. Frankly, I found the vast majority of them to be a class act. The following remarks by Craig Phillips make that point.

ACP: Now the other thing, as state superintendent of North Carolina, I made more big-time friends, people who I got to know through all of the things that happened, than I could possibly ever have done any other way. And during that time, I was in every chief state school officer's backyard at least once, and the wives got together; and that didn't have anything to do with any of this stuff, except that that's what makes good things happen.

RSC: I was just thinking about when Hal talked to me about this particular interview, and he asked if he could come meet with a person who could represent the Southeast, you know, state adoption states, pretty much like Laufenberg did in California. I called some people and concluded that you would be the best person to really represent what Hal is looking for in the state adoption states.

ACP: Well, you're very kind, and I'm not sure I deserve that, but if we made an impact, we made it because we had great folks in this state. We had reasonable folks, and this is why we were able to deal with you textbook publishers.

Education is a lifelong process, whereas *schooling* occurs during only part of our lifespan. How responsibly society discharges its schooling, which requires only a fraction of a total lifespan, establishes a society's education norm. The foundation years—actually the first three years of the schooling experience—are key to the success of all that comes later.

Parents who responsibly prepare their children for school, *responsibly trained* and *experienced* teachers who know what to do with the children when they get them, and proven instructional materials that responsibly address the teaching/learning process are the key ingredients to a successful beginning in one's schooling.

The state textbook adoption process did much to forge public schools into meaningful entities. They are the pacesetters for the curriculum found in today's public schools. They wield a big stick in the makeup of our textbooks. Given that influence, today's textbook publishers, in large part owned by foreign conglomerates, must conform to American educational standards. The educators whose comments appear in this chapter, only a few of the total number interviewed, amply attest to their know-how and dedication to education. There are others coming along just like them who deserve a chance to prove themselves. Toward that end and in the best interest of schooling itself, we all would be well served if the self-interested and special-cause "do wellers" backed off.

We have discussed the various rewards and warts of the state textbook adoption process. From the outset there has been a clear public intent to educate our kids, and nowhere more so than in the state adoption states. Limited financial, transportation, and educator resources existed, yet the citizenry provided school buildings, teachers, and textbooks, often with a measure of personal financial sacrifice.

The diverse makeup of our mushrooming, ever-changing population posed a unique challenge to providing, in the sense of instruction and training, school for all of their kids. Public schools were developed to serve the vast geographical reaches encompassing different economies, from farming to manufacturing, and a coast-to-coast state adoption-based swath resulted. The powerful, pervasive influence of those states on publishers' textbooks and the nation's entire public school curriculum is rarely recognized elsewhere in the nation. The public schools must take in all comers and educate them in an increasingly complex environment created by such forces as technology and society's changing customs and usages, which often become a given in our activist culture.

From the outset of the state adoption movement, a state's call for the listing of textbooks prompted immediate action among textbook publishers. The publishers responded for many decades with author-created submissions in numbers far exceeding the lists' call for the number of different texts to be adopted. In recent years, however, an odd twist in the relationship between the large adoption states, primarily, and the textbook publishers has developed. Conglomerization, much of it foreign-based, has gobbled up textbook publishers and reduced opportunities for author-based textbooks to proliferate. As a result, there are few truly author-created textbooks published for the public schools at the same time that more, not fewer, different, unique, and meaningful approaches to the teaching/learning process are urgently needed in the schools for our diverse population.

An informed understanding of the basic schooling problems facing educators appears to be outside the comprehension of the public schools' critics. There is no one-size-fits-all solution to the public schools' charge to educate all of our children. The never-ending litany claiming improved education results from increased financial support and the synergies of conglomerization rings hollow in the face of continuing discontent. What is needed are informed and insightful schooling tools for improving the teaching/learning process and teachers trained to know the importance and use of them. Granted, education must be funded, and in large measure it is. However, what goes on within the classroom matters most. Much of what's offered by critics reminds one of the old saying that such talk is tantamount to washing one's feet with one's socks on.

The fundamental skills requisite to a basic education, particularly at the elementary school level, where the school process matters most, are not negotiable. There is no royal road to learning. The skills that everyone, without exception, must master to read with meaning, to do mathematics with comprehension, to speak and write coherently, and to be a productive person in our society are known. Hard work as their achievement may require, those fundamentals must be mastered by everyone going through the schooling process. The basics are known and how to teach those basics is known, as the authors, editors, and educators make clear throughout this book.

Textbooks written by proven authors and edited by trained editors are a given if we are to ensure quality in the nation's public schools. We cannot stand still in our effort to improve our schools, for we are not living in a static society. Therefore, new ways to affect schools must be developed into the future, just as in the past.

The state adoption states are where the aggressive action is and has been. They have been influential and effective catalysts for the textbook publishing industry. When publishers and educators cooperate, the result is an alliance of state curriculum committees, authors, editors, researchers, and teachers dedicated to honing the schooling process, including textbooks, over years of classroom use and revision.

The state adoption states appear to be the prime catalyst influencing the teaching/learning process. But with the emergence of numerous start-up, author-based, entrepreneurial textbook publishing houses, it is hoped that publishers will once again take a leadership role in the process.

CHAPTER 5

What Was It Like to Revise a Reading Program?

A Group Discussion

On June 16, 2001, I invited to my home a group of Houghton people who had been much involved with the Reading for Meaning program that later became the Houghton Mifflin Reading Series. The group included William Durr, long-term lead author of the program; Nancy Sargent, lead editor of reading for many years; John Ridley, head of the reading department; and Carol Case, director of advertising in the School Division. All of us had known and worked with Paul McKee, the author whose ideas inspired Houghton's enormous success in reading, and all of us were grateful to have been enriched by that experience.

It is a tribute to the author-centered philosophy of Houghton Mifflin that when Paul retired, Bill Durr was able to pick up where he left off. Bill had the help of Houghton people, like us and many others, who were willing to follow him while providing him with what we had learned and inherited from Paul. The following is an edited version of the entire discussion.

HTM: We decided to launch the '71 revision of the Houghton Mifflin Reading Series. How did we go about doing that?

NS: I was at the company when the editors were revising the series for the '66 edition. Then it came time for the '71 edition, and, Bill, you were there, and Paul McKee was beginning to end his career. We were trying to think of ways to move Houghton Mifflin forward, to do some things that would be educationally sound and yet would be innovative. What kinds of things would you take from a core of material that was working—*a basic philosophy that was working*—and turn it into something that would move us forward?

We looked at a program by Bill Martin called Sounds of Literature, published by Holt, and we were looking around at other things and looking at what we had. We began to have this idea of putting something together that looked more like stories and was less stiffly written. We were looking for the first time at trying to move out, without dumping vocabulary. We wanted it to be more kid-friendly and more teacher-friendly. It just seemed like basal publishing was over here, and storybooks were over there. We had sound, good literature, but it was heavily adapted.

HTM: Bill, a few years ago, we met at your house in Lansing, Michigan, and I asked you what was it like to be the lead author of a multimillion-dollar textbook reading series, and you spoke about not trying to reinvent the wheel, but instead to do additional things.

WD: The day before yesterday, before I left Lansing, I got out the '66 edition of the readers and the '71 edition at the same levels and compared them. And the thing that just hit me was something that the editors were responsible for—and that was the complete change of format in those materials. The readers prior to the '71 edition looked so dull, no color in the teachers' editions and no white space on the page. And Nancy and her people absolutely changed that. The new '71—thirty years ago!—are just beautiful. They're colorful; there was lots of space, lots of interesting things for the kids to do in them.

I thought that was one of the most dramatic changes in the material. There were lots of little things in the beginning, but the overall look of the program was drastically better in the '71 edition.

NS: We had the benefit too of involving a lot more art and design. Before, we would just have these long sessions where we'd sit around forever and talk about where Jack and Janet were standing and where the trees were. But it somehow didn't relate a lot to what kids would find exciting. We were trying to find a way that there would be some excitement. So, based on what we saw in the Sounds of Literature, which wasn't even a basal program, we began to think creatively.

We chatted with Bill. I remember talking with coauthor Lucile Harrison, who thought it was a terrible idea, because she liked the way it was and she thought we could mess it up. Bill was very supportive and Paul McKee was supportive but he was always wondering if we might make it fancy, but not a very fine reading product. And I think keeping a program's integrity is the overriding job of the author, because I think editors and designers could go wacko. But somehow or other, if you can hold the bottom line of making whatever it is work and do the job and also do some pretty creative things, then you have a different kind of publication.

HTM: Please describe the innovations to me and how they related to the basic thrust of the series. There are two elements that we are looking at here. There is the all-important method of unlocking (decoding) new words and reading independently. And then there are the innovations you're describing, Nancy— better ways to teach through improved content and design. But it was crucial that the integrity of the program's word-analysis skills be retained throughout all of this, was it not? Certainly, retention of the word-attack skills was crucial in the thinking of the sales force.

WD: The basic context/letter-sound association was still there, exactly the same, but there were alterations in it. For example, Paul always had apoplexy if you'd talk about putting vowels down any lower in the developmental sequence of the series than he wanted them to go. We looked to the research, and we found that the kids were not bothered by being introduced to vowels earlier. And so, in the '71 program, in terms of the word-analysis strategy, vowels were moved down to lower grade levels because it just seemed like the thing to do. I thought it would help the little guys.

So most of the changes are very minor ones like that, but minor changes for the benefit of the child that research supported and that the editors and authors agreed were desirable for the kids.

HTM: The Dallas Office reading consultant, Dolores Rowe, recalls going through a Texas state adoption campaign with all of its travel. Dolores, the sales representative, and you, Bill Durr, would meet with the teachers' groups, then get into the car to travel to the next stop; Dolores would ask if somebody else wanted to drive. No one did. And she'd say, "Then I'd drive, and Bill would be in the backseat continuing reading through children's stories that had to be read for possible inclusion in the revision. Bill would then send his selections to editorial, letting them know which stories would fit into the basic teaching/learning process of the series." Certain stories were appropriate, certain others were not, and, Bill, I don't know all of what you were looking for, but you knew, and you spent hours doing that job.

WD: Yes, I don't know how they did that before. Nancy would know. But it seemed to me that the editors had worked out an extremely good approach for selecting content, because everybody was involved. Everybody that was in the construction of the program was involved and reacting to every single selection, reacting to whether it was appropriate to the interest level of the kids, whether it was appropriate for the reading level of the kids, and whether it was quality literature. And the editor would send stacks of those stories out, and everybody involved would react to them; that was taken into account before the final selection was made.

NS: And that process is the strength of the program—that so much goes into the review of which stories are in those anthologies. That they're not just randomly placed there—they have a purpose. There's some integral thing that's being dealt with there, whether it's some kind of a sound skill needed to identify a new word, or a comprehension skill, or a study thing. You just can't present this lovely little story, then just say we're going to think about cause and effect. So that's one of the strong features of the program.

In '71, we brought Jean LePere, a literature expert, in, and she sat with us while we wrote the pre-primers. She wasn't there every minute, because she had to teach, but she would come in time after time while this group wrote those pre-primers to a controlled vocabulary that had to match the skills sequence. And she had a wonderful way of saying, "No, it doesn't feel like that," until we would get it to the right place.

WD: That controlled vocabulary, Nancy, reminds me about the vocabulary study that Houghton Mifflin commissioned that was quite unique in putting together the pre-primers, remember?

Because they did a fabulous study in which teachers and librarians were asked what books children liked to read on their own, and then these were winnowed down in various ways. And the ones that were left were analyzed; the vocabulary was counted to determine what words were most essential in teaching children. This was unique. It was little things, that people may not have even been aware of, that helped children become better readers more quickly.

NS: There were several studies. One study we did with Jean LePere and people in the office. We set up a whole host of librarians who became a resource for the study. And then a word study of the high-frequency words was done at Brown University by a Professor Kucera. And we had, through the basis of that study, a way to look at frequency of vocabulary in a much more profound way than we had done it before.

JR: It's like part of when you buy a house. Your first impression and why you buy it: maybe you're thinking of buying a place to live in without necessarily knowing what really went into it, what makes it stand, what makes it be sturdy. It's those bricks, like the vocabulary study, that the end user wouldn't necessarily know, but the benefits are basic.

HTM: John, you're hitting on a key point that must be made when selling a reading series to educators, parents, and the press. It's the hidden structure that makes a series work. If you don't have those fundamentals built into the series, then the pupils are less likely to become effective readers. If the teachers do not make use of those learning tools, then the school district fails to get a proper return on their investment. You can bring in the company's reading consultants; you can bring in the editors or even an author, all to little avail if the classroom activity excludes attention to those bricks. The company would not have spent the millions of dollars it spent on consultants over the years if it hadn't been amply clear to us that teachers who effectively implemented those fundamentals got results. And so that's part of the struggle.

Many reading programs published concurrently with Reading for Meaning came up over the horizon, sometimes with a big splash, and a few years later you couldn't find them. What happened? What was the difference?

NS: Up to then, people had been going along, doing much the same thing. It was a big change, for example, to conduct a word study with librarians, that you would basically tamper with what was held as sacred, particularly in terms of early basal reading. That you would adjust the word load, that you would categorize words differently; the art and design was very different. But the idea was that you could walk in and do that. I think the only way we felt that we could do it was based on the fact that we had begun to do it in '66.

At that particular time, Houghton Mifflin was taking steps to be more innovative, and a lot of other publishers were, up to then, following everybody else. But you had to support it a lot with pretty sound background, or our own field people wouldn't sell it. We had fewer problems with customers than with our own field force—who came to believe so firmly in Reading for Meaning. You've got to sell to your own people first, and that's why a lot of this work was done.

HTM: An unusual relationship within the company was the author/sales representative/consultant relationship. Bill, I would be interested if you would speak to it. There were many, many salespeople who had great working relationships, as well as friendships, with our authors.

They all knew Bill Durr. They all talked with Bill Durr over dinner and in the car traveling from place to place. They felt that they were not just privy to what you stood for, Bill, but also what was in your books, and that they were part of your program, because they made suggestions. They didn't feel that they were only salespeople.

WD: Oh yes. In my opinion, this is a result of the quality of the sales force. I mean, those were good people, you know? And it was very easy to interact with them, and they were very quick to ask questions about the program. They really would. Sometimes quite specific: "Why did you do this at level four?" Because they wanted to know. As you said, they had feedback into the program, and they were married to the program.

CC: Going back to the question of moving the vowels down, one of the comments that Hal Donelson, the Nebraska salesman, made was that after '71, the principles of *Getting Ready to Read*—that is, the consonant letter-sound association in context—was not carried on up into the study skills. That was his perception.

Getting Ready to Read was always the foundation of the program. You started out with that. You got used to the idea of using context and consonant letter-sound association, and then you continued using that technique in the later grades. But Hal Donelson felt that you didn't carry that on as strongly as in the past.

NS: Well, in order to have a program based on research and innovation, some new things had to be moved into the program. Then, as new things started to move in, there was sometimes a sense of others being diluted. The consonant letter-sound association in context was a very firm foundation that went through anything that had to do with decoding familiar words. And then there was a point in the third grade when we made a transition from word study to using other skills. It was a very thoughtful passage that was carried on. It was less obvious than it was when I started to teach, when the only thing you saw in the teachers' guide was the decoding side of instruction.

WD: Our belief was that you begin with single-consonant letter-sound associations and context, and that this will work only with words that are known to the child orally. It won't help you decode a word or understand a word that is not in your meaning vocabulary. But you need to progress from that, and you get to the stage where you use phonograms—for example, *et.* Not just a single letter as a basis for decoding words that are in your meaning vocabulary. You get to a place where you also use syllables as a basis for decoding words that are not in your oral meaning vocabulary. And so you have to teach how to get meaning by using meanings for word parts, or get words from the dictionary.

So it wasn't that we abandoned decoding; we built on it and went forward from it to higher and higher skills in terms of getting words, dealing with words. But of course study skills—this was always, in my opinion, the part of Paul McKee's textbook that was unique: the importance of study skills. And that was in the program. The direct teaching of study skills. And it progressed when it was necessary for the kids to begin to study material.

JR: I remember sessions when Bill and Nancy, in particular, would go over the scope and sequence charts. There would be endless discussion about the refinements of those fundamentals until you got all the details right. That really had to happen, for it would be very easy to gloss over the key items. You two had some real discussions about the placement of some of those skills. You hammered it out in very careful discussion.

NS: That was a very thoughtful way of doing our job, as opposed to some of the things that happen where you just look at a big list of items, and then just sort of slot them into different places. The approach where you would say, "We start here, and then put the structure together," was necessary. It was a very complex system requiring careful thought when you pulled something down, or you moved something around, or you added something in. And all the way along, there was always the question of: why would you put it here? Why would you put it there? But in a way, I'm not at all sure that today in publishing, that kind of thoughtful discussion goes on, in terms of where things should be placed.

It's invaluable to revising that you teach editorial people how to become reading experts so that they develop a firm knowledge of reading instruction. It's critical to the success of the reading series that they don't feel, "I just work on this kind of book, and I can put together a teachers' book for third grade, but don't ask me what happens in the fourth grade." Or, "I'm in the fourth grade, but don't ask me what happens in kindergarten;

I have no idea." In our system, you were so much involved in these conversations with authors and research that you really learned a big piece of teaching children to read.

Whereas in recent editorial consulting work, I have discovered that management and editors don't believe you have to have that knowledge in a company, that all of editorial does not need that kind of expertise.

WD: Nancy just made the point that you don't just throw something in because you've got space for it. Teaching how to use a dictionary is a perfect example of how you have to use a sequence of steps. You don't introduce a whole dictionary to a child at any level. You teach him how to use a dictionary to get a single word meaning, how to use a dictionary to get multiple word meanings, how to use a dictionary to get pronunciation. And those all have to build on each other.

CC: Nancy you used the word *system,* which made my ears perk up because I think "system" equals the "teaching/learning process." The point you're making is that everyone in reading editorial knew the system; therefore, it didn't matter whether you were talking about the sixth grade or first grade because it was still the same system.

NS: When you'd reach the level of having impact on the book itself, you had to have this sort of knowledge so integrated. When you looked at something, you had some of the same expertise as the authors. Otherwise, editors just edit out things. I worked on the '66 edition with Paul McKee. And I came out of teaching the first grade, and I thought I was brilliant. And I would cross out things. Then I would send it to Paul, who would write, "No, Nancy," and he'd just put the whole thing back in, or "No, leave it in, because ..." There would be these thoughtful notes. I don't think that happens now. It's known by a few people, but it's not known by many.

HTM: Nancy, your comments bring to mind the present-day California-based problem that exists for the publishers of elementary school textbook series. The Curriculum Commission unloads the wagon, covering all the components to be taught, but not necessarily giving them the careful sequential placement to which you refer. It's not dissimilar from the teacher we have all encountered who proudly proclaims, "I use a lot of different things, and isn't this wonderful? I don't want to be a captive of one program."

They have a disregard for, or perhaps an unawareness of, the fact that sequential development of skills is important, so they lose that advantage. Now reportedly you have people sitting on educational standards or Curriculum Committees determining that we'll put into our specs this skill or that skill, but they are not looking at them as a sequential assemblage that you weave into the process of development.

JR: A curriculum is, in some respects, not unlike a play, where the playwright has in mind an end result of what's to be accomplished onstage, now called the reading series. But it has to be crafted well enough that the actors are able to interpret what the playwright wrote, and the audience understands, through the actors, what it was all about. The analogy there is, the authors and editors craft a play. The teachers have to be the interpreters of it. And the kids only get what it was that you, as an author, intended, based on how well you were able to put that on the page.

I think where the theater analogy falls apart is that the publisher doesn't mean it as a literal script. But basically, the teacher comes to understand the philosophy of the program by the way in which it is expressed. And so you get patterns of understanding, and you can then communicate that in how you work with the youngsters.

NS: Everyone would say, "We do the best job of teaching kids to read." But I think there was a mind-set that every single skill must go into having a child become a motivated reader and master enough required skills so they can do the job. There was, however, less attention, initially in our program, paid to a lot of peripheral activities that the teacher could do, because the dilemma we saw in the classroom was that the teachers were not aware of the *basic* ingredients that build a reader.

What you had better be doing—and I think you better be doing it now as well—is putting the essential pieces down, so that someone can walk through the program and deliver what's critical in a way that is imaginative, and not just "thrown in." You could, for example, talk about the word *mosaic,* you know, and get way off the target. But I think if you're a good teacher, you don't get off the target.

My niece, Tanya—her teaching job was in Brockton, Massachusetts—and she had second graders who couldn't read. She had the teachers' guide for another program, and she was wandering through the first unit, going through everything suggested in the manual. And she said to me, "We're doing that, but they're not reading." I said, "They *can't* read, for pete's sake!" She and I just took the teachers' guide and marked it all up. We just highlighted the key pieces; forget this, and go back, and do this. And I thought, "That's the part that was strong in the beginning that has become more and more diluted."

HTM: We had a reading series that had been in existence since 1949. It had been revised a number of times and continued to be revised after the 1971 edition. You, the authors and editors, did not work in isolation. You constantly sought out the latest and best research on the teaching of reading. You brought to Boston editorial many leaders in the discipline. Bill, you had the task of being the discussion leader, and, Nancy and John, you too had to keep the meeting on track. People should know more about that, for this procedure is a marked contrast to the idea, often voiced by critics of reading programs, that a reading program is the result of a few people sitting around in a publishing house and conjuring up something to publish.

WD: This business of bringing in experts seemed to me to be quite productive. It gave us ideas that we might not have thought of on our own. We would select people that were supposed to be— that we truly believed to be—experts in reading, particularly people who were knowledgeable about recent research. Most of us were pretty hip on what does research say, as opposed to what someone thinks.

HTM: Could you underscore that statement, Bill? For it focuses on a major problem. Tragically, so much of what I read and hear today is merely what somebody thinks, rather than being based on research and analysis.

WD: I digress, for I've got to tell you this story. In my presentations around the country, I would frequently say to people, "What you need to do is teach according to what research proves, not what somebody thinks." I'd frequently say, "It doesn't matter what George Spache (former president of the National Reading Conference) thinks; it's what research proves." Except in Salt Lake City, and I had gotten the idea that maybe somebody really liked George Spache—and I had better not say that. In Salt Lake City, I said to the teachers there, "You know, what is really important is what research says. It doesn't matter what Joe Smith thinks." Joseph Smith was the translator of the Book of Mormon and a founder of the Mormon Church, headquartered in Salt Lake City, Utah. Needless to say, we didn't get that adoption.

One of the things we did was to bring in a dozen or so people, and we tried to minimize the number of Houghton Mifflin authors, actually, because we were there to listen, not to contribute to them. And we had good people.

JR: What I was struck by, too, was we deliberately brought in contrary points of view to test ideas. I'm thinking in particular of the contrast between, let's say, Hugh Schephoester, a colleague of Paul McKee's in Greeley, Colorado, and subsequently a Houghton reading author, and his Mastery of Learning orientation, and the people who were committed to the whole language approach.

WD: A perfect example.

JR: In later years, we would do this before every program. It wasn't a one-shot deal, and we got a lot of great information from a group like that, as opposed to what any one individual could bring to you. And that, to some extent, helped shape future programs. It couldn't be to a large extent, because you couldn't agree with both whole language advocates and Schephoester. But it was valuable information on what we knew about teaching reading.

NS: This kind of discussion among people who are reading educators, plus some of the editorial staff and our own authors, meant that we all would share some kind of thought or an idea. I would walk out of that room and think, "Aha, this is a clever thing to do." You had so many bright minds working together, kind of puzzling out things. In fact, it was a great gift, I think, to editorial, because in a way you didn't have to sit and wonder if you'd thought it through. You just sat in that room, and people would say, "I believe that, but I don't believe this." And sometimes you just came to this impasse. Then, realistically at that time, some people would pick one kind of program as opposed to another kind of program.

Whereas nowadays, everybody wants the same kind of program to deliver all the differences that used to exist in separate programs. For example, Economy Publishing Company's reading program was known to be a heavily phonics-based program, whereas we, in our Houghton program, had phonetic elements plus comprehension—a more holistic program. But I think that those symposia helped to shape where we were going.

JR: A side benefit—but it was all quite unintended—was that it was an incredible recruiting tool. We had several ways of doing the testing-out part, and we should probably talk about that. We would be able to test the mettle of these people to see whether they might become part of the author team. But even if they didn't, and most didn't, the symposia gained that Houghton Mifflin credibility in the academic community. I mean, they had never experienced anything like this. Actually, a bunch of professors from various universities getting together to explore an in-depth pedagogical issue doesn't often happen. So we enabled that to happen, and it was incredibly beneficial to them as well as to us.

As a result, I think that's one of the reasons why we never had any difficulty recruiting good authors. But it's the credibility that we established as a company that believed in serious research with high integrity.

NS: I think they had thought publishers were not reading educators; they just put out books for kids. But when these people participated in these discussions and saw how the structure was built, they began to feel like they could really use these programs to teach reading. And it moved them into the process, whereas before, they were outside, on the outside, commenting on it.

WD: In relation to what John said—and what you said too, Nancy—there were, and still are, many professors out there who think that basal readers are just trash. So there are people out there who can do you a lot of damage. But they knew we weren't all bad. We really are concerned with what they thought and knew about teaching reading.

You know, one of our strongest supporters, not Houghton Mifflin's strongest supporters but of our approach, is Jeanne Chall, the reading expert and coauthor of the Dale-Chall Readability Scale.

NS: John and I and others would go to the Harvard School of Education and talk to the graduate students, and she sometimes would invite me to lunch. She said to me, "You know something? You people from Houghton Mifflin know about reading."

WD: Did she? I didn't know that.

NS: And that, from her, was an incredible compliment because I don't think she thought many people did.

HTM: Not unrelated to what we've just been discussing, each year I would travel out to South Bend, Indiana. I always looked forward to those trips to the Notre Dame Reading Conference. The conference was a three-day professional program during which educators from all over the country were invited by Houghton Mifflin to hear about new and important issues in reading education. To this day, when I talk with people in educational circles, they inform me that that conference was one of the best and most effective learning experiences they ever encountered. I should not use the word learning, for the experience was broader than that—it was inspiring. Educators valued hearing about what was going on in reading, and then returning to their districts, and knowing they were bringing back something they could use. I recall the one time we had Ernie Boyer, former president of the Carnegie Foundation, out there. Remember that? And just before he was leaving, after he gave his great talk that first day, I said to him, "I wish you could stay around," and he replied, "I wish I could stay around too, because this looks like a meeting where I'd really get something worthwhile out of it."

WD: Oh, Notre Dame had a number of advantages. I've often wondered how expensive it was. It must have cost Houghton Mifflin a pile of money. But as you know, we would have selected educators, selected by salespeople, usually to try to impress somebody to help get an adoption, quite honestly. But we would contact them, and we asked them to indicate areas that they wanted covered. And they voted, and quite literally, we set up, say, twenty small groups maybe, according to what they wanted. And always they got into the group—there were a number of meetings—they got into the group they wanted. And the groups were run, I think entirely, by Houghton Mifflin people.

JR: Yes, but sometimes by customers.

WD: That's right, I'd forgotten. But usually by Houghton Mifflin people. So they learned additional respect for Houghton Mifflin people. "These people know something about reading, because they can answer my questions. This is what I wanted to know about." It was always a delightful experience, just a great experience.

JR: It was analogous to what I said about the symposium as a vehicle for talking together that they wouldn't have otherwise.

WD: Yes, yes.

JR: There were people from all across the country talking about topics of mutual interest in a very congenial but serious way to learn from each other, and learn from authors directly. You know, you authors and editors were with these people twenty-four hours a day, and they got to ask the burning questions that they had directly to Bill Durr.

WD: And it was amazing how many times we would get the response in this interaction that they found out: "Well, other people have the same problem that I have! I didn't know anybody else had this problem."

HTM: That's a point that various educators have made to me. That it was reassuring to find out that their problems were not unique to them. They compared notes, and they departed feeling that they could try out new ideas.

JR: I think there were about 125 customers, but there were also about 100 Houghton Mifflin people. The sales reps were there; the authors were there; editors were there.

WD: The reps came and watched over this person that they had sent from North Dakota or wherever.

HTM: You would have educators from all levels, superintendents and others.

WD: That's true, yes.

JR: I remember something that Bill insisted on: that it not be a commercial. And I remember the first time that you bowed to a request, Bill. It was sort of impromptu. We were coming out with a new edition, and people who were there were very much interested in it. But we kept the purity of it, if you will.

You could go to sessions where there was no reference to Houghton Mifflin, or you could go to sessions where, in effect, you were preparing yourself for "selling" the Houghton Mifflin program in your district. But you were able to go through the whole conference without hearing a Houghton Mifflin commercial at all.

WD: But still, for Houghton Mifflin, all the responses and answers to questions involved the philosophy that we had in our program. But we tried not to say, "If you look at *Getting Ready to Read,* that just explains the whole thing." What we did better achieved the goals that we had. Notre Dame has a mystique about it— just walking down the mall there.

JR: Well, astonishingly, the dormitory experience, as opposed to fancy hotels, built camaraderie among these people who initially were a little apprehensive about being in a dorm. But then it became a joke, and then it became a bonding experience. That was just the dynamic.

HTM: I always remember that scene when I would register. Along with the registration forms, I think maybe it was Jean Muller, one of our consultants, who gave you a washcloth because the dorms didn't provide such things. You got a registration form and a washcloth.

JR: That's almost symbolic of the attention to detail. You knew that you'd get a washcloth.

CC: One thing I noticed about Notre Dame—and I think all of this may have helped—is how quickly people became friendly with each other. And we did simple things like a cookout. Not necessarily a fancy dinner, although there was a big dinner at the end. But at the cookout, people just sat around chatting, playing volleyball. It was really neat.

HTM: Notre Dame was a great asset in building good relations between customers and Houghton Mifflin. How much of the customer feedback went into the books?

WD: I don't think very much. Do you, Nancy?

NS: No. I would say that it was more a process of building a knowledge base among people who would review the program. Not to say there weren't people there who would have ideas or things to share, or criticize, you know, very strong criticism. And in a way, it's always good to hear that. The thing that did happen, though, because people came from all over the country, is that people learned what the trends were in all the other places. You could be sitting there and know that in this place they were doing one thing, in another place they were doing this or that. They gave us a good sense of what was happening nationwide.

WD: They were there for input rather than output. So yes. I don't remember any specific—somebody might say, "Well, that teacher said so and so," but, no, it was an output kind of thing.

JR: However, there was an opportunity for firsthand customer contact, and through that getting a sense of what their issues were. You know you just kind of absorbed that information, and it was useful at some point. And you certainly got a sense of what the hot topics were. You know, if you found a session oversubscribed, you had a sense that something was up.

HTM: Bill, I keep looking at all those notes you have on the pad before you.

WD: I tried to list some of the differences between earlier programs. Nancy, correct me, if you will; I don't think that literary skills were a part of the previous program. And in '71 we started a very direct strand teaching literary skills, starting with something as low-level as "Is it possible that this story really happened, or did the author make it up? What do we call stories that the author makes up?" That kind of thing, which was an added dimension to the program, that was pretty unique. If it was widespread with other programs, I was not aware of it.

And the other note I have here is that we had initiated a program of different levels of comprehension that we had not had before. It seemed to us that simply teaching comprehension was not specific enough, so we had—in fact, in all the selections of later grades our discussion questions were labeled *literal comprehension, interpretive comprehension,* and *creative or evaluative thinking.* You might ask a child, after he'd read a story, "What did Tom do on Tuesday?" We might ask at the interpretive level, "What season of the year was it?" when it was not told in the story, but the kids were not going to school. The garbage got to smelling because it was so hot outside. And so you'd take that to ask, "What time of the year do you think this was?" Or a critical and evaluative question such as "Do you think children should be required to help around the house?" So you can, I think, right from those questions, see quite easily the different levels of thought that are called for here, which I think was pretty good. It led to greater depth in reading than simply something that up to that time had been called *comprehension*. So I thought those were some things that were new in '71 and very desirable to help kids.

HTM: During the period when all of you were active, Houghton Mifflin markedly expanded its presence into the educational market. The Houghton Mifflin Reading Series was a major contributor to that success. It became very obvious we had something that was totally unique in textbook publishing, and that was author involvement. Author involvement, from research through publication and into sales, by getting our authors out into the field: no other company ever was able to match us.

There was that relationship between the authors, like you, Bill, and all of us company employees. We were a closely knit team. We were out in the field, as well as attending to our respective responsibilities, and also doing what authors and publishers do to create publications. We had people who could function well in that kind of an organization that was not highly structured. And I don't think the competitors ever quite got a hold on how that happened. We had authors who could represent publications to customers, yet do it professionally.

That was hard work, as you well know, going around to one school district after the other. The authors had a huge role in moving Houghton up into a leadership position. That's my take on it, and I shall be forever grateful.

JR: No question about it.

CC: And did the authors for other publishers' programs do the same thing?

NS: Eventually, they used them more.

WD: Yes. I don't think they did before, though.

NS: I think eventually they had to because otherwise we were going out with a voice of really helping teachers to understand what reading was about, which gave a lot of credence to the power, strength, and depth of the program, and then they had to be in the same ball park.

HTM: They never matched us for two reasons, as I see it: (1) their authors were not as involved in the company as ours, and (2) many of them were not equal to the challenge.

NS: With some people they'd stand out, but then it was also the incredible commitment of the authors that Houghton Mifflin had, that they were willing to do that, because a lot of people aren't really that willing to do it.

WD: I've got a map on the wall at home that I'm very proud of. It shows that I gave a presentation in all fifty states.

HTM: Plus Europe.

WD: That's right, in Vienna. I'm very proud of that.

JR: Yes. The practice became very large. Actually managing that process became a major assignment, because we tried to find authors who had the intellectual capacity to bring to the process. And so we started to develop an author team that had several people who could begin to do that work. Initially you were it in reading, Bill, and then Hugh Schephoester came on.

I remember at one point, the speaking requests came through me, and there were hundreds of them. When you look across the author team, I always felt guilty about the workload that was there; the load on you, Bill, and on Jack Pikulski, the reading author that eventually followed you as the lead author, was just really, really tough.

HTM: I doubt most non-publishers, and maybe some publishers, have much insight as to how the author/editor team functions day by day in just getting a program out. There's author Bill, over here, bringing to editorial materials based on his research, knowledge, creativity, and experience. There is editor Nancy, over there, bringing her editorial expertise to bear on the task of publishing author Bill's manuscript, and doing so in ways that meet company standards, as well as winning acceptance in the marketplace. So how does it all come together?

NS: In advance of starting the undertaking, the author and the editor spent endless time and endless discussion in shaping and really constructing the model of what the publication was going to be, and we also spent a good long time creating a vision that would really hold the whole project together. I think in a way for both of us, we understood at the outset, although things evolved, what we were trying to do and where we were headed. Then we outlined how it would be done. The construction part of it was the key part.

WD: Nancy, I can remember sessions in a room where there was a blackboard, and you had written things down on the blackboard, and we'd talk about this topic, then that topic, for a while. It's preplanning I'm talking about.

NS: I remember one time, Bill, we were in a room with giant tables, and we had all these skills. We were trying to get them into the program where they should be, and we were saying, "Oh! It's like constructing the Fleet Center here in Boston." I mean, you really have to work a lot. And the pieces: some don't matter much and some matter whole a lot. And if you don't have that kind of expertise, then you tend to push some unimportant thing to a big place. Or in the process, you dump things into different grade levels, and you don't do a good job and put things where they need to be.

WD: In talking, you adopt this sequence we just discussed. You don't just stick this in here because you've got room for it. The question always was: Is it necessary for this particular skill to build on a previous skill? And does this skill prepare for something at a higher level? And that was always a basic question. It just didn't happen in some place, for you needed to preplan so you could place skills in the sequence that you had in mind for the proper development of the program.

NS: We all had to come to an agreement that at least some key authors and editors had to look at everything. And there was a way that, as Bill said, the stories were all read by the authors and by school librarians, so we had a lot of feedback.

That really kept a cohesive picture of a program from the beginning to the end, whereas I think a lot of publishers send out grade 2 to somebody, and grade 1 to somebody else. At Houghton, Bill and I insisted that the authors and editors look at the whole program over and over and over again. That's what holds a series together.

CC: When you talk about the preplanning, I can see how very important that would have been in '71, because you were going to make a big change. How did that work when you did the next revision? Would you say it was equally rigorous?

NS: Always was, don't you think?

WD: Yes, and with this additional input that we talked about from the groups a while ago.

JR: Even though you weren't starting over, you were dealing with the processes again. You know, nothing was so cast in stone that you didn't take another look at it. You really tested it so that you didn't simply by default continue something; you did it quite deliberately. So in order to scrutinize that, you put it to the test again.

HTM: Would you agree that one of the great strengths of a carefully preplanned series even in revision, such as we're discussing, is that as a result of the process of trial and error in the marketplace, through use in the classroom, a resulting value is that of a honing process. These programs are really honed to a fine cutting edge for, after all, they are used in thousands of classrooms across the nation.

NS: Right.

HTM: Today, as I see curriculum standards being set by states and bypassing the process you have been describing, I have a feeling we're losing that invaluable honing process. Now we have locally appointed committees setting up curriculum standards. One such group does the work one year, then another group comes five or six years later and changes it. You lose the continuity of a publisher author/editor group working through revision after revision.

WD: Yes, I can share an example of that with you. We had skills lessons in the pupils' books. Instead of the teacher telling the child how to read a newspaper, there would be a skill lesson in the book that taught the skill. And one of our skill lessons was SQ3R—the time-honored Survey, Question, Read, Write, and Review—about how to study something. And in the honing process, we asked, "Why don't we present our lessons using the SQ3R technique?" We still had lessons on how to read a newspaper, but now we taught that lesson in the kids' book using SQ3R, and we did that in every single one. So that's no great big, enormous change. The lessons are the same, but the way they were structured and taught went along with the way we said lessons ought to be structured and taught.

NS: Another piece of it was that there was a lot of decision making about how to deal with current trends and fads. A lot of decisions had to be made about how to put something in, but not to put everything in. In fact, early on the assignment was to keep the job of teaching reading simple enough so that you could do it in the time that was allotted and also to make provision for kids that were going to go faster and slower. We made decisions based on our own feeling of integrity. We weren't subject then to these big lists coming from the states.

Just by pushing down the standards on all of the things, a lot of space is taken with stuff that's somewhat peripheral. I once said, "We ought to put the teachers's guide information in two colors, and make the red part of it the part that you need to do if all else fails." But I think we used to make more decisions. "If this is in, okay—well, that's out." Not just "This is in, and we'll add this, and we'll add this." We did start to add more ancillaries, but in the program we tried to keep the integrity of the simplicity of the plan.

HTM: You rendered the complex simple. Outstanding authors and editors had the ability not to muddy up a work with a lot of bells and whistles.

CC: I have a question about task forces. I remember attending one meeting at Notre Dame; it followed the Notre Dame Conference. We all sat in that huge room, and there were quite a few salespeople and consultants there. And we had big sheets of paper, and people would write things down, and then we'd run around the room and move those sheets. How did you treat that material? How seriously did you take that input?

NS: I think you had to attend to it. I would say that I think because the field people were selling the product in their own areas, they were very concerned about local issues, and they would quickly bring forth items that we didn't have but someone else had, or something that was a problem.

On the other hand, they were creative people who had very good ideas about some things to do. But in a way, you had to take a look at it, and extract from it what you needed, and then just say, "You know, there isn't anything we can do about the program that's out there now." We can consider this for the future, but it was taken as observations and not as something that you absolutely had to take from each person and react to it. John, do you agree?

JR: Yes, I agree with that. We recognized that it's very hard for the reps, who are dealing with the day-to-day, to think three years ahead. Our challenge was always to try to think, to project. I think that also we, in our own minds, thought of those meetings in terms of that not being the place to make decisions. You couldn't have a discussion and say, "Let's have a vote," even though I think some of the sales reps wanted that to be the case. You had to keep that perspective. This was a place for gathering information and thinking through where we're going, but it's only one piece of input. It was not a decision-making body.

CC: And was it a little bit of public relations too? In other words, kind of making the field people feel that they were on board in this? You brought them in repeatedly.

NS: You brought them in when you started to construct the programs, and in a way through that process, they did begin to buy in. Sometimes they would find places where they would have concerns, and you'd have to consider determining that we are not going to do this anymore, or we will continue to do it.

JR: I think the use of the task force has evolved over the years. I think early on you got a sense that you had to involve key salespeople and consultants, because you want and need them to be your advocates once the program is published. You want them to be knowledgeable about it. You needed to have them buy in. The sales force is your first customer. And they *were* your very first customer, in essence, in the case of the task forces.

Publishing a reading program isn't just done in a kind of petri dish, where you can be in control of the situation. Sometimes something happens, but it's an outside force. You had nothing you could do about it; it just happened. In Kalamazoo, Michigan, we had the suit against the use of federal funds to buy educational materials that were deemed to be sexist. Our program had been chosen for the district, and it was the one that was attacked. There was no way that we could avoid dealing with it. Not that we wanted to, necessarily, but it was a disruptive—very disruptive—thing. I always felt in the long run it was beneficial, because we came to a conscious awareness of what needed to be done relative to sexism. And I think we responded better than others did, because we were on the spot.

And Bill, I so vividly remember when you and I went out to Kalamazoo to deal with that situation, and I think on balance it came out pretty well.

WD: We had been taught all our lives that using *everyone* uses singular, and the singular was always *he*. "Tell everyone that he should sit down." And now you couldn't do that anymore because they counted the number of times the word he appeared.

JR: It led to us sitting down and literally going over material—you know, the devil's in the details. That's how you work these things out. I remember one person saying, "You know, I think maybe you've gone a little too far in this." This was somebody who was making the protest. She said, "You've made every single bus driver a female in the entire program." Another one was when somebody said, "How can you stay with *ringmaster?*" And she said, "I've been hearing *ringperson* lately." And I think everybody kind of looked at each other and said, "No, we have not been hearing *ringperson.*"

NS: The other thing that we did as a result of that was we adjusted some of the content. And I don't remember exactly what it was, but John probably does. Do you remember the illustration that we redid? What happened with that?

JR: Well, it was a mother in a domestic setting. And initially she was ironing, and we changed the illustration to …

NS: Wallpapering?

JR: Wallpapering, right. But we actually had her wallpapering incorrectly, from the bottom up! Nobody noticed, but we changed it in the last edition; I think that she was painting.

NS: It was so funny that we worked so hard to get this woman doing something that was a really hard task.

JR: But it's really only to make the point that the content had lots of demands placed on it. It wasn't just children's interests. It wasn't just other chestnuts. It had to deal with societal issues that related to racism, sexism, etc. And it was a very, very complex task to choose that content while having it deal with all of the skill issues that it took. As you said, "It's like building the Fleet Center."

NS: And there must be a lot of decisions on what you can do within the integrity of what you're publishing and what you're not able to do. There are certain things you just don't do. But I think sometimes in some of this, so much is bowed to that it becomes a matter of not doing the main job, which is teaching children to read, and the content must support that. But when the content of the literature gets so overpowering that the reading suffers from it, then you shouldn't call it a reading book.

The other thing that we attended to was time: realizing that the teacher had to do the task in the length of the period allowed for this lesson at different grade levels. We constructed our materials around that and put them in a framework. As you know, we would talk about additions that were peripheral versus those that were critical.

But we no longer can do that in the present programs, because we now have the state guidelines from places like California and Texas. There is so much of everything they specify that if you read it just to yourself, you go crazy, because you know that no one could ever do it all.

And yet I think it was thoughtful on our part to put in a plan that teachers could really implement. But now, because of the state guidelines that come down, everything but the kitchen sink is in there. Then a lot of times I think arbitrary choices are made, and then you have to question whether those are choices related to the teaching of reading or just what everybody likes to do.

HTM: What would you do if you were going to do it all over?

NS: When I was at Houghton just doing some of the small projects on a freelance basis, I would be saying, "Take that out! Take this out!" But people said no to me, because they're up against a lot of ...

WD: Up against checklists.

CC: Hal frequently refers to the occasion, Nancy, when you spoke to the Associated Industries of Massachusetts. And you said to them, "We know what is required to read, and we know how to teach it." My question is, don't we still know how to do it? Why are people not doing it? Or maybe they are doing it.

NS: I think people are doing it, because kids do learn to read. We know how to teach people to read, and we must put it in a structure that is simple and basic enough that teachers can find it and follow it. But now teaching reading has become more complex, because of what's imposed upon teachers is this structure from the state specifications and the testing requirements. You may know how to teach someone to read, but you've got to throw in all this other stuff because of the state and because of the testing. And in some cases, I think a lot of teachers don't know how to teach kids to read. I mean, that's the truth of it. I think we've had a simple system. Now the system isn't simple. I think there ought to be tons of other kinds of things to help people understand the process, if that's wanted, but then a guide marked up identifying the things that must be taught. *"Please do this."* It's just like anything in your life: you have to make some priorities.

WD: I've always felt—and this may be sheer conceit—that even people that bought our reading program—and we talk about the construction of this being so careful and based on research—does not necessarily mean they're not going to use a hammer to try to cut wood. You know, "Oh, is that a teachers' guide? I didn't know that came with the program. I'll get around to it someday." I really believe there are many, many teachers like that.

CC: Remember the famous Denver Study? That was conducted back in the sixties, and its purpose was to determine, if children were exposed to *Getting Ready to Read* in kindergarten rather than waiting until first grade, would their reading abilities be better, worse, or unchanged by the time they got through fifth grade? It turned out they were better, which of course made Houghton very happy. We decided to do a story about it for *Timely Topics*, a newsletter, which we used to put into *Instructor Magazine*. I went out to Denver, Colorado, and interviewed a number of teachers. And oh, they loved it. They adored Paul McKee. Everything was wonderful. But then they were telling me about how they were teaching, and I thought, "I don't think this is the way things should go." Even though they loved it, and perhaps it was working, they truly did not understand it.

NS: But they didn't have so many outside choices to make around the reading. The thing about it is the state mandates this, but it's almost not thoughtful. You say, "So they can write, but teach them to read. Provide a place where they have to learn to read."

Writing and making a diorama are lovely things to do, but they don't teach them reading.

HTM: Millions of people—literally millions of children over a period of time—learned to read through the use of our reading series.

NS: And we viewed it as the building of something that mattered, rather than just marketing a product line. A product line is more the case nowadays because there are so few people willing to put up the money just to put a reading program together. There used to be what, fifteen or sixteen different publishers who put out reading programs?

In the far future there probably will be another fifteen or so small publishers who start to do something worthwhile, and then they all will be bought up by conglomerates and foreign companies too.

HTM: Fortunately for education, from what I hear, there are small publishers emerging. They pick a spot or a niche, develop a new idea, and go with it.

CC: Picking up on your point, Nancy, about doing something really worthwhile: I did go to one of those Paul McKee sessions out in Boulder, Colorado. I always refer to the experience as "sitting at the feet of Paul McKee." Many years later, I was at a Houghton Mifflin gathering. It was probably about this reading program, and Paul was long gone. And I said to somebody that I had done this, and I felt as though I should spend the rest of my life convincing the world it had to learn to read the Houghton Mifflin way. And the person said, "And you have."

HTM: As did we all. What better note to close on? I thank each of you for once again giving your time and energy to publishing and our long-standing friendship.

CHAPTER 6

A Generation of Great Creators

Publishing Children's Literature

"I don't want you to like all of our books."
—*Walter Lorraine, publisher,*
Houghton Mifflin Children's Books

Walter Lorraine's publishing achievements earned him a reputation as an editors' editor. His ability to perceive the difference in the elements that make up quality children's literature drew to him authors and editors of like uniqueness. The list of children's books winning Caldecott, Newbery, and other awards for Houghton is impressive. According to Anita Silvey, "Walter's department was one of the most creative in children's book history. Now I'm talking as the editor of *The Essential Guide to Children's Books and Their Creators*. Only Viking in the thirties and forties, Harper in the fifties and sixties, and Houghton in the seventies and eighties ever rose to this kind of excellence in the field. Walter was literally finding the next generation of great creators, publishing their first books, and publishing all of their books."

It is not a reach to state that the children's literature editorial group and their authors were as one with the school textbook editors and their authors in implementing Houghton's strategy to publish to educate kids. To read this chapter with meaning, it is important to have a clear sense of the differences and similarities between the two. Proficient young readers master the requisite basic skills for decoding new words, as we have read, through an organized teaching/learning process. And that critical achievement must be accompanied by skills techniques for obtaining meaning from the material being read. Both accomplishments are essential to the success of young people through-out their lives, and textbooks are carefully crafted to perform that task.

Today's technology is taking us into a visual world, to be sure, yet as printer Rocky Stinehour observes, "Certainly the techniques of getting into print are changing very rapidly [but] … the nature of reading is constant and always will be." Print, we must bear in mind, consists of established symbols used first by the writer and then by the reader. A form of coding followed by translation takes place. The way in which words are put together conveys the writer's intended mean-ing. The reader decodes the symbols to determine the writer's words and then seeks to comprehend the writer's intent.

The second phase of the translation process goes to the core of the public's unhappiness with today's educational shortcomings. While widely discussed in the news media, the charge of academic regression is only partially accurate, as is evident when the impressive records of stu-dents entering college today are examined. Nor, to be sure, are all school systems performing poorly. The abilities to read with comprehension, to create one's own mental images as one reads, and to reach closure are but a few of the comprehension skills often cited as the shortcomings of today's children right up through college. These educational assets— indeed all of the higher-order thinking skills—do need to be improved. Quality children's literature can and does contribute to that goal.

What follows documents that claim, but clearly *not,* at the expense of reading enjoyment and creation of a love for good literature. In the process, the necessary differences between textbook content and children's literature are easily identified.

Chris Van Allsburg, author of numerous successful children's books, including *Jumanji, The Polar Express,* and *Garden of Abdul*

Gasazi, goes directly to the matter of vocabulary control, making clear how words are chosen to be used in stories written for children. He leads us into a fascinating but complex, highly creative writer's world of words and pictures and how they become stories.

CVA: And so I just started writing the story, but never making any compromises in what I wanted to say, but always being fairly careful about the language that I used, so that maybe not an earlier reader, but a relatively young reader, would be able to handle the story itself. And it would be easily accessed by young children who have had it read to them.

Somebody asked, "Well, gee, did your editor give you a list of the vocabulary words you could use for seven-year-olds and eight-year-olds?" And I replied, "No, no, no, no." The challenge is to never allow yourself to misrepresent your idea by a desire to use language that is going to be appropriate for your audience. It's always to find a way to say it with their vocabulary in a way that doesn't deform the idea that you have.

That was always my goal, and that's what I did in *Gasazi.* And I sent the story to Walter Lorraine, and Walter approved of it. I don't remember that there were any significant editing comments on it. Among other words of wisdom Walter gave me was, "You know, a picture book does not need a lot of descriptive language, because you are supposed to be doing that with the pictures. And essentially, anything that is either described in the pictures or may be inferred from the pictures should not use up text, because what you want to have happen is that the two carry the burdens of storytelling, or carry the reader along by working together, by both doing things, and that the illustration is not simply a redundant addendum to the text."

Chris defines a very different undertaking and ways of going about it from those of reading textbook author Bill Durr. Counterproductively, seemingly in the collective minds of the news media and various pundits, reading textbook publishers continue to bear the Dick-and-Jane legacy of fifty years ago. Actually, Houghton Mifflin authors and editors for decades have combed libraries' and publishers' lists seeking to find the best of children's literature for inclusion in our reading series. Still, and realistically so, there exists the necessity of selecting stories that can become part of a teaching/learning process ensuring pupil mastery of the decoding and comprehension skills programs.

Significantly, it was the reading skills program and the efficiency of its presentation through our teaching/learning procedures in which they were embedded that won and held the series' leading market share. It was the company's cash cow. Then somebody in Houghton's School Division suggested that since we have many leading authors of children's literature in Houghton's Trade Division, let's propose to their editors that their authors write stories for the company's reading series. Through the fine cooperation of the juvenile trade department and the school reading department, the suggestion became reality, as Anita Silvey explains.

AS: Jim Marshall, I know, did a lot of that writing, and I know Susan Meddaugh did too. Yes. It was just under a little different direction. Jim Marshall is the most creative author I've ever seen, worked with, or known. I mean, we published books at Houghton that Jim did on cocktail napkins. I'm not kidding. He could sit at a dinner party and create a book. You could take it back to the office and you'd realize it had all the potential of a book. You know, it needed something here and there, but he really had that kind of spontaneous, creative urge. And for him the School Division would just set different parameters, and he would create around them. It was an exercise of a different kind, so it was never a problem.

But I don't think until then—maybe I'm wrong, you know this better historically—but there had been a certain real distance between what was done in trade and what was done in school. And I think of the seventies as the beginning of people looking and saying, "We've got this great wealth of talent, and they're writing for children; they can write for children in a text-book as well as they can write for children in a trade book."

And it gave trade authors revenue of a kind that we couldn't provide for them in trade publishing at that point. You didn't make that much money as a beginning children's book author. So we were able to use many of our beginning authors to make some money they could live on, and the School Division got an even better reading series as well.

The authors and editors of our elementary textbook series understood that good story content is important, and they sought out the best in published children's literature. It soon became common practice to purchase the "subsidiary-rights" from other publishers and use these stories in the reading textbooks. Logically the law of supply and demand created sharply escalating fees for stories suitable for inclusion in textbooks, just as such fees had impacted the now nearly defunct, but once widely adopted, high school literature anthologies. The intensity of the search for outstanding stories in short order drove subrights fees to levels exceeding the cost parameters publishers could absorb while offering textbooks compatible with state and local school systems' lean textbook appropriations.

Anita's reference to "a certain distance between what was done in trade and what was done in school," beyond the normal in-house rivalry, speaks in part to the issue of subrights. Some in Houghton wanted trade authors to be paid less for a Houghton reading series entry. Helpful as a general discount might be to the authors of our reading series, and also conceivably to the corporation, there also exists the corporation's contractual obligation to obtain the best subrights fee for each author's publications, and that amount often comes from outside Houghton. This refers directly to the concept that being an author-centered house entails more than merely claiming so. Commitments and priorities must always be observed.

Walter Lorraine describes how he operates as the outstanding editor of children's books he is:

WL: I look on my experience in Houghton as an honor to be able to do what I like doing best. I can't imagine myself ever having done anything else in a lifetime. I've been at Houghton doing books all of my life. I don't regret it.

After my Naval experience, I went to an art school, The Rhode Island School of Design in Providence. I already had a job lined up when I got out, with U.S. Steel of all things. Houghton had an opening. I decided to interview for it, and I figured I could spend a couple of years with the intelligent folks around Houghton Mifflin Company before I went over to Paris and sat around in the bistros and talked about art.

But then an interesting thing happened. The problem of making a book, the idea of it and the structure, was so intriguing to me that it kept me making books all these years. I believe I was the first person that came into the field who had a deliberate and direct art background, which struck me as very strange because in many children's books, the art and illustration tell most of the story.

There was practically no one that I encountered in those first years who knew one small thing about fine art or visual art as such. So I had no competition. That's why I excelled in doing what I was doing. I believe the official title of my first job was production manager of children's books, but I was really a designer and art director in the children's department, when the department was made up of only about five people.

This was in 1952. It made it very easy to get my way, as it were, with the design of the material. The idea of compressing thoughts and feelings and facts through a particular format has always intrigued me. It has intrigued the people that I've worked with who have been successful.

People these days talk about the computer and say, "You can't take one to bed with you." But I don't think that's the important difference. I think the important difference is the timing. With a book, you can vary your timing every other second, which you cannot do with a computer. You might be able to program it or push a button at a particular time, but you can change the time of reading even in mid-paragraph. And so, always a book suits the reader more than the reader has to suit the format.

A book is a particular personal voice, an observation, and compression of the way the author really feels about something. People have often asked me, "What kind of author do you want to publish?" Or, "What makes you decide to publish this versus that?" I say, "For me it's very simple. I always try to publish people who have something to say. And if they truly have something to say, and they can adjust to that form of expression, then you have a successful author and a successful publication." It's almost a one-to-one thing, the way I, at least, generally think about it. It's a means of putting down an idea and conveying it to the reader. I usually think of the reader as really pretty much one person.

One time years ago, we did a series of editorial ads in *The New York Times.* I did one with the headline, "I don't want you to like all of our books." And that was a very important consideration. If you try to publish for everyone, you will generally miss everybody. We published, at least in those days, for a minority readership that had some rapport with the content or could follow the author's reasoning. We were publishing for a specific audience. And in doing that, you had more creative work.

I wasn't trying to reduce everything to the most common denominator, and so essentially I published for a special readership. And if you have enough of those readers who would pay you money for the books, and it was more than what the book cost you to make, you had, in my opinion, a successful publication. It was more of that philosophy than the kind of numbers game that goes on these days.

HTM: How did you apply that philosophy or approach to author selection? You worked with David Macaulay, Chris Van Allsburg, Jim Marshall, and many other people. How did that play?

WL: I think of that as playing out in a similar fashion to my personal professional experience. Houghton allowed me to create things that intrigued me and that I was personally very interested in. I think it's almost that simple with the authors. It was usually just a sense that this author was very enthusiastic about a particular idea or a subject and was anxious to express it to someone else. It's hardly any more or less than that. Mostly, creative people are neurotic, and they are trying to resolve those problems. It's a theory that if you equate creativity with unusual association, if as a child you make all the right associations and smile when Grandmother gives you a kiss and that sort of thing, then you grow up in a conventional manner, etc., but you don't reach out for an unusual situation to save your soul. So you are looking for unusual association.

Mostly these authors are looking for that. They are alienated, as are we all, and they are looking for a way to relate. They want to express their idea to a receptive readership. As another example, in those years after World War II, there were a lot of creative people working in more commercial, applied art, such as advertising, who were making a lot of money at the time. Certainly books didn't pay that much. But I got a number of those involved with book work because they were bothered by the ephemeral nature of what they were doing. They looked on books as a more lasting statement of their feelings.

HTM: I hear constant reference to authors being creative, but just saying they are creative doesn't really tell you much. Sometimes I have used the words *the unique factor,* to identify that additional something. It isn't just being creative in the usual dictionary sense, for you have to go a step beyond that. I think that is what I hear you saying.

WL: Yes. That one is a little more difficult to put your finger on. But if you take somebody like Chris Van Allsburg, his reputation is as a very accomplished fine artist. In fact, most of his early work was in sculpture and in fine art drawing, but the basis, really, of his thinking is narrative. His sculpture always had a narrative content theme to it. It was rarely an experiment with spatial or color relations. That's why he fit into books so well. He was more a storyteller than a fine artist.

If you take someone like David Macaulay, David is the most creative fellow that I know, although on the surface he seems little more than a hail-fellow-well-met, ordinary guy.

He can take the most unseeming thing and relate it in such a clear, concise manner that it's extraordinary. His ability to take very, very complex subjects and focus in on what is essential to making them work is David. David and I, through the years, have enjoyed a lot of most creative exchanges. We would lunch at Locke-Ober's when it was in its heyday and discuss ideas back and forth on all sorts of subjects.

David is a master at making a reader look at something in a fresh but effective manner.

HTM: There is an account about your early meeting with David Macaulay. It has to do with gargoyles. Is it an accurate account?

WL: Sure. It's an accurate account, and it gives an example of what I've said about how you work with an author. David had submitted what was a conventional, but a quite good, picture-book idea. The story line was about gargoyles that came alive. In discussing the idea with David, his obvious interest was with the cathedral itself. That was the only impetus that he needed. "Chuck out the gargoyles and do the cathedral, because that seems like where your interest lies," and *Cathedral* was born. He did the work in a very brief time and with wonderful enthusiasm.

That was the beginning of his construction books. That's how it happened. It was obvious that he really didn't care that much about the gargoyles. He was more concerned with his feelings about the world and life, etc. The cathedral book allowed him to express those ideas. His skills are certainly unique and in a direction all his own.

Now let's hear directly from David Macaulay.

DM: I started trying to put some story ideas together, and, at the encouragement of some friends of mine, I called up publishers in Boston. I came to three places, and I showed them story ideas. Right from the beginning Houghton Mifflin was different from Atlantic and Little, Brown. In addition to a rejection, I always got encouragement. They wanted to see the next thing that I did. And that meant a great deal.

Finally, I had this notion of a gargoyle beauty pageant—a fantasy set in the Middle Ages. I remember sitting down with Walter and Melanie Kroupa, and we had a conversation. Basically the consensus was that I didn't need the gargoyles. I didn't need the fantasy element. My half-finished drawing of the cathedral was more interesting than the fantasy. So I thought, "Oh, boy, you just want me to do the architecture?"

I came back to the studio, got out my Pevsner *History of European Architecture* from school and looked at it. I sketched a dozen pencil drawings on tracing paper, showing the cathedral growing, and then I did details of masons working. In the end I made blueprints of them, stapled them together, and suddenly I had a large book. I brought this to Walter, and we laid everything out on his table. I told him the story as I saw it. We got to the end of the story, and Walter said, "Okay. Let's do it." And that was the beginning.

One of the most important things to me about the conversations I have with Walter is that Walter never directs me. Walter just asks questions, and it's in the questions he asks that I find myself thinking, "Well, I never thought to ask that one." And he doesn't give me the answers. I don't know whether he even knows the answers. But he certainly knows the questions.

HTM: Your account of meeting with David and coming to realize where his real interest existed reveals, I believe, another side of the truly exceptional editor, and that is, editors have to be skilled in reading people. You sensed that there was an underlying desire on the author's part to do a different book from the gargoyles. You were able to read David well enough to suggest that he follow another course. You have to be a bit of a psychologist sometimes as an editor, don't you?

WL: Yes, that's probably true. But there is one thing that I do not lack, and that's conviction. I have a clear sense of what's of interest to me. The gargoyle book would have been okay. God knows I've published enough material that would fall into a class of what the gargoyle book would have become, but the other was more exciting and a newer direction. And so it was, I suppose. I haven't thought about this before. I suppose in a way it's exciting to have somebody join with you in exploring what's outside the conventional. Those are the authors that I worked with best.

Anita Silvey explains how Walter's convictions and style translated into everyday practice within Houghton's children's literature editorial group.

AS: You see, what we were hunting for at Houghton—this was the way Walter trained us to think. He said, "Go to New York if you must. I mean, if you've got to go to New York, I'm not going to stop you from going. If you're going to—and maybe you have friends and you want to see a reviewer, and I can't tell you not to talk to anyone, but don't spend ten seconds trying to figure out what they're doing. I don't even want it to cross your lips what they're doing. I am not interested that they're developing a biography series for the four through eight age group. I could care less.

"What we're doing is finding individual voices with something to say of their own. And I don't care if no one else in the industry is doing a book like this. That's not what matters. What matters is they've got something to say." I would sometimes mouth off my *Horn Book* truisms and say, "Well, with the development of a bibliography," and he would say, "I don't want to hear about that development. It's not important. Is this a publishable book without it? Okay?"

And it was such good advice, because what it meant was that a list was being developed that was its own, that was idiosyncratic, that was individual. And that, in point of fact, would outsell everybody else's list because there weren't books like that anywhere else.

Let's say "Goosebumps" were the rage—and you weren't doing the second "Goosebumps" series. You were doing something completely different. You were completely on another tack. And you weren't running the same way as the herd. I was trained to think as a contrarian publisher—as a contrarian investor. You were hunting for things that were slightly different from what the herd was doing. If you got it right, you made out like such bandits, all of you, because you were the only voice there.

Anita, Indiana Hoosier she may be, is speaking about children's trade book publishing and while doing so clearly defining the long-time culture that existed across all of Houghton Mifflin from editorial to shipping. The company's first outside director, a member of an old Yankee family and senior partner of a prestigious Boston law firm, Richard Nichols, counseled me as Houghton's CEO never to lose sight of the values that made the company great, nor should I manage the company to please the financial analysts, for "if you do, you'll lose the company." The Houghton publishing culture was too deeply engrained for me to attempt to manage otherwise. My years of service in the company while it was still privately held, however, had not fully prepared me for the inherent dissidence I encountered with many financial analysts who often seemed quite uninformed as to the basic tenets of book publishing, especially textbook publishing. The revenue fluctuations inherent in the state textbook adoption scheduling and a mindset focused on the mechanics of publishing books without understanding that we were editorial-centered, not printing-centered, and what that mission required of us never quite reached some of them. Theirs was more of a commodity orientation.

I recall well the analyst who visited my office one day and informed me that speed-reading was the coming thing in reading instruction for children, and as a publisher of a reading series with a large share of the market, I should get into it.

I pointed out that one entrepreneur after the other had been hawking speed-reading products before and since my days as a salesman and that not one of them had enjoyed much lasting success. So I thanked him for his suggestion but said that I had no intention of spending corporate dollars and author/editor resources on a speed-reading product. The analyst informed me that perhaps he should stop following Houghton Mifflin.

Try explaining to that analyst and others like him that within the company, a number of editors were always working on such publications as *Snowflake Bentley*. Keep in mind Walter's admonitions to Anita about finding out what others are publishing.

HTM: I often think about what you were doing with children's books—the authors, the artists, and the editors—with these beautiful illustrations coordinated to the story. You couldn't depart from the play.

AS: That's right. It can't depart from the basic sense that was created initially.

HTM: And this is an integral part of publishing that I doubt many people appreciate or realize how complex it really is. You, the editor, had to see and feel what the author wanted. You had to see that the artist and everyone else got it, including the marketing and salespeople.

AS: Well, we all had to get it, because if everyone didn't get it, then you didn't have anyone carrying that vision forward. I was very fortunate at Houghton in children's editorial for I saw two such periods. I saw Walter, and I was fortunate to have that for a few years myself. Such publishing operations work well when the operation is just so seamless you don't even know it. You're not even working toward it, because you're just all there together. You share a common vision, or that the publisher communicates, I guess, enough of a common vision, and everybody can sign on to it in some critical way.

HTM: You're really describing what the true editor's job is, aren't you?

AS: Yes.

HTM: It's far more than correcting misspelling and grammar. It isn't somebody that just goes to parties and long lunches. It's somebody who has that uncanny ability to get inside the author's mind.

AS: And pull something else out.

HTM: And then to see that everybody else involved understands that "something" to the degree that everyone functions in a way that produces a great book.

AS: A great book, and also together with some of that enthusiasm. The best example that I have in my own publishing time—and we should talk a lot about the books from the seventies, because I'm much more objective on those. It's harder to stand back on what you published yourself more recently. A superb senior editor, Ann Rider, brought me a manuscript and she said, "It has been rejected elsewhere; I love it. It's just exactly the kind of book I want to publish."

But then she said, "I'd like your thoughts on the market because I don't know if there's any market." And it was a biography of a man who photographed snowflakes. And Ann started to talk about what she'd do with it. She had a vision for it. And the vision was absolutely right.

And she said, "Well, what about marketing concerns?" And I said, "Ann, they'll know about him in Vermont, and we just have to make a good enough book to get the other forty-nine states." And that's pretty much my vision of marketing. I mean, if you make a good enough book, things will follow in turn. And she worked with the author, and what she realized was that there was a nonfiction component, and there was a story component. She could weave them together in a different way.

And she pulled out of that author a whole other manuscript than the author initially saw. Ann had a vision for an artist who was wonderful, and our art director loved Ann's idea. And they started to work together. But it was an average book on the Houghton Mifflin list. It was a book about a Vermont photographer of snowflakes, after all. We had problems with some production, and some art had to be changed. And, as publisher, I said, "Look, we're going to do everything for this book that's necessary." We treated it like it was a Cadillac. We treated that author and that artist like they were Cadillacs, even though we knew they weren't—at that moment they weren't.

And the work was *Snowflake Bentley*. The book, of course, was to go on and win the Caldecott. It has been one of the most successful Caldecotts of the last decade. I believe that one of the reasons it won the Caldecott is because the book was treated with the same respect that a Chris Van Allsburg book would be treated, the same that a David Macaulay book would be given. The author and artist were given their due in the process.

HTM: When a publisher says, "Yes, we will publish your book," the publisher has a commitment to give its all to that author, no matter what.

AS: That's what the publishing commitment is. You don't say, from the beginning, well, we're only going to say—what would have been my estimate for *Snowflake Bentley*—7,500 copies? Mary Azarian, the artist, was known but not well-known. Jackie

Martin, the author, was known but not well-known. You wouldn't then say, "Well, because it's not going to sell many copies, we won't do anything for it; we won't print it on the right paper; we won't fix design problems; we won't give it attention." My vision of a publisher is that if you're enthusiastic enough about that book to give it a contract, then you see that process through.

The intellectual and aesthetic faculties of hundreds of thousands of students were, and continue to be, enhanced by *Snowflake Bentley.* No commodity-type pursuit here, such as the Goosebumps series. It's just an act of shared faith and gut intuition from the editor through the corporation into the CEO's office.

The monkey celebrity *Curious George* was created by the widely known Reys, gifted authors repeatedly honored for their literary achievement. Recently it has made appearances ranging from decorating department store cash registers to a balloon in parades, as part of a foreign corporation's plans to reap the benefits of literary synergies. Synergy exploitation is not publishing, at least in the dictionary sense of "a person or company engaged in publishing printed material." How was it that *Curious George* reached such a high level of public recognition and popularity that he became part of a global commercial glitz? Walter Lorraine describes what it took to build the *Curious George* mystique.

WL: Curious George always worked within certain rules. Rey was really a very, very intelligent fellow. You can see the appeal of the book: Curious George is like a little kid who gets into trouble all the time, and he never knows why, but it always works out for him at the end. So it's satisfying; it gives reassurance to young readers.

The other thing is that Curious George never did anything that a real monkey could not do. He never talks; he never swims, for example, or does anything like that, at least as far as I know when I was working with the books.

There is an integrity about the work that's solid. The book is in content, if not in format, as fresh today as it was in 1943 when it was first published. But that's because the story spoke directly to the kids. At one time, if you were a kid and you asked another kid, "What's a good book?" and they said, "*Curious George,*" it was an infallible suggestion. The work got passed on down through the generations. And the reader never hit a bad book.

HTM: So to you, the original idea was just expanded and became a series.

WL: Yes, rather than planned as a series. Some authors plan a series, such as Harry Potter. One wonders whether the fifth book will have the value of the first. But I've only once deliberately done a series, and that was the North Star Books. It was a history series. Although I've done a number of books that became a series, such as the Anastasia titles by Lois Lowry, I never believed in planning one.

With titles such as *Rotten Ralph,* or *Lyle the Crocodile,* or *George and Martha,* the books build on one another as the enthusiasm comes to the author. A series is often planned to make money, but creative authors are not doing it for the money or anything other than to express the idea of the book. If you take a book like *George and Martha,* a picture book that's very simple and direct, by Jim Marshall, it is the greatest statement on relationships that I know of, including all those long-winded adult publications.

I'm not sure the readers of this will know the book, but when George pours the pea soup into his loafer, it's just wonderfully symbolic of one person relating to another.

"It isn't really the technical stuff; it isn't the wordage, the wording, the format, necessarily. It's that leap between mind and mind." Recognition and appreciation for the innermost workings—values—of the writing/reading process culminate in adult trade editor Ruth Hapgood's few words. She cuts to the quick of the publishing process.

The full meaning of Ruth's words, the act of reading with meaning so definitively discussed in this book, is demonstrated in the following interview with Walter Lorraine.

HTM: There are those I've interviewed who talk about the difficulty of finding the right person to be the illustrator. An illustrator who can really put into pictures from the author's message—one who gets the right relationship. You must have dealt with that challenge many times over a period of years.

WL: Yes.

HTM: And it would be interesting to hear your views.

WL: Well, I handled that the same way I would with an author. I would never just take a written piece and give it to an illustrator and say, "Here, illustrate this." I would always ask the illustrator if he would like to illustrate it. And then we'd negotiate terms and other details after that. The illustrator has to have some rapport with the content. If I find that's true, then I let the illustrator go ahead. I make certain that the author and the illustrator never meet so that the author can't influence the illustrator on how to present the material. If the author wants to do that, then the author should illustrate the work himself.

What's in the author's mind is not necessarily what's on paper. The only thing that should be influencing the illustration, at that point, is the written piece itself, and not the background of what the author was thinking about.

And if the author was thinking about a young lady with black hair, and he doesn't say "black hair" in his text, and the illustrator feels it should be blonde, then blonde it is.

HTM: Did I hear you correctly that you didn't want the author and the illustrator to meet?

WL: That's correct. I keep them apart just as much as possible. In recent years, there is more and more pressure to get them together, and I'm older and weaker, but during the most creative years that I had, I was able to keep them apart. And I think it's appropriate.

The illustrator should be able to bring his experience to the writing and interpret it. That will give more dimension to the book rather than the author pushing at his or her elbow to make artwork to the author's specification. If the author wants to do artwork, that's fine, and they should do it. They don't have to be an accomplished technician, but should be expressive in visualizing the written word. In fact, even there I have lots of theories, Hal. I'm opinionated, I suppose. But I would bet you that every good writer, every good author—adult, children's, whatever—has done an awful lot of artwork between the ages of maybe three to four and about seven. And it's visual art because at that time that's the form of expression that is most comfortable to them. They are true artists at that age. They don't mess around with technique. They express their ideas as directly as they are able through whatever means they have at their disposal. I would bet you that most writers have done a lot of artwork at that age.

So art, you see, for me is more an expression of an idea or of a story. It is just a different means from words but to the same end. I used to keep the authors and illustrators apart because the illustrators, in order to be creative, should not do only what the author tells them. They should be bringing their own experience and inner feelings to the work.

HTM: That the work generated.

WL: The work generated, yes. Back a number of years, when *Island of the Blue Dolphins* came out, I was involved with a lot of fine art painters. I decide that, being an art director, I would involve them in book work. I asked one if he would do the jacket for *Island of the Blue Dolphins*. He was excited to do the work.

He read the book and started to do some paintings. They were wonderful paintings. He did about four or five different works that would have been lovely in an art gallery, but they had nothing in the end to do with the book. He just used the book as a stepping-off point into his own world. Rather than trying to go back and interpret the book, he was just using it as an inspiration to go in his own direction.

That's not what I mean by allowing the illustrators to express their own ideas. They have to have a rapport with the idea that the author has expressed.

HTM: When the *Island of the Blue Dolphins* manuscript arrived in-house, there was discussion whether it was a work to be read by children or adults. Once the printed copy arrived in the bookstores, we found that people of all ages were reading it. Much attention is given in bookstores, schools, and libraries to classifying children's books by age level. How do you see it, Walter?

WL: I've done a lot of material that has created a so-called controversy whether it should be for children, like the Macaulay books. I look differently on what's for kids and what's for adults. I think all the material needs to be is accessible. And to make it accessible to a child, all you have to have is that it cannot contain anything that has adult experience or knowledge. Otherwise, you can cover everything, whatever you want to name. And a kid can relate to it okay.

As an example, we had an adult editor who became quite a good poet. His poetry got good reader response. But it was all based on fable and ancient stories. It would have been most inappropriate for kids, because they would have had to have a college degree to have enough knowledge to appreciate them fully. On the other hand, for Robert Frost you don't need that. You can experience it directly as long as it's accessible material.

Macaulay certainly does create books for all ages. We have always had our categorization of title that said "all ages." But the category that I feel is most confused is that of young adult. You can find a book that's listed as young adult for children that is bland and unrealistic, and then you can have another one that wouldn't make it through the censors in Boston for adults, but it's still all listed as young adult. There seems no way around that. It's just one of the things that you hope that the book will survive, I guess.

So this is how prestigious books for children come into being. The gifted individuals who write and edit them are dedicated to making credible literature of lasting quality available to generations of our nation's children. Accessible in school and public libraries, and in bookstores, these books support the teaching/learning process crucial to every child's well-rounded education.

But the benefits do not stop there. There is, too, the pleasure factor that results from developing a fondness for reading that can serve for a lifetime. And what parent and what child ever loses the sense of sheer joy and important one-to-one bonding of a child's book read and reread? Early experiences of that type provide a kind of family glue that is never forgotten. *Calico, the Wonder Horse* with those unforgettable characters, Stewy Stinker and Snake Eyes Poison, will never be forgotten at my home.

CHAPTER 7

Using What Pupils Know
to Teach New Concepts

Mathematics Instruction

Mathematics instruction shares with reading a crucial function in the elementary school. It too is often the object of criticism and proposed failsafe cures. Numerous personal accounts are heard about our youths' shortcomings in making change at checkout counters, with an accompanying call for a return to traditional mathematics instruction. Pupil mastery of the foundation skills integral to successful elementary school instruction in mathematics, as in reading, is a given.

Individuals who, as the saying goes, are playing without a full deck often make the *dumbing down* charge. The critics of our public schools should remind themselves that the schools are obligated to educate all comers in an increasingly diverse nation. In my chapter on testing, the impact of the *open-door policy* legislated in many states, giving all high school graduates entry into the state university, necessitated development of new college entry tests. These tests enabled universities to expand their curriculum to include entry courses—often at a remedial level—adjusted to accommodate the requirements of enlarged and less academically homogenous freshman classes. Textbooks written to meet this new market followed, but courses and textbooks for the rigorous courses of long standing continued. Just as the GI Bill opened the doors to greater educational opportunity for more of America's population, so too did the action of these states. The laudable inclusiveness of these actions broadened course offerings to serve a justifiable purpose.

Instruction, in the classroom and in textbooks, for both the most and the least able, is necessary if we are to meet our nation's educational objectives. Unfortunately, misinformation, combined with unacceptable performance by some educators and textbook publishers, provides validity to the claims of these critics, but they should not be regarded as the only show in town.

Some years ago, an officer from a large financial institution came to my office, seemingly unaware of the wide range of student abilities just mentioned, obviously convinced that all textbooks had been dumbed down. His purpose was to address—correct may better describe his intent—the error of our ways. He spoke at some length. In due course, I pulled our widely used, second-year algebra text from a shelf and suggested that he look through it with an eye to identifying sections he found in the dumbing down category. That exercise was followed by a session with our geometry text. He was obviously struggling with texts more advanced than he had used. I refrained from pulling down the advanced math text. The point had been made. He thanked me and left. It was obvious to me then, and remains so now, that more should be done to communicate the full nature of the challenges faced by educators and textbook publishers and what is being done to meet them.

Mathematics textbook author and former dean of the University of Kansas School of Education, Lee Capps, graciously agreed to discuss mathematics instruction and teacher education. As his publisher, I had ample opportunity to obtain the measure of his authorial contributions to Houghton Mifflin and, importantly, to the achievement levels of the elementary school children using his texts.

Lee's telling analysis of mathematics instruction and university schools of education shows what it takes to ensure a meaningful teaching/learning experience in mathematics.

HTM: Lee, here we are in Lawrence, Kansas. And thanks for your fine hospitality. It's great to be here with you.

LC: Well, thank you, Hal. It's been, first of all, a long and rewarding relationship for me. To understand how I got into publishing—you'd like to think that you have control over your own destiny—but I suspect a good part of how I got there was I just happened to be born at the right time.

When I was doing my graduate degrees at the University of Minnesota, modern math was just beginning to make its entry into the modern world. Of course, Sputnik and other things had a great impact. The point is that I came through college at a time when I grew right along with the movement, as opposed to someone who'd been around a long time and had to change their mind and be convinced about the value of modern math. My mind and knowledge evolved with the movement as time progressed.

Something I noticed early on in my growth was that it became easier for me to understand the mathematics that I knew based on the modern math approach. That was probably a key factor in my role as an advocate.

I had studied with some excellent professors when I completed my Ph.D. About the time I graduated, the peak of interest in the modern math movement existed. But there weren't any supporting mechanisms and materials, and there weren't a lot of people around who understood the entire picture very well, probably including me. And there was very limited experience with introducing it into the public schools.

In my first job, which was in California, I was asked to give a few talks on modern mathematics and to explain some of the basic concepts and the goals: what we were trying to accomplish, why we were using set theory, and what did that have to do with the whole process? In that explanation I tried to point out that we really weren't doing anything new in mathematics. It was going to be new to the elementary schools and to the secondary schools. But the material had always been around. It was just that we had never really called it by its legitimate name, and we'd never really introduced it to students in the way of emphasizing the structure of mathematics as opposed to just how do you manipulate equations. After a few of those talks, I soon found that I didn't have enough time to meet all of the requests. Obviously there was great demand and need for communicating the "movement" to the public, teachers, students, and parents.

Having had training from a professor who was very much a proponent of concrete materials, using manipulatives and hands-on materials for instruction, it occurred to me that this was a golden opportunity to show how one could use these devices to teach teachers basic ideas about the structure of mathematics and have the students learn much more interesting mathematics.

For example, one of the first experiences I remember in doing in-service work with our 1967 series was that people had trouble teaching missing addends: two plus what number gives you five $(2 + \boxed{} = 5)$ in equation form? Teachers were claiming first graders couldn't do that. I had taught such lessons with first graders, and I knew they could do it. But it was one of these tasks where sometimes you stumble along until you discover what the problem is.

Suddenly it dawned on me, after I had been confronted with this problem several times, that teachers were not using concrete aids. They needed to put out a stack of two objects, then ask a child how many more do you need to add to that to make five objects, and then have the child stack up the three more to be added, and then translate that model into an equation. They were trying to teach just the equation. They would say, "Okay, this is two, and here's a plus some number—let's put a box there. And so what does that equal?" With the modern math approach, you had a model available to show what happened. I would say, "Well, we've put three objects in that box, and that gives us the five." When you teach that equation using models, young children understand it very clearly because they have both a tactile and visual connection to help understand the abstract equation.

As a result of that experience, I began to realize that these teachers were not using manipulatives to teach these basic concepts. And the young learner, being so visually hands-on oriented, didn't have a chance to understand the abstract equation. Young children cannot abstract as an adult can. That brought us to the idea of how to combine the new mathematics and manipulatives into teaching structure. And how we would use specific modeling situations—where models represent the mathematical ideas, particularly the more abstract ideas—so that children can understand them. That seemed simple enough. It's easy enough to prepare your materials. But there are numerous ramifications when you make a decision like that. A major concern is the question: are all the teachers capable of using the materials? That became the major issue and challenge. Equipping teachers with high-quality instructional materials must be followed by massive amounts of in-service work to learn how to use the materials appropriately.

In Santa Barbara, I found that I wasn't really happy with the professional climate. It was the period when California had eliminated teacher training as a major at the undergraduate level. At that point, I decided that someday I would help write some math materials that students and teachers could use to learn mathematics effectively.

When we moved to the University of Kansas, where I'm located now, our home was adjacent to Dale Scannell's, who was already writing tests for Houghton Mifflin Company. He knew about my work with modern mathematics, because at Kansas I was teaching courses practically every night of the week on this new development and what was going to be needed to make a successful transition. He was interested in me, and he was already associated with Houghton. And it was through him that I became involved and met, well, first of all you—Hal Miller—

when you were, at that time, the regional manager of the Midwest Geneva, Illinois, Office. At subsequent meetings, once in Geneva and once at Dale's house, in our conversations I expressed to you my interest in doing this kind of work (writing and in-servicing a modern mathematics textbook series). Fortunately for me, and I hoped for Houghton Mifflin too, they had just successfully published a highly popular secondary mathematics program, known, probably, by most people as the *Dolciani algebra*. Their problem was a lack of foundational materials at the elementary school level to build readiness for people to go into their high school program. In that sense, it was a golden opportunity. The Dolciani algebra was extremely popular. It had captured probably seventy-five to eighty percent of the U.S. market.

But Houghton Mifflin at that time did not have an elementary program. So from their perspective, it was necessary to make a major financial investment to prepare such a program, and they wanted to make sure that it was not a traditional program. They wanted something that was tailored to fit their secondary programs. That is how I became involved in the writing process. Arthur Clark and, I think, probably Dick Gladstone, came to the University of Kansas, and we talked. The next thing was numerous trips between Boston and Lawrence and arranging to launch the elementary program. That's how I became involved. It has been a tremendous learning experience for me and equally gratifying.

HTM: Lee, we also had one other elementary math author, Ernest Duncan. After you met with Arthur Clark, Dick Gladstone, and others, including Manuel Fenollosa, they were bound and determined that you become the one who could bring the necessary practical school experiences to the program.

LC: One of the things I remember saying to you and to Arthur Clark and Dick Gladstone was that I didn't see how it would be possible to put together the best elementary mathematics program and market it successfully unless you built a strong supporting team to help teachers learn how to use it. It was my opinion that this was an obligation an author should be willing to accept. My experience with other people was that most authors didn't relish the idea of going out into the field and talking to teachers. To me that seemed to be the only way we were ever going to make this new math program, Modern School Mathematics, work. I saw this as an opportunity for Houghton Mifflin and for me. We could have constant feedback for revisions.

HTM: You were fully aware that many teachers had limited training in the teaching of mathematics. The teachers' colleges were not teaching the fundamentals. There were and are exceptions, of course, but on balance across the nation, they were not giving the teachers the nuts and bolts of what they needed in the classroom. Publishers, if they wanted their published programs to work— and Houghton Mifflin had found this to be the case with our reading program—had to develop teachers' manuals that supplied that missing ingredient in their background. Otherwise the program, no matter how good it was, didn't work. You brought such crucial components to the math program.

LC: You observed earlier the fact that students can learn all the rote mathematics in the elementary grades and then fail in algebra. A major reason for that happening is that we don't use the power of the whole number system and rational number system to make the connections to algebra. The NCTM Standards now place major emphasis on the need for these connections.

For example, if you add two fractions, you can find the common denominator and add the numerators. Algebraically the way we do that is to cross-multiply, and sum those two products over the product of the two denominators.

For example,

$$\frac{3}{4} + \frac{6}{5} = \frac{15 + 24}{20} = \frac{39}{20}$$

Well, that's the generalized algebraic rule: if you have a number $\frac{A}{B}$ plus a number $\frac{C}{D}$, then it's AD plus BC over BD. Teachers rarely make that connection to algebra when they're dealing with fractional numbers. The literature sometimes refers to this as *anchor-based* instruction: use what students know to teach a new, but similar, concept.

If we would make those connections between fractions and algebra, then students would too. It became clear to us that these were things we had to deal with in developing our elementary program.

That's the type of information we started incorporating into the revised 1972 manuals. Our argument was: "Look, if you learn to do these processes with fractions and you emphasize these connections, then when you get to algebra, it won't be such a mystery to students why those *letters* behaved the same way the *numbers* did in fraction examples." That was, to me, the essence of how you're going to improve mathematics instruction and learning. Surely, the new movement wasn't inventing any thing new in terms of mathematical discoveries. Sets had been around for ages, but it was new to the elementary school.

We began to realize that this lack of structure was a major factor in why students fail in algebra. They often fail to understand the structure of the number systems alone, and how they work, and their properties. So how could you expect students to succeed in algebra, except for those few bright ones who would somehow be able to manage it? And often, many of those who succeed are equation manipulators and often can't explain why an equation works. Interestingly, we subtitled one of the early editions Structure and Use.

HTM: A while ago I stated that teacher-training institutions across the nation generally do not do a very good job of training teachers. I'm wondering if a fundamental problem isn't that the institutions do give teachers a course in math or reading, but they don't get down to helping those teachers understand the fundamentals, such as those you're talking about.

LC: Yes. I think it goes back to that, Hal. I think that number one, you have to understand the needs at the time. When I came to the University of Kansas, we had 640 majors in elementary education. Preparing those students was a permanent faculty of five people and with about ten or twelve or fifteen graduate students assisting. We weren't doing an adequate job. A good portion of my time each spring was spent trying to tell students they weren't going to graduate or we weren't going to recommend them for certification. (At which point they would write letters to the governor and practically everybody else.) There was such a demand for teachers that all of these programs were overloaded in elementary education. Equally important, colleges lacked adequate personnel to do the preparation. That was part of what was happening in the sixties.

Even if you wanted to teach teachers all of the basics, how could you do that? My first class at Kansas had 147 students in it. It was an undergraduate math methods class. That became a real problem. Our approach to that over time was to have a limited enrollment. We now prepare fifty to sixty elementary teachers a year. That's all we prepare. We can be much more selective, so we have really competent students. The majors in the elementary education program right now are second only to the science majors with their entry scores into the university—really very bright people. And they are there because they want to be there. With thirty students a semester, we can now do things we never could do with 140–160 students. You're right, we weren't doing a good job. But at the University of Kansas, that has changed. We were one of the first five-year training programs in the country.

There are still the "degree mills" out there that are pouring out teachers with minimal mathematical knowledge and less-than-ideal experiences in teaching the concepts. This is self-defeating, in my opinion.

HTM: I don't mean to sound political, but when the federal government advocates placing 100,000 new teachers in the classrooms, as

though numbers alone will solve the problem, without also providing for their proper training, one must question the action.

Those who have been in the trenches, be they authors,
publishers, or teachers, understand the teacher training and
preparation assignment you're talking about. The government
seems to fail to give thought to this central ingredient.

LC: I think it's a matter of oversimplification of the idea. That if
you reduce the student/class ratio, things will happen. Now
that could work, that system could work, because we probably
have a million teachers sitting out there who are currently at
home not working, and we've had probably that many who
have left and are in the insurance business and taken other
jobs. And there are some qualified teachers out there, good
ones. But they're not the ones that are going to take those jobs.
It's going to go to new people who don't have the background
and experience.

Even in the sixties, we had those large numbers because
there was a shortage of teachers. There is no longer a shortage of
teachers; there are many teachers available. The problem is, you
need to get *qualified* teachers, and that's the word that's always
missing in legislation: qualified, well-trained teachers.

And your comment about adding new teachers to reduce
class size involves a critical caveat. Research on class size shows
achievement gains only if teachers modify their instructional
practices.

HTM: Qualified teachers and teacher-training institutions must
become a prime legislative objective.

LC: I think we're getting better-qualified people into the profession
over time. Back when we were doing the modern math movement, there was a parallel movement in teacher education that
required teachers to take at least a couple of math courses. When
I first came to Kansas, of that 640, maybe forty would have had

a math course. The rest would have never taken a math course at the college level. Currently our undergraduates must complete two or three math courses to be an elementary teacher.

We make these changes, but that still doesn't guarantee understanding. You still must know how and when children learn mathematics, and you have to understand that completely.

HTM: There were those times when you as the author, who thoroughly understand what you are trying to get across in your series, encounter an editor who thinks that he or she was improving what you have written by changing the illustration because it looks better or played better on the page. So even a publishing house, in which you have trained people—many of them editors with years of experience—can still come up short in comprehending the central ingredient which you, the author, are trying to get across in the manuals and/or the pupils' books. I believe I'm presenting that difficulty properly.

LC: Yes. I think that's a very important issue. A typical example in mathematics—and this was a decision we faced early in the game—was format in traditional primary textbooks; all computation practice examples were in vertical form. Seven plus two $\left(\begin{smallmatrix} 7 \\ +2 \end{smallmatrix}\right)$. We made the decision to introduce equation format: three plus two horizontally (3 + 2). Why? To reinforce left to right eye/hand reading readiness for algebra. Calculus, and most other secondary mathematics and beyond, use the horizontal format as well. It's a simple thing; it's not difficult to do. But when you introduce this material in the classroom, the teachers says, "Oh, this is too difficult; they can't do it this way." That was easy to defend. I would say, "Well, how do students read? They read from left to right. The equation is naturally left to right." You should be asking, "Why are we doing it vertically?" We should discard that, if we're going to discard anything. I think that traditional practice is part of the difficulty in implementing change.

So editors, in well-meaning ways, often will try to change, even rephrase a question you asked, when you've asked that question hundreds of times and know exactly how a student can misinterpret it, and you phrased it the way you did because you know that will avoid—is less likely to be misinterpreted. Sometimes we'll change it, and they don't understand. Now if it's grammatically incorrect, fine, fix it.

Then there is the problem of changing artwork. That was one of the things I noticed the most. Oftentimes the artwork didn't illustrate the concept as intended. The original artwork was designed to tie to the concept, and by its placement, with regard to the equation. Placing the art above or below the equations can facilitate the connection between the equation and the art. Illustrations can facilitate linking the symbolic and diagrammed representation. This is a very important factor in learning and understanding, often missed if one doesn't fully understand the process intended by the authors.

HTM: You're getting to one of the fundamental considerations within the overall conduct of a publishing house. The authors and the editors have very different jobs. And an editor working with you developing an elementary math text—that editor really has to be tuned not just to the manuscript, but also to all of those background considerations you have been discussing.

LC: The task was to communicate with that editor, and the editor had to communicate with you. You had to be somewhat compatible in your philosophy. If you weren't compatible in the philosophies, it really became difficult. I think what editors often had to recognize is, "I, the author, have the power to change this any way I want to. Obviously, the last decision is going to be mine. I cannot compromise the clarity of the presentation of the concept."

On the other hand, as an author, one must listen to what the editors are saying. Sometimes an author must rule against the editor and vice versa. In general, both should be trying to look at the issue from the learner's point of view as opposed to the point of view of "Let's get the material out." Too often deadlines get in the way. You get in the crunch of time, and people stop thinking about the learner.

And if author and editor are not working together, the product changes—loses its integrity. That is what I see happening in the current publishing world, where much of the material is farmed out to be produced; there is no author input; everything is left to the editor. The editor doesn't have that same necessary knowledge of how the content gets delivered in a classroom with a teacher and twenty-five children. And so editors can easily make decisions that will lead to trouble in delivering that page or that lesson to the student.

One of the positives that drew me to Houghton Mifflin in the first place was it's author-centered publishing. We were listened to, very respectfully. Not always did we get what we wanted. But I think when we had strong arguments, we succeeded. There was never a problem with that. And to me this is the power behind good instructional materials.

It concerns me today that we prepare so many materials without what I would consider well-versed people in the fields with sufficient subject knowledge and teaching experience. Experience was always my strong suit. I had taught in the elementary school quite a few years and was always considered to be an excellent teacher. By looking at a lesson, I could often tell where there was going to be a problem, where a student is going to be confused. That was one ingredient where I worked diligently to add to the creation of the lessons and manuals. But having been involved in teacher training, I wanted to expand the teachers' edition to explain to teachers why they're doing specific things and how it connected to earlier and later mathematical concepts. If teachers know why they're doing something, they are not as likely to object to it or to skip it.

HTM: Now, unfortunately, it's a case of what goes best in the market-place. In the earlier arrangement, editors had to understand what you authors were creating. At the same time the author had to understand that there are elements in the printing and marketing functions that are important. You have to integrate these two forces. It's inevitable that there is occasional conflict. But if all parties understood the ultimate purpose of the under-taking—and in my opinion it is the responsibility of the publishers' senior management to ensure that is the case—then most times the end product entering the marketplace represents both parties' considerations. The acid test, then, is: did the pub-lication ever get sold?

LC: Exactly. And I think that's part of what happened to us. We came on the scene when it became possible to do four-color printing. That was a decision we made to implement in our materials. The initial thought was: "Well, we'll use lots of color and make it look great." As authors we said, "No, no, wait a minute; let's think about this. We want to use the color, but we want to use the color and art functionally to teach ideas." That worked beautifully, because we were working together saying, "Okay, now how can we illustrate this concept so that the art and color provide an impressive image, but their use also facilitates clarity of represen-tation of what we are trying to teach mathematically on this page?" It's functional art; it's functional color, functional use of color, to support comprehension of the idea.

But going back to your idea of a systemic reform, reform-ers talk about bringing the curriculum into alignment, and publishers have a big responsibility to be sure that curriculum is in alignment. Research that I'm doing right now in vocabulary provides an example: NCTM (the National Council of Teachers of Mathematics) states, for example, "Mathematics is a language; you must learn the language to be literate." I say, "We really should be doing this. Students should master math language and be conversant with it." Nowhere can you find a list of math language for use in mathematics textbook series. What words and symbols should first graders know? What words and symbols should second graders know? That's what the researcher, Pickreign, and I did. We tried to establish a mathematics word and symbol list by grade level.

We went through and scanned five different first-grade textbooks, and then we scanned another five second-grade textbooks, and up through the sixth grade. We scanned all of the vocabulary and symbols into a computer, built a dictionary, and completed lists of words that occurred in the textbooks. Now there may be other words that need to be there that aren't there; we don't know that yet, but you have to start. It is interesting to note that there are numerous such lists for authors of reading books, but not for most other subject areas.

Now why is this important from a publisher's point of view? Recently I had a master's student do a study on a fractions chapter selected from five different textbooks. In one of those intermediate grade textbooks, the word *reciprocal* never occurs. How will a student ever learn the word *reciprocal* or what it means, if it never occurs in the instructional materials? Now, was there a lesson in the text that relied on the concept of reciprocal? Well, the context was used consistently when teaching division of fractions, but the word *reciprocal* itself never occurred in the book. So the student couldn't see it in print. Now what you hope is that the teacher would have used that word. But still, where do they see the word? If it wasn't in print, and all she did was talk about invert and multiply, students don't even know what the word looks like or how it relates to the term *invert*. They may know what it sounds like, but most students need to see and hear the word at the same time for reading recognition. What happens when the students who have not seen this word meet the term their first time on a standardized test? Most often, they don't comprehend the term and hence the item.

What is the purpose of this list of mathematical words at each grade level? My argument would be that publishers would be well advised to take this list, program it onto their computer, run it against their lists of words they're using in their textbooks, and see if they have all of those words and symbols included. If there are words missing, a keyword like *reciprocal,* it should be included, or students have been shortchanged. This is a simple change publishers could make that would be a great contribution to students' acquisition of the mathematical language and improve the matching of language in textbooks and standardized tests.

In math, we tend to pay no attention to this problem. Part of the problem is the list hasn't existed until now. The idea of the list is not that you drill the socks off of the students to master these words. Rather it is to ensure that publishers could say, "Let's be certain that we have all of the mathematics terminology first graders should know built into our program."

Another perfect example of that comes from that same study in fractions. The only time any fraction terminology appears in the textbook is in the fractions chapter. It doesn't occur anywhere else. So there's no chance to systematically review the terms and keep them in the students' spoken and written vocabulary.

One of the new developments is that there be a focus on reviewing concepts and vocabulary regularly to keep terminology fresh and alive in the students' minds. With assistance from technology, it has become possible to do this much more consistently. How long would it take for a publisher to match their material against a master list of first-grade words to determine if you had included all of them in a first-grade program? It wouldn't take long at all, but it would improve tremendously the quality of that product.

The end result is that the pupil sitting in the first-grade chair, when taking a test, would have a better chance of scoring well on that test, especially a standardized test.

That is a critical part of the achievement problem in the schools of America. Students don't know the words on the tests, their mathematical terminology. Therefore, they don't know what the question is asking. A prime example I can refer to is the simple test question that appeared on one popular standardized test: find the sum of two and three. If you take one hundred randomly selected students who miss this problem and you ask them what is two plus three, ninety or more of them will tell you it's five. But they don't understand the word *sum*, S-U-M. It's just missing for them. Often they confuse it with the other some and are totally confused.

Another example is that teachers often do not use the words *common denominator* or *denominator.* Many children don't understand what those words mean, because teachers refer to the denominator as the bottom number. The substitute language does not help the students learn the mathematical vocabulary; instead they are learning a substitute vocabulary that has no mathematical meaning. The term *bottom number* doesn't involve understanding what a denominator is.

HTM: The State Departments of Education developing their own tests and texts should heed your words.

Some years ago, I sent a letter to eight different Houghton Mifflin editors who had been very successful in seeing to the publication of works in trade and in education. I asked this question: "How come you have been extremely effective as an editor in bringing forth very successful publications?"

Arthur Clark, the editor with whom you worked, was insistent about the terminology you choose and how you used it.

LC: I think that's correct. I don't see how an author could succeed without an editor. At the same time, I don't see how an editor can succeed without the author, because the author often has knowledge about the subject that the editor doesn't have. The editor often has knowledge about things like grammatical expressions and ways to state information, and the best terminology to use. And often editors know which words are being used on standardized tests, or which is the most acceptable usage of a word. An author might not know this.

I think it's the blending of those two minds that really becomes a powerful ingredient. Then there are those who tend to focus too narrowly. One has to possess a "bear trap" mind to keep all of those things in proper focus. That is where we as authors are less experienced. We keep a lot of elements about the content knowledge on focus, but we don't keep some of these other elements of communication in mind. Editors are expected to have some mathematical knowledge, but they must possess their own special knowledge. For example, how does this concept become reinforced through artwork? How does this entire lesson lay out in terms of page format? That, to me, is an invaluable thing that no author could do alone. A strong author–editing team is critical to the production of high-quality material.

HTM: Publishers and authors must constantly revise materials to provide the current copyright dates schools demand, meet the competition, and, of course, use what authors have learned through new research and classroom use to improve their publications. It isn't a case of just revising, as some people claim, so sales can be increased.

LC: We made a decision that there were at least two things we could do. One was to deal with the changing environment. A perfect example of that would be technology and calculators. Certainly in subsequent revisions, we had to include calculators in instruction and use them appropriately. My personal feeling is that in the area of mathematics we still don't do that well. In some ways, education has been completely missed by technology in terms of using it to teach students. While students get experience with technology, we haven't capitalized on it as a teaching medium. So we knew revisions of our first editions would require inclusion of calculators.

But even more importantly, we knew that in the marketing and revision process that if you don't address the concerns, the problems that teachers are having, then the revision has not met its purpose. Somehow, you must know what to do about this. Maybe it means deleting something you're doing now or switching it around in sequence.

An example to illustrate this was our coverage of addition and subtraction. Based on research, we taught addition and subtraction together, so that students would have an in-depth understanding of the inverse relationship. This is a powerful concept that helps in memorizing the basic fact families as shown below:

$3 + 2 = 5$, so $5 - 2 = 3$ and

$2 + 3 = 5$, so $5 - 3 = 2$.

Again, connecting to algebra, you see that:

$A + B = C$, so $C - B = A$ and

$B + A = C$, so $C - A = B$.

(This is another instance where we fail to help students see the connection of the inverse operation in arithmetic with the same operation in algebra.) Well, from working with people in the schools, we soon learned our next revision would need to introduce the two operations separately, no matter how solid it was research-wise; past tradition wasn't going to allow the combining of the two. This was a case where we had to decide: do we want to risk everything and stick with doing it our way and leave the book to sit on the shelf, or do we want to say, "Okay, let's go back and separate them out, satisfy the teachers, but find the compromise position that allows us to bring the two operations back together later"? Compromise is among the most difficult things to accomplish and still focus on quality content presentation.

My experience with editors was that those editors who worked the material in the field were the most effective. Often editors relied on information from other people. Sometimes it was from representatives; sometimes it was somebody they talked to at a meeting. My own feeling is that this is all second-hand information. The problem with that is that you get into people's personal preferences rather than focusing on really valid problems and solutions.

Since I had a huge investment in this program, I wanted to be out there in the classrooms, seeing how it was being used. I didn't enjoy having teachers being critical of the material and hearing about their problems. On the other hand, when they were open and often blunt, I understood the problem. Then I could really talk rationally about why we must consider a change. We have to change this, because if we don't, we're going to fail in the classroom.

Now if a problem was mentioned infrequently, I think I was astute enough to say, "Well, that's really not a problem; there's one teacher who is unhappy about it." But if I went to fifteen different meetings over a period of several months and heard the same concern, I knew we had a trouble spot, and we had to come up with a solution for that in the revision. And that to me was a critical thing about being "in the trenches"—that's the element about teamwork that's hard to beat.

As an editor, one cannot sit in Boston and know the true significance of a problem. Nor can a rep traveling his territory know if it is a national problem or a local problem. You need someone who is working in all areas of the country and in direct contact with teachers and administrators. That is where Houghton's consultants are very helpful. The company's policy of having math consultants work in the schools where they can see and hear firsthand what was happening is a valuable resource. Consultants were doing very much the same thing I was doing, but on a regional level.

HTM: Understandably the editors can't know all that's happening in the classroom, but aren't the salespeople on the cutting edge, for they're in there trading blows with all kinds of people?

LC: They know the front edge of the problem, but they don't always know what is happening beyond that. You mentioned how publishers must keep changing as they revise, and that you have to meet change and embrace it. As an author, issues I would never think of became apparent as I worked in the schools.

As an author, you often don't think about how a state adoption list can impact what you must do. If you sell in a state and they specify some obscure requirement, you must meet that requirement to qualify for listing. You must publish a textbook that has a lesson included on Roman numerals. If you can't claim it is included in your program, that is a tally against you in the evaluation process and can lower your score in qualifying for that list. Many state lists have specifications of that nature, which usually are the remains of tradition and failure of states to update their criteria regularly.

It was fascinating to me how such unusual specs could enter into the adoption picture. In the end you are challenged creatively as to how can you take that requirement and integrate it with a concept you are already teaching. To make it a valid, worthwhile learning experience for the child, rather than just a window dressing, is the key to quality material. It is one thing to say, "Here is one example with Roman numerals," but it is quite another to say you have done something to teach Roman numerals and to give the students a feeling of the historical significance of the idea and how it relates to place value. This occurs over and over as you work in the field. You cannot learn that subtle information any other way than by working and dealing with your clients.

Another thing that I am researching currently is this statistical fact: as many as sixty-five percent of the words in the glossary in a mathematics textbook don't occur in the textbook itself.

It's absolutely astounding. You would wonder why that happens. I have some suspicions as to why that happens on the publishing end of it. It is a problem the publishers must address; nobody else can change this. We must realize that when you farm out the glossary preparation and somebody compiles it without looking at your manuscript to build that glossary, there is bound to be a mismatch. You have many words in the glossary that are not used in the text. That is poor pedagogy. You want most of the words in your glossary to match what you're using in that particular book. This is a crucial element publishers must consider in terms of their materials. These are things that we continue to discover, and we must address them in preparing materials of high quality.

HTM: The development and publication of a textbook series is an expensive undertaking. Most textbooks have traditionally been published for a single national market. The economics of subdividing a program into a half dozen different series are prohibitive. Customer calls for distinctly different subparts to be integrated into the program without destroying its basic tenets take a lot of doing on the part of both the authors and the publishers. The basic concern I've always had about such action is the likelihood of it disrupting the sequential buildup of the basic skills the author structured into the series.

LC: It's popular for schools to say, "We're going to write our own program, have everything tailored just the way we want it." They say, "Well, give us access to your materials, and we'll take the pages and use the ones we want." Then when their test scores go down, who do they blame? They blame you because "You didn't have the materials we wanted when we made the decision."

You almost have to have a national program if you're going to fit the assessment programs that are out there, because those represent national programs. It makes no sense to enter into a national testing arrangement and compare yourself to other schools on a national test when you're teaching a regional or local curriculum.

You can adapt your curriculum, but you very well better meet national standards, for you are so judged. That's what the systemic reform movement is all about. It says, "You had better bring your curriculum into alignment with the testing and assessment that's going on out there, if you want your students to be measured fairly and appropriately." Most foreign countries have a single national curriculum and a single national assessment program, and isn't it interesting that they always seem to do better than we do? And to some extent, I think part of our problem in achievement of mathematics and reading is that we have local control. Education is a locally controlled thing. If Lawrence, Kansas, wants to teach the Siberian Revolution, they can do that. They have a right to do that. But the problem is, no standardized testing program is going to pay much attention to that. If they omitted American history to do that, the students are not going to do very well on an American history exam. That is what systemic reform is about: that we must align our curriculum and assessment nationally or we will never maximize our potential in education.

That is what my vocabulary research involves. We must have some basic agreement as to what is basic. That doesn't mean you can't adapt your curriculum and include additional things. But you prioritize the basics before you do the fancy stuff.

In neglecting a basic curriculum, the result is that children suffer. Publishers have always been the ones who have helped specify a national curriculum with their materials. You try to meet the needs of Florida and Texas and so forth, but most publishers haven't done it at the expense of every other state in the Union. Other states might not like something that's required in the California curriculum, but California does not have everything it wants either.

HTM: Recently, the head of teacher training in a college informed me she would never think of training her students to use a single basal series. "Every teacher should be able to find his or her own way." I inquired about the fundamental word-identification skills and comprehension skills that are required to be a proficient reader: "How can you be sure the fundamental skills are taught?" Young teachers trained to do whatever they want should know about these things, yet that seems not to have crossed this instructor's mind. Experienced teachers, particularly in the primary grades, will tell me you've got to have an organized basic set of skills to teach if you're going to be sure that they are being taught. It's the fundamentals of such subjects as math and reading that must be addressed in an organized manner and not left to chance.

LC: We're big on teaching students to think and thinking skills and so forth, but let me tell you, you can't think without knowledge. What a lot of people have done in these sort of classy movements that we've experienced is to say, "Okay, you don't need knowledge to teach reading anymore. All you need to do is have good literature, and kids will learn to read." They still have to have the ability to identify words. They still must know the difference between an A, a B, a C, a D, an E, and an F. Those are still basic things. And what we've done to some extent is to give our teachers the impression, or allowed it to persist, that one can throw out the basic skills that we know are critical.

HTM: You can't learn how to read without knowing the components of a reading act, which involves letter recognition, sound association—all of those things. And the research is replete with evidence that students often lack these fundamentals and don't become good readers.

If we go back to your earlier comments when you were discussing two plus two or the sum of and recall that just the change of one word means all the difference between a high percentage of proper answers and a lesser percentage, then the argument we are making becomes very clear. Certain fundamental understandings, even as to your terminology, are part of the learning process.

LC: I think that says it. What you said has reminded me of what often happens with teachers when we make a curriculum change or a revision. For example, the new literature movement in reading has somehow carried along with it the message that we are throwing out basic skills. We're not going to teach those anymore. The same idea was true when we went back to using manipulatives in math. It was, we're going to throw out all this emphasis on basic knowledge, like basic facts and all that. We have reduced some of the excessive focus on computation, but it has not been eliminated. Somehow teachers pick up the message: "Now I don't have to do this anymore—that is, teach basic knowledge."

What happens in education is an inability to maintain a centricity and then change around the edges. Every time we make a change in a curriculum area, we go whole hog to the left or to the right. We just don't stay around the center lane. We make these wild swings and the message becomes: we are not teaching basic facts any more in math; we're in modern math now, or we use manipulatives now, or constructivism, or whatever.

In the modern math movement, one of the mistakes we made was in conveying the movement to the public in general.

We tried hard to introduce the correct mathematical terminology, and it somehow became: "All they are doing is teaching students new words." (And difficult words in the opinion of many.) We were not teaching students math. I think people misinterpreted what modern math was about. Then lack of achievement had an easy scapegoat: modern math.

Another thing is that, with all of our communication mechanisms and the media and its power, it's easy now for almost anybody to get a hearing. Malcontents are more likely to request a hearing than somebody who is happy.

California is a perfect example of that. How many times have they adopted a dramatic change in the mathematics curriculum and then moved back to basics. These wide swings are a challenge to preparing sound educational programs. If the issue is that one of those approaches is better, if back to basics is better, then why do they keep moving away from it each time they go back to it? This circumstance often leads to public cynicism about all educational change.

HTM: What were your editorial-related experiences as an author?

LC: Well, I think the secret in our case was that the editorial people had responsibilities farmed out among the authors. They had a very well-organized system where we got to see each other's material. So if I'm writing a lesson in the second grade, I know what somebody in the fifth grade has done with the ideas in my lesson. I know a little bit better how to prepare. I think we did a better job in that area than probably the average publishing house would do. It was never just the editor who looked at your materials. Your coauthors also looked at it. Now I say I assumed they looked at it. At least I think all of them looked at it in terms of what they were writing. They may not have looked at every lesson you wrote, but they knew when they were writing something on fractions, if they wanted to go back and check what was done back in second grade, that they could do so. This helped consistency in the materials so the learner could see the connections from level to level.

There were numerous times where we had to change a lesson when someone said, "This won't fit with what we're doing in fifth grade, or vice versa." That becomes a very important element in terms of achieving consistency in a program, thus helping the learner learn it. It sometimes can be such a simple thing as using the same model that you used in your earlier lessons with the skill reviewed in later lessons. If we used Cuisenaire rods at the second grade or some kind of a rod arrangement, then it was useful in the fifth grade on the first lesson in fractions, to use those rods again to bring the learner back into play in connecting to fractions. Then you can move forward and develop your more unrelated concepts.

HTM: The reality is, if you do not have strong editorial input and if the coauthors do not coordinate, then you're back to outsourcing.

LC: Sure.

HTM: There must be a team effort to understand one another, or the authors lose track of what they are about, and continuity is lost.

Would you be willing to summarize your thoughts about what you did through your relationship to the publisher and vice versa, and the significance of what that combined effort achieved for the long-term welfare of the nation?

Obviously, you achieved success. How do you feel about all of that, knowing that along with all that you achieved, your efforts unquestionably had a significant impact upon future generations of the nation?

LC: Yes. That's a hard one, because trying to measure what you've done is really elusive in this business. I think about the fact that when we had sixty-five percent of the business out there in that elementary program, thousands of minds were being shaped every day by material we had put together. It's what they did with that knowledge, and who knows for which of those students it made such a significant difference so that they went on to be leaders in other fields. It's difficult to track that. In some ways, it is almost a stroke of fate, but you know it had to make a difference.

Probably the biggest difference it made was in me as an individual in terms of my perspective. I often thought about that as I talked to my colleagues at the University of Kansas about administration and the administration department. If we were talking about how school finance works, I would ask, "Well, how does it work in California?" Or, "How does it work in Florida?" It was amazing to me that they really had no comprehension of this beyond their local area. It was the incidental knowledge I picked up in all of my travels that was invaluable to me. It gave me a whole new context and perspective that I had never had before. I always felt good about it—I guess it's selfish in a way—but I always felt good about what I, myself, learned in the process.

I guess the greatest satisfaction I get out of the process is that mathematics scores haven't declined significantly, if at all. If you think about that, at first you ask, "What's the significance of that?" And I think when you think about all the people at the low end of the mathematics achievement perspective (spectrum) that are in school today that were not there thirty years ago, we have held our own. For example, all of the non–English-speaking students. What has happened with test scores is that we've added more people than we've ever had, yet we've been able to maintain our own. I would like to think that we deserve a little credit for that.

If you look at the mathematics materials that are published today, I can show that many of those ideas were ideas that we generated in our programs to begin with. One big idea that I hope still has promise is the vocabulary project that I'm working on now. I still hope to have that research make an impact on math instruction. And I would hope that maybe publishers would be interested in using the list to monitor their publications for consistency. I can't help but believe that if you gave teachers a list of words and said, "These are actually keywords in mathematics that first graders or second graders have to know," teachers would be certain that students knew these words. To be sure, there would be teachers who would misuse that list. But far more of them would use it appropriately. I think you know who started the message on language and vocabulary in mathematics. We did at Houghton Mifflin. As an authorship team, we started that message. It was one of the things we picked up on as we were going along in our revisions. I take great pride in that.

The experience I had with the reps and consultants was equally rewarding. They were very professional people. Much knowledge was exchanged with them. It was always just exchanging knowledge. It reminds me of the old adage: "If you find a job you like, you'll never have to work a day in your life." That summarizes my feeling well with regard to working with Houghton Mifflin. I never had to work a day in my life. I like what I'm doing and just always enjoy doing it. And as I said last night when we were at the table with my family, had I not done that, we wouldn't have this home, and the family would not have had all the experiences they have had.

So there is great self-satisfaction. Even though there were sacrifices to begin with, I say that is part of the "game." It's been a rewarding experience, and you've been a big part of that, Hal.

This chapter has provided in essence a rare backstage visit with a leading author of elementary school mathematics textbooks and dean of a leading university school of education. Lee's account is a model case history of the author/publisher relationship. It demonstrates clearly that textbook series do not just happen; rather they are based on a combination of dedicated hard work, research, full awareness of the teaching/learning process, and, significantly, the author's one-to-one involvement with educators across America.

The all-important need to provide elementary school teachers and their pupils with carefully structured texts ensuring sequential development of the basic skills—the fundamentals—is amply demonstrated. What's given is practical, down-to-earth information that, once made known, can reassure educators and parents alike that our authors and the house of Houghton placed educating children at the top of our priorities.

Here again, as in Chapter 5 on reading, the importance of sound instruction at the elementary school level, ensuring mastery of the reading and mathematics basics, is made obvious. Lee describes what is needed to master mathematics and how to teach it. Clearly, much has been accomplished toward that end in the schools and textbooks, but much more needs to be accomplished. One can only hope that the present willingness of proven successful authors to pass along this treasure trove of know-how will induce new waves of authors and editors to carry the work that comes before them to new heights. That end can best be served by the authors and editors of the future working in creative, innovative, author-centered publishing houses dedicated to publishing works focusing on properly sequenced fundamentals at the elementary school level.

CHAPTER 8

Kill the Messenger

Standardized Tests

The years from World War II through the 1980s are regarded by many knowledgeable educators as the "Golden Age of Testing," for during that period, publishers' norm-referenced tests were taken by millions of national elementary and secondary school pupils, and the results put to good use.

This chapter contains seven sections: (1) "Testing Fundamentals"; (2) "Authors and Friends Who Greatly Mattered"; (3) "Diagnosis: The Business of Testing" (the core purpose of commercial publishers' tests); (4) "The Ability to Learn and to Cope: Testing IQ" (reasons for responsibly using intelligence tests—cognitive ability tests); (5) "Testing the Tests" (commercial tests were critically evaluated by competent authorities, plus survival in the marketplace); (6) "The ACT–SAT Controversy" (a primary-source account of how the American College Test came into being, challenging the Scholastic Aptitude Tests across much of the nation); and (7) "Ensuring Enlightened, Responsible Use of Test Scores" (an insightful account of the uses and misuses of tests by the nation's senior test consultant).

Testing Fundamentals

With every testing program, it is necessary first to determine for what purpose the tests are to be used. It is equally important to determine the fundamentals observed in their development by responsible professionals and their subsequent evaluation by qualified reviewers.

The achievement tests developed by Houghton, for example, were designed to obtain test scores to improve instruction, thereby assisting teachers and pupils in the teaching/learning process. The tests were based on the best published research on school curriculum and developed by leading educators in subject-specific fields and in tests and measurement. The test questions selected for use had survived extensive item reviews and analysis during item tryouts. The final items were then used in standardization procedures involving thousands of pupils from across the nation. This thorough process ensured test content representative of the nation's instructional focus. The authors spared no effort to ensure that the tests measured what they were purported to measure—that they were valid tests.

All of our tests, in the areas of cognitive abilities (intelligence tests to most readers) and achievement, produced valid and realistic score-discrimination indices across time. Simply stated, the tests, through their numerous revisions following extensive use over the years, created a database against which each revision could be assessed. This asset ensured that the results were realistic—not indefensibly high or low due to test construction flaws. Additionally, this broad distribution of scores—the growth curves, for example—provides a useful means for analyzing differing student needs.

The major test publishers' publications are norm-referenced. The data collected at the time of standardization are what distinguish them from classroom teacher tests, unit and chapter tests that accompany textbooks, other commercially prepared curriculum materials, and various state-mandated tests. Standardization programs are planned by the author and implemented by the publisher. Scientifically structured, the standardization samples require administration of the tests to a carefully selected sample of pupils representative of the nation's population. Briefly, the school sample adequately represents all geographic regions, districts ranging from the smallest to the largest, urban and rural systems, and the full spectrum of socioeconomic status. Parochial and private school samples are also used. Both fall and spring standardization samples are obtained, thereby providing an all-important tool for teachers to use in determining where additional instruction is necessary at the time in the school year when they were identified.

In our culture, it is considered an insult to be classified as "below average" in any trait or ability. Hence, norms, which place half the student population below average, are viewed almost as deplorable as racism by some people. Laypeople often fail to realize that tests can do no more than provide a sample of the legitimate tests that instruction has prepared children to perform. Even the best teachers cannot adequately review such a sample and state confidently what performance (score) a slow learner, an average learner, or a fast learner will attain. When samples of intellectual tasks are undertaken for the first time, we simply can't determine from logic or inspection alone how the full range of individuals will perform. Norms are the only satisfactory way in which performance can be meaningfully described.

One might say that tests developed in this way provide a kind of preventive maintenance rather than allowing weaknesses to accumulate, only to be identified at a later date when a pass or fail is the outcome.

There are numerous contributors to the composite curriculum in place across America. Test developers must take them into account. In Chapters 5 and 7, reading textbook author Bill Durr and mathematics author Lee Capps define the importance of their textbooks in providing elementary school pupils with carefully structured programs to teach the skills basic to each discipline. And critical thinking skills are not ignored. Often referred to as higher order thinking skills, these are the cognitive functions beyond mere recall of information. Their mastery requires students to retrieve information and then interpret, infer from, classify, analyze, or compare it. In Chapter 4 the influence of the state adoption states on their own curriculum guides and in turn on textbook publishers' publications is discussed. All of the above are influenced by the subject matter standards published by such professional organizations as the National Council of

Teachers of Mathematics, the International Reading Association, and the National Council of Teachers of English.

Obviously, the demand on author/publisher teams to publish valid tests capable of measuring what's being taught in the public, parochial, and private schools is extensive. The developers of established test publications obviously benefit from the accumulated statistical data and curriculum content knowledge acquired over the years while working with the various contributing entities. Lest we forget, kids graduating from high school enter national-based competition. That competition comes in the form of college entrance examinations, civil service tests for police or fire duty, the military, or a host of other challenges for which a full and complete education is important.

I have yet to be dissuaded from the belief that it requires the combined resources of authors in major universities and established test publishers, operating over an extended period of years, to ensure acceptable norm-referenced testing programs for use with the nation's school children.

Norm-referenced test authors and their publishers easily relate to the tale in Greek mythology of the luckless messenger who upon informing the king that his army had lost a crucial battle, was rewarded by the exasperated king's order to kill the messenger. The scores yielded up for a school system, following administration of a publisher's test, can, and often do, constitute an unwanted, even if needed, message. Reaction then takes the form of, "Let's use a different test." The test publisher's antidote for "kill the messenger" is trust. There can be no tolerance for tests seeking commercial, political, or similar leverage. An individual's test score, just as an individual's blood sample, subjected to the test, analyze, and prescribe process by one's doctor, must be complete in quality and reliability.

Authors and Friends
Who Greatly Mattered

I regard my years as head of Houghton's test editorial as the highpoint of my publishing career. The roster of test authors with whom I worked, the tests published, the positive impact these publications had on the teaching/learning process, and the lasting friendships created, all combined to establish an author, university, publisher family.

I've often felt a tinge of nostalgia for that wing of the University of Iowa, called East Hall, and the people I met there. It was where E. F. Lindquist, the senior author of the Iowa Tests of Basic Skills and the Iowa Tests of Educational Development, and his colleagues were housed when I first met them in 1957. Throughout this book, I've made frequent use of the words "the unique factor," sometimes adding that the great authors I know could render the complex simple. That "East Hall Gang," who excelled in creating intellectual properties, so qualified.

E. F. Lindquist (Lin) was the East Hall leader, not by decree, but by his sheer ability, intellect, and personality. He didn't have to tell you he was good—you instinctively knew it. That statement in no way detracts from the other members of the group, for no one individual, no matter how gifted, could accomplish all that was developed in the East Hall setting. Operations of that magnitude, if they are to achieve ultimate success, require meaningful cooperation, participation, and the backing of able, often selfless, colleagues who provide enabling support—people such as Iowa University's President Hancher and others.

There were far too many people at the University for me to write about each one. Later in this chapter, the reader will get a sense for what various authors were like through interviews with A. H. Hieronymus, author of the Iowa Tests of Basic Skills, Leonard Feldt, author of the Iowa Tests of Educational Development, and Dale Scannell, author of the Tests of Achievement and Proficiency. I use the University of Iowa setting, where many of our test authors resided, but it is equally the case that other authors located in other settings, including Teachers College at Columbia University, created environments of like nature. It is only through intense effort on my part that I'm refraining from writing about all of the others. Unfortunately Father Time added his restraint, for I would much liked to have interviewed, at the very least, Robert Thorndike, coauthor of the Cognitive Abilities Tests (CogAT), and Maude Merrill, coauthor of the Terman Merrill Tests of Intelligence.

My earlier use of the word "family" is not used lightly. There is no more deserving individual than Freda Hieronymus, who on numerous occasions graciously and competently hosted husband Al's generous invitations to Houghton personnel to come to his house for large social functions. The 5:30 A.M. fried chicken breakfast with all the trimmings for Manuel Fenollosa, the many large-group dinners, the late-night musical gatherings, and just plain old bull sessions over a bottle of beer were all part of it. How Freda found the time and energy to see to these successful activities, I'll never know. She was always smiling, friendly, and interested in our conversations. This was in addition to a family to look after and a major role in the renovation of downtown Iowa City, Iowa. There is no way I can adequately state in written words the impression and warmth of feeling Freda's hospitality and attention made on the Houghton sales representatives, editors, and other authors from across the nation who spent so much of their time away from home. Freda made a big difference to the total sense of family we all treasured. Nor can there be any question but that knowing both author Al Hieronymus and his family in addition to his test publications that Houghton Mifflin salesmen went forth not just intent on selling the tests, but also preaching the gospel about the core values upon which the tests were constructed.

Al Hieronymous tells about the joke Houghton's reading series authors, Lucile Harrison, Paul McKee, and certain colluding Houghton accompanists played on Professor J. B. Stroud, coauthor of the Harrison/Stroud Reading Readiness Test, on his first visit to the McKee's home in Greeley, Colorado. On the occasion of my first meeting Stroud, there snapped into my mind an image of that learned, courteous, slightly irreverent, and fascinating professor in Ross Lockridge's great novel—one of the best novels ever published, in my opinion—*Raintree County*. The Harrison/Stroud Reading Readiness Test, written to be used for the Houghton Mifflin Reading Series, captured all of the clarity, directness, and logic of the McKee reading series' word identification skills. It was so professionally structured as to have value as a test for use with all pupils, whether or not they were using the McKee series.

You will see, from the following, yet another reason why I enjoyed being with these people.

HTM: Al, you had a collection of great people here at the University, all of whom were memorable individuals. I remember Professor J. B. Stroud being at your house for dinner one night, when he started telling his many amusing stories. I guess he was kind of a role model or mentor for you, wasn't he?

AH: Oh yes, absolutely. I remember the most interesting story concerning—now wait a minute. Was it Bill Spaulding? No, it wasn't. Did you have somebody named Marvin back in the history of the company? Out in Colorado?

Anyway, Stroud went out to Colorado to visit—to address some sort of a conference; it was one of McKee's conferences. Lucile Harrison and Jim Stroud were represented there for the Harrison/Stroud Readiness Test. So, Stroud traveled out for it, and when he came into the Denver railroad station, some old character that was dressed in beat-up clothes and had an old hat on his head, met him. And he asked, "You Stroud?" And Jim allowed as to how he was Stroud.

This character had an old beat-up truck, and he said, "I'm supposed to pick you up and take you to Mr. McKee's house." So then, he started talking about all the work that he did around the place for Mr. McKee, and he drove and drove and drove. Stroud said, "It took forever in that old beat-up truck."

And they finally got to McKee's house. And when Mr. McKee met him at the door, everybody just laughed their heads off. They thought that was the biggest joke. They had set it up. Whoever it was was a Houghton Mifflin big shot!

So, Stroud went inside. And he said very soon after he got in, there was a gorgeous lady coming down the stairs. So, Paul McKee introduced her as Mrs. McKee. And Stroud said, "You fooled me once, but you're not fooling me twice. You can't be married to anybody that looks like that!" But it really was Mrs. McKee.

HTM: That was typical of the company for years. I shall always remember all the humor around the place.

AH: Oh absolutely. Well, this wasn't a joke, but I remember once when Manuel Fenollosa got into Iowa City down at the railroad station at five o'clock in the morning. I met him, and we went for a "typical Iowa" breakfast, which consisted mostly of liquids and fried chicken, and I don't remember what else we had—out at my home. Lindquist and Stroud and many others were there for the breakfast.

HTM: Manuel has since told me, "All the lights were on in the house and everyone was there. I thought, 'What's going on here?' Here were all these people and they served fried chicken, the whole thing, for breakfast." That experience just lasted forever in his memory.

Make no mistake about it, however, every one of the authors knew his profession and was very demanding about getting things right and that requirement encompassed editorial. I recall to this day my feeling of total abject depression when Lindquist and Hieronymus returned to me the marked up copy of several paragraphs I had written about some long-forgotten topic for inclusion in their test manual. Al Hieronymus once said it all when he responded on my behalf to the inquiry about my test construction credentials, made by some professor whose name I don't recall. I do recall that the professor had me in his crosshairs. Al answered on my behalf by saying, "Hal doesn't know all that much about what goes into test construction, but he knows what to do with tests, once he has them." A lesson learned that I never forgot. Publishers in an author-centered publishing house make it possible for authors to be published, but we are not the authors—both parties are needed.

A no-nonsense, no phony-baloney approach to the business of the day prevailed in East Hall. It was friendly, helpful, and focused. Here is a story Don Beggs, an East Hall Ph.D. and president of Wichita State University, told me, about his first meeting with Al Hieronymus and Paul Blommers, another Houghton author.

As a young student, Don was sent by a university dean to East Hall to find an advisor. Two names had been given to Don—Paul Blommers and Al Hieronymus. The observation had been made that of the two, life might be a bit easier working with Paul.

On the scheduled day, Don arrived early in the East Hall office area and took a seat in the hallway. Shortly thereafter a person Don did not know arrived, entered his office without speaking and then, in a few minutes called out in his no-nonsense way—Al had served as an officer in General Patton's Army during World War II—"You, out there, are you Beggs?"

DB: So I was waiting there for Paul Blommers, and Hieronymus called me and said, "Come on in, sit down, and let's talk." There I was talking to the man that I'd been told was the hardest and to avoid, and he was being so nice. He had so much common sense, he knew the area, and so forth, and he looked at me, and he said, "Who are you working with on your assistantship?" I said, "Well, no one." I said, "I went down to see the assistant dean, and he told me to come down here and see if any of you were interested in working with me." He says, "Want to work for me? What do you say to that?" And I said, "Well, yes, I'd like to if you think I can do the job for you." "Well, yeah, you can work for me." And so, it wasn't five minutes later Blommers came in, and Al Hieronymus said, "Hey, have you met Beggs?" "No." And Al says, "Well, you can talk to him, he's going to work for me." So, that's how I met Blommers and Hieronymus.

These authors were real people. One gets a sense for the human being involved through Al Hieronymus' following story:

AH: One of the things that Paul Blommers (author of *Elementary Statistical Methods in Psychology and Education* with Robert A. Forsyth, Houghton Mifflin, 1977) provided was an office. He had a big office and he had a big table in there. And so we always used to meet for coffee in the middle of the morning: Lindquist,

Feldt, Blommers, Hieronymus, and Edberg, who was the chief engineer on our project to develop the high speed test scoring machine. Also John Dolch, you know, he was the son of Edward Dolch at the University of Illinois. He got a Ph.D. in psychology, and he was also an electronics genius. And then later on he became the first head of our University Computer Center. And then Bob Ebel, author of *Essentials of Educational Measurement* (Prentice Hall, 1986), who also became a Vice President at Educational Testing Services. So, we were all around the table, every morning, to talk about things.

We used to argue quite a bit. I told you about Ebel proposing topics for discussion—to get something that was more or less controversial. We kind of ganged up on him too. We kind of took turns working him over. The biggest single issue that we always fought about at times—and kept coming back with—was his defense of true/false tests. He loved true/false tests. And most people didn't like true/false items. You know, a true/false test is a multiple-choice test with two responses, and it's either yes or no; it's either right, or it's wrong. And there are very, very few important issues in life for which the answer is true or false. There are almost none. It's almost impossible to come up with what I would consider to be a good true or false item. Because the question is— or the answer is—almost always, "It depends." And so, he claimed that when you're building a multiple-choice item with only two responses, why then you can specify what it depends on. And he defended that to the death. He defended it in the last measurement book he wrote. He convinced Dave Frisbee, who was a co-author with him on the book of the inherent beauty of true/false items. Or at least, out of respect, Dave went along with him!

Diagnosis:
The Business of Testing

Now, getting on with the business of testing, let's draw on some just plain "horse sense" from another test author, Dale Scannell:

DS: Hal, when I taught measurement courses, I always used the example of a sign that I saw in a dentist's office one time that said, "To see is to know. We X-ray, because to see is to know." They X-ray your teeth to make sure that they'll find all the cavities. And I think about measurement in that same way, that the tests are going to help the teachers see, so that they can know what to do with their students and make their instruction more effective. And that was the guiding philosophy.

Most professions rely on increasingly sophisticated test applications. Today's technology enables geologists to penetrate through several miles of water and ocean floor as they search for the location of petroleum deposits to bring the oil to the earth's surface.

Doctors administer a blood test when conducting physical exams as part of a procedure to discover the state of one's health. If analysis identifies a problem, corrective action is taken.

Test, analyze, and prescribe; many professions share that triumvirate of procedures. To find out your weight, you step on a scale. To check your height, you use a yardstick. The standardized tests discussed here are used in a similar manner. To find out how you are dong in school, the scale, the yardstick, and the test all tell you something about yourself. Therefore, it is important to establish the difference between the commercial tests and the state-mandated tests used to determine a minimum competency.

With many state-mandated tests, if you don't get a passing score, you will not advance to the next grade in your school, or, as a senior in high school, you can't graduate. There is nothing new about that pedagogical approach to education. The New York State education system, with its three-hour-long Regents exam, required students to pass, if credit was to be given for each course taken. It is not difficult to understand the motivational impact of this practice on teachers and students alike.

A major weakness in the NYS Regents system was the absence of carefully constructed tests for use in the elementary schools, revealing early on where learning difficulties exist so that those weaknesses could be addressed constructively. The quality of the teachers and the teaching/learning process conducted at the elementary school level, grades 1–3 in particular, largely determine the quality of a child's educational foundation. That foundation in turn shapes what occurs over future years in school and thereafter.

Both state-mandated and commercial tests affect the educational standards of school systems, for after all, test content is based on a body of knowledge, which becomes known to those who administer the tests. A key question then is who, how, and for what purpose that body of knowledge was chosen. We need to know if the tests used in any school program are valid and how well the achievement scores obtained in a school district compare with national norms. It is not beyond the realm of unintended consequences for school systems to stray outside, or worse still, remain moribund within the existing parameters in today's fast-changing intellectual climate. Therefore, a testing program without benefit of the national component has its limitations.

During my early test editorial days, I rode the commuter train to and from Boston and regularly shared a seat with a friend—a lawyer. One raw New England morning as the friend sat down beside me, he began complaining that he had experienced one of those seemingly never-ending school board meetings the night before. He went on to tell me that many parents were complaining that their children were not getting what they, the parents, thought they should be getting in their classes.

The superintendent, according to his account, claimed that the schools were giving the children what they needed. The suggestion was made that the schools should use a commercial achievement test. The superintendent responded, "Those tests do not measure what we teach."

The lawyer asked, "Since you're a test publisher, tell me what it is you put into those tests. What do you test?"

I responded that I was not going to sit there and attempt to describe what we test, but I would bring an Iowa Tests of Basic Skills booklet with me that evening, containing tests for grades 3–8 and go through the test with him.

That evening we went through it. When we finished, he looked at me quite upset and exclaimed, "But that's exactly what the schools should be teaching, in fact, are supposed to be teaching. I plan to speak to the matter."

Reportedly, there was a substantial Donnybrook at the next board meeting. The school system in question was then and remains a good system, but apparently had gotten overly committed to social skills at the expense of fundamentals.

"Minority Students Treading Path to Private Schools." So read the headline for an article in *The Boston Globe* (February 16, 2002, City and Region, p. B4). The parent in the story goes well beyond the observation that merely measuring the level of her daughter's content mastery is adequate. She speaks to the central thrust of the testing triumvirate—test, analyze, and prescribe. As the dentist advertised, you find the cavities, then you fill them.

> Taft, who took her daughter out of public school three years ago, said Markeysha (her daughter) is getting terrific grades and learning a lot. In comparison, a relative who remained in public school is falling behind in grade 7 and isn't reading at grade level.
>
> Taft believes that large schools are unable to pinpoint problems, and they don't have enough teachers to give special attention to students who need it.

Well said. Tests "pinpoint" the problem, and the teachers who use the test results are able to analyze and prescribe.

A repeated theme used by critics of commercial norm-referenced achievement tests is the concern that the tests, if used, will lead the school's curriculum. That thinking reflects an absence of knowledge and understanding about test construction procedures. In actuality, it is the purpose of the developer of the test to measure what the schools are teaching and what experts say they should be teaching, and not the reverse of that. Here is the response test author, Al Hieronymus, gave to my question about "leading the curriculum":

AH: No matter which test you build, make sure that it represents what it is that the teachers are teaching. But more importantly, it isn't just what the teachers are teaching, but it is what the best programs have to offer. And so we've always looked very closely to national curriculum organizations: National Council for the Social Studies, National Council for Teachers of Mathematics, the International Reading Association, and the others.

We've always kept very close tabs on those elements—on those organizational matters. We've always had those materials, and we've always had somebody on our staff who was in close touch with them, who was a member of the National Council for Teachers of Mathematics, and so on.

So, we've covered that reasonably well. And we tried as best we could to reflect what you would call the *ideal program.* Now sometimes those *ideal programs* were pretty far out. And you remember what happened when they got into modern–so-called *modern math.*

But we also, of course, have to be able to reflect what the teachers are doing, so that the teachers won't look at the test and say, "Well, that isn't fair." And in some ways, you might say it isn't. If you're a parent and they ask your kid to do something he hasn't been taught, you say, "That isn't fair." But the next question you ask is, "What should he have been taught?" Because one of the most important things that you get out of tests, is not what the kids know, but what they don't know.

And that's what prompted all of the switch in philosophy from end-of-year testing to testing early in the year. When someone asked me about the ideal time to test, I always said, "Third or fourth week in October."

The notion there was that teachers have a couple of months to learn each child's characteristics—to form some pretty definite impressions of what the child can and can't do. It's a good time to be giving him or her some good, solid, reliable test information. And then he or she has the rest of the year to do something about the deficiencies that showed up. And, of course, that's still a part of—at least my—instructional philosophy about what the tests are all about.

In the test manual, I said, "We've always tried as best we could to tread the narrow line between best practice and what is being taught." And it's just that simple, but it involves a lot of judgment.

HTM: Both the authors and the publisher must be aware of all that is going on in education across the nation. Most of the textbooks are a reflection of what state guides call for.

AH: Oh, yes. Now I used to emphasize in the sessions, both with Houghton's field representatives and with the customers, that we think of these tests as a model for what children should be learning. The University established our curriculum laboratory. And then at the curriculum laboratory we spend a tremendous amount of time analyzing content and looking to see what was taught in each textbook series by grade and time of year. And we also talked about the fact that some of the best instruction the kids get all year is the time they're taking these Iowa Tests of Basic Skills. That is not lost time; the kid sees what it is he's supposed to be learning. And it does represent the objectives—if you want to call them that.

One of the most difficult sections in the manual for administrators that I ever had to write, was that business about making comparisons of the averages, because you don't want to encourage the wrong kind of competition. But, on the other hand, you want to get valid information to use in making educational decisions. Just try to write that down in the manual so it's meaningful for the school administrators.

HTM: I read and hear, with some measure of dismay, the testing controversy currently going on in Massachusetts. The state created a test that basically rates the schools and, in reality, the teachers. And I don't see anything much being done about the tests analyzing the pupils, in the sense that we're discussing.

AH: I know exactly what you mean. Concluding that the schools do a good or bad job because of what the kids do without taking anything else into consideration. You talked about the guy on the school board—the parents, I think, have been our biggest supporters.

I know that's true in this state. Now, whether it's true nationally—I would guess it's probably also true. I think it's very important that the results be reported to parents and pupils. And that was why—I don't know whether you remember or not, but the *How Are Your Basic Skills?* pamphlet.

HTM: I remember it well.

AH: We insisted that one of those be provided with every answer sheet.

HTM: We packaged it with the test answer sheets.

AH: And the customers had to take them. And I said, "If they're not going to use them, then they're going to have thrown them away. And they don't like to throw away things that they've paid for."

HTM: Mostly they used them.

AH: And that was very important, because that was supposed to be used, you remember, before testing. The teachers were supposed to get those things out, pass them out to the kids; the kids would see why these tests were given. And then she collected them. As a matter of fact, at the end, I usually asked, "Now, do you know how your skills are—where your strengths and weaknesses lie? Well, now we'll find out."

And then after it's over with, they got back their profiles, and, also, we hoped that they would be sent home—or better still, be used in parent conferences. And with your publishing cooperation, that was a good part of our program.

The comprehensiveness of the development of the tests, including the nation-wide examination of educational curriculum standards, as just discussed, was made possible and facilitated through a singular arrangement, combining the resources of the University of Iowa Testing Program and Houghton Mifflin. It required a major investment to develop, publish, sell, and service the Iowa Tests. A royalty is paid to the University and the authors as part of the total undertaking.

The mobile nature of the U.S. society argues for achievement tests constructed on a broad-based, consistently updated test item pool. Achievement tests unable to rely on such a resource over time may well lose their content validity. The concern that the ITBS might lead a school system's curriculum in the face of author Hieronymus' remarks leaves more to be explained by the challenger than the challenged.

The ITBS, published for use in grades K–8, might, according to some educators, be less prone to lead the curriculum than tests constructed to be administered at the senior high school level.

Well, let's see about that. I sought out Dale Scannell, who I'm proud to tell I signed up nearly one-half century ago, then at the University of Kansas (later he was at the University of Maryland), as the head author of the Tests of Academic Achievement and Proficiency, and repeated the charge to him that tests lead the curriculum at the high school level. His response follows:

DS: The tests were not leading curriculum. They weren't imposed on schools. The tests were trying to reflect what the schools were doing. And we thought that if we could sample broadly the mainstream of the curriculum, and if seventy-five percent of the test items were appropriate in a given school, that was pretty good.

And along with that, our philosophy also always was, "We do important work for you, but we don't do everything that's important for you, and you've got to do your own. There are some things we don't cover in our test that are important in your environment, and you need to find ways of documenting how well you're doing with those things." I hear people say that tests are imposing on us what we have to do. And that's just the opposite side of the coin that we were working on.

HTM: I hear and read many such claims. Either through their lack of understanding and knowledge, or for other reasons, people make statements, which are not at all accurate and often are damaging to those they claim to be helping. Unfortunately, many educators and much of the public believe them.

Dale, are there differences between the make-up and purposes of your high school test and the elementary school test?

DS: Yes, there are a couple of differences. Because of the fact that elementary schools are pretty much self-contained classrooms, you've got a teacher who's teaching most of, if not all of, the subjects. And at the high school level, you've got individuals obviously who are going to be teaching their own content, and they have the kids in the class for only an hour a day—so that makes a big difference. The teachers at the elementary levels identify more closely with the kids because they have them all day. And the teachers at the high school level are not as interested in knowing how their students are doing in all of their subjects. If you were an English teacher, you are not very much interested in what pupils are doing in math. There is more of an emphasis at the high school level on what the administrators and the counselors can do with that information.

As you know, we started out with tests that were really heavy doses of content. We couldn't take a basic skills approach like the Iowa people did in their elementary battery, because by the time kids get to high school, you expect those skills to gel and to be used. But even though there is an emphasis on a more mature use of those skills, skills are still important.

And when we recognized that our original heavy dose of content was too much, we went more toward a skill approach, but within an area in more depth than you would at the elementary grades. We found then that kids did better on the test, teachers liked it better, and administrators liked it better.

Just thinking back, talking to you, brings back the various kinds of pressure that we went through. At one time, the pressure was minimum competency. That came up as the term that everybody was pushing—*minimum competency.* And states started to develop tests that were designed to assure somebody that all the kids were at that minimum level. Well, the teachers did such a good job of responding to that pressure from the public that they forgot that you can also help kids to learn beyond a minimal level and that you ought also to focus on getting them to grow optimally.

And so, it was late when we got into the higher order thinking skills. When the higher order thinking skills became popular, a response had to be made. Well, we did a couple of things with the TAP at the high school level. One was to create a score in each, math and reading, that would reflect whether students were minimally competent or whether they were at a level where you could make a reasonable projection that they will be able to read the kind of things that high school students read and to do the kind of math that high school students should be able to do by the time they graduate.

In 1978, we created a score that was derived from—it wasn't a different test—it was derived from the tests that were already in the test battery. And the score reported was *yes, no,* or *maybe.* So, when we said, *yes,* it meant that a student had reached an acceptable level—or, *no,* they had not gotten there—or *maybe,* they're not there yet, but they have a good chance of being there. And that called attention to what the teachers in the schools needed to do if they had kids that were in real deep trouble. They would be able to respond and help kids get to that level before they graduated.

Another one of the scores that we produced was the applied proficiency skill score. And it was built out of items from math, reading, language arts, and study skills that were real-life oriented.

Well, like whether or not a kid can write a business letter. They need that competency in real life if they're going to apply for a job. So we drew items of that kind from the test and came out with an applied proficiency skill score. Even though you've got an academic emphasis at the high school level, it's still important to know whether or not kids can function in the society in which they live. And that was what that score was supposed to do. So without increasing testing time at all, we produced a *yes, no, maybe* for minimum competency, and we produced an applied proficiency skill score, which, probably for the high school chemistry teacher didn't mean very much. But for the counselors working with the kids, it meant a lot.

The Ability to Learn and to Cope: Testing IQ

That East Hall assemblage of individuals was awe-inspiring and by no means were all of the topics they discussed at the lower intellectual level of true or false tests, although it seems even those tests had their higher order aspects.

Within days following my arrival from New York Office sales to Boston test editorial in 1957, I was informed that the prestigious Binet test was being revised, that Terman had died, and that his co-author, Maude Merrill, would soon make the trip from Stanford University in California to Boston to discuss the revision with me. It was my good fortune that Maude turned out to be a gracious, understanding lady as well as a fine educator and author, and the 1962 revision found its way into publication. This was accomplished, thanks in large measure to test editor Stanley Osgood, who received his Ph.D. at Stanford University under Louis Terman. Stan was the soul of our test publishing activities for many years.

Franklin Sherman Hoyt, editor-in-chief of Houghton's Education Department, 1907-1935, persuaded Ellwood P. Cubberley, chairman of the Department of Education at Stanford University, to evaluate manuscripts for the Riverside Textbooks in Education (RTE) series. Cubberley recommended publishing Lewis Terman's *Measurement of*

Intelligence, believing publication of Terman's book would enhance the reputation of the RTE series. Terman had revised the works of Alfred Binet and Theodore Simon, who had established an intelligence scale. Published in 1916, the text and test materials saw to Houghton Mifflin's entry into standardized test publishing and, yes, the IQ (Intelligence Quotient). Terman's tests were drawn on extensively in 1917 as the U.S. government developed tests to assist in the screening and assignment of military recruits during World War I.

IQ is a much-maligned, sensitive topic. It has, nevertheless, become a familiar term to the layman as well as to professional educators, and the term is frequently found in newspapers and popular magazines. Theoretically, the range of IQs is from zero to 200 or more. Since the norm is the level of development of the average child of a given age, it follows that the average IQ must be 100, so long as these norms are kept up to date.

Over the ensuing years tests developed to measure an individual's intelligence quotient, cognitive abilities, or such other moniker as someone might designate, have encountered the proverbial buzz saw from some quarters. The IQ, standard age scores, and other spin-offs, however, have not only prevailed, they have thrived and are useful tools for educators.

Why? There are numerous well-founded reasons, so let's get down to real cases and learn about some of those reasons. I turn to Francis Laufenberg, former superintendent of the Long Beach, California, schools and later President of the State Textbook Commission. Lauf responded as follows when I raised the subject of IQ tests with him:

FL: Well, first of all, being a counselor in the Los Angeles schools, and in a junior high in an impoverished neighborhood, it was more of a hands-on thing, and not too much of the esoteric thing, except to give the Binet and the Wechsler. We mostly gave the Binet for legal reasons, and that's why you had to be trained and certified, because the test was often used in court for various reasons, such as a child being expelled, or sometimes for special education assignment. In order for the test to hold up in court, the person who had given it had to be certified. And, of course, I don't know how much you know about the Binet, but it takes at least two three-hour sessions to do it properly.

In fact, I might say that I always remembered the experiences, because it was very educational to me from a psychological point of view. The one part of the test that sticks in my mind is the section that was called "vocabulary." As you know, the Binet is designed so that the child doesn't necessarily have to be able to read and write. Whereas with the written IQ tests, the great fallacy is that the child who isn't good at listening to instructions or can't read and write well, doesn't know what he or she is doing in the test.

But the Binet tries to avoid that problem. On the vocabulary, however, what always used to astound me was that you would get this child in the testing room, and the first question was. "What is an orange?" If the child was of low mental ability, when you asked that question, he or she would answer, "You eat it." Or, "It's round." Or, "It's got this orange color." But you would get this other child and ask the same question, and the response would be, "An orange is fruit. It's a citrus. It's got this rind or peeling on it." And they would go into such detail about an orange that you could hardly shut them off. You would see this literally leaping at you, this unusual mind that is still just beginning to develop, but already this particular mind had absorbed a mass of detail, whereas this other child's mind had seen only the surface things that are needed to just get along in life.

In fact, that experience impressed me so, so that I regularly told principals, who had never been counselors, or never did anything with testing, "Everybody that ever becomes a vice principal or principal should be a counselor first to get this experience of dealing with children, and seeing what goes on in their minds."

HTM: Not every child is a genius and not every one is way down in the pits. There's an in between, and we should be aware of those differences as we go about seeing to all children's education.

FL: Right. There are fifty percent above and fifty percent below 100 IQ ...

HTM: You can't have everybody above the average.

FL: No, but remember, they are all out there driving on the freeway.

Again, as with the achievement tests, the intent, the focus, is on seeking information that will provide valuable knowledge about a testee to bring focus and insight to educators' decisions and actions that can make the teaching/learning process successful. Such tools are needed in the educational endeavor.

Cynthia Essex, Supervisor of Secondary Programs at the Perkins School for the Blind in Watertown, Massachusetts, along with her colleague Sally Boyd, graciously made time for me to conduct an interview about tests and testing. Some weeks earlier, I had been privileged to visit this fine school as a guest of Sally Boyd. During that tour, I observed activities in a few classrooms that reminded me of the Stanford Binet, as we referred to Terman's test. I made mention of my observation, and Cynthia spoke to my observations at a later time.

Why you may ask, include information about use of the S/B in a special educational institution such as Perkins? The answer is simply to demonstrate how important the IQ score is to the teaching/learning process in any setting and the extensive efforts to which proven senior educators will go in their efforts to obtain a child's intelligence quotient. The IQ score can be an important contributor to the test, analyze, and prescribe triumvirate.

CE: I've been at Perkins since the '60s. And I have been involved in the educational division here for about that period of time. I've also been in administrative positions for a lot of the time. I've always had an interest in testing and research, so I've been involved in some of the testing that went along over that time period. Historically, with Perkins, the first you hear about tests actually involved the Stanford Binet Tests and the Binet, of course, was developed about 1916.

There was interest in trying to adapt it for handicapped children, and during the '20s, there was a movement to adapt it, and they produced what they called an interim form, which was based on the Stanford Binet. They used that interim form with a large population at the school. And I'm not exactly sure how that all turned out. I think there probably was some abusive use of that test, some decision-making around that test where they felt, well, the student really isn't educable, the student is educable, and so forth.

One of the huge problems in this field, which has always been there, and will be there, is the fact that there is such a low incidence of—visual impairment—such a low incidence of handicap that you have a lot of trouble getting a good normative sample, given the limited population at Perkins School and similar institutions. And furthermore, your population is spread out in a way that makes sampling even more difficult. There aren't necessarily a lot of registers that list all the visually impaired students in one age group, for example. So, just to find a good sample, you have a lot of difficulty even knowing where kids are.

There was one large attempt to norm group intelligence tests that I know of. That was done here at Perkins, and the person who was in charge was Karl Davis. In the '40s and '50s, there actually were very large numbers of kids in a six-to-twelve age range who were visually impaired literally from birth.

He wanted to do it because there were no intelligence tests available, and in fact, there still aren't, but the objective was to develop a test using real objects that would actually measure the nonverbal skills of visually impaired kids. Most of the nonverbal skills tests involve pictures, they involve coding, they involve things that are paper, pencil, and they take vision.

HTM: And the purpose was to obtain an IQ?

CE: Yes, for the very same purpose you theoretically should be obtaining them anyway, to think about this kid's performance in school. And as far as I know, the IQ is considered a predictor of school performance, so it's useful. And then there is a lot of feeling that if we can look at this score, then we can do two things— one, we might be able to help the kids in class—that was one thought. The second was we might be able to say this is why we are having some of the difficulties we're having, or this is why the students are having some of the difficulties they are having.

Given the independent status of the Perkins School, even in the face of the unique educational challenge the school faces, there exists leeway to experiment with tests and test scores. Cynthia, her predecessors, and her colleagues continuously searched for a reliable means to determine the intelligence quotient of the children in their charge. Aware that Perkins administered a specially prepared version of the Stanford Achievement Tests, I inquired about their possible use of the combined achievement and IQ scores.

CE: I think there was a lot of correlation between the kids' results on Binets and on the Stanford Achievement, published by Harcourt Brace Company. I think there was a fairly high correlation, except maybe in the math area, that was always a problem.

One thing, though, I do know, is we didn't really have a good sample—so, we'd use the sample we had anyway, and we've used it ever since then to test our kids. And all of the studies that have been done kind of correlated with vision kids' IQs and with achievement results that I know of. We did it religiously every blessed year, and we got the results back. I do feel there is a high correlation between most of the subjects.

The other thing that we would get, and it was always fascinating to me, is if we had a kid who maybe tested low on the IQ test, then tested high on the Stanford Achievement, nobody would ever quarrel with that kid going on in a more advanced situation. But if you had a kid who tested high on the IQ, and tested low on the Stanford, we would continue the kid in the same group of kids. So, it actually probably had a good result.

It didn't penalize the kids whose IQ didn't match their achievement, and it probably helped the kids whose achievement did match.

HTM: That's a good point. I don't think I've heard that approach mentioned before, but it should be.

CE: Yes, yes. Those achievement test results have been used to consider kids as perhaps more able than we originally thought, or perhaps more able than they show in a classroom situation. You could have a kid in the class with a teacher who shows a tremendous incompatibility, might I say? Or you could have a kid in class with a teacher, where the kid wasn't a talker, and maybe that kid is getting everything that's going on there, you just don't know it. And then you give him an achievement test, and wow, he's at the top of the group. What do you say to that? We say, hey, we missed something here.

HTM: That's right.

CE: Move that kid some place else, see if he does better. So, that's another thing that we looked at. Always we looked at that. I think that was probably a good use of that test.

Testing the Tests

I always regard the IQ and achievement tests scores, when both tests have been administered and their results evaluated, as a school district's veracity test. Consider the questions a school system's administrators, the school board, and the parents might justifiably ask when their school district's average IQ for the entire district is well above 100 and the achievement test average scores are at or below average.

Given Houghton's long history of publishing IQ tests, going back to Terman's 1916 publication, later the Henmon-Nelson Tests of Mental Ability, the Lorge-Thorndike Intelligence Test, and the Thorndike-Hagen Cognitive Abilities Tests, there existed within the company a strong commitment to this sector of test publishing.

To appreciate fully what follows, I believe it is necessary to provide first some background information about the interviewee, Leonard Feldt.

Rutgers University was the home of Oscar Buros, the widely recognized elder statesman in the measurement world. A positive learned review in his *Mental Measurements Yearbook* was the Rubicon to be crossed by every author and publisher of standardized tests. It is difficult to challenge the often-repeated postulate that the existence of Oscar Buros and his *Yearbook* was a contributing force to the "Golden Age of Tests" as authors and publishers alike endeavored to publish tests of quality, ensuring a positive Buros review. Commercial publishers' tests were subjected to such a review. Awareness of that review serves as a major force in ensuring quality. One might reasonably suggest that all other tests, even today's state-mandated tests, be subject to a comparable review process. Given the information in this chapter, I am at a loss to understand why parents do not insist on such a review process for all mandated tests administered to their children. The Buros Institute exists to this day and may be visited at its website on the Internet.

Leonard Feldt, a research assistant working on Buros' fourth *Mental Measurements Yearbook,* in discussion with Buros, was informed that Rutgers did not have the course work required for his Ph.D. and was then given the suggestion that Leonard seek his degree at Princeton, Columbia, or the University of Iowa. Through great good fortune for the University, Houghton Mifflin Company, and many others, and E. F. Lindquist's persuasiveness, Leonard took his doctorate at the University of Iowa, and then he remained there. He brought with him a deeply ingrained respect for and adherence to integrity in test construction. It would be unrealistic to assume that all test authors, including the most widely recognized and highly respected among them, always read from the same page. They held deep-seated, but often divergent, beliefs about tests and testing. The measure of these individuals over and above their own contributions was that they could respect one another personally and acknowledge the rightful existence of differing but well-founded beliefs as my following exchange with Leonard demonstrates:

HTM: Leonard, there is a story I can't resist asking you to tell about. Manuel Fenollosa and I were in the old Del Prado Hotel in Chicago attending a Chicago Office sales conference, and Lin and Al had been invited to attend the meeting. In due time Manuel said, "You know, Lin, we ought to have a triple-norming program. The Lorge-Thorndike Intelligence Tests, the Tests of Academic Progress, and the Iowa Tests of Basic Skills should all be normed on the same national sample."

Manuel and I were aware that Lin and Bob argued about the value of differences between the two types of tests. We both were aware that comparisons of scores for ability and achievement tests are meaningful only to the extent to which they measure unique elements. In essence, Lin wasn't opposed to intelligence tests so much as using them for purposes that are better served by achievement testing, which incidentally was behind his criticism of the SATs (Scholastic Aptitude Tests). I understand from Al Hieronymus that in all of Lin's writing he said that "aptitude or ability" needs to be taken into consideration in interpreting achievement results—especially in interpreting group averages.

LF: Yes.

HTM: We all ended up here at the University of Iowa for a meeting to work out a triple-norming program. Leonard, you were present at that meeting. I had test editor Stan Osgood with me. Also present were E. F. Lindquist, Bob Thorndike, Al Hieronymus, and Dale Scannell. The discussion became complex as this informed group engaged in doing the job right. I still remember partway through the meeting when Bob Thorndike leaned over at me and whispered, "Hal, do you understand what's going on?" And I responded, "No, not really." And Bob said, "Don't worry, we'll take care of it."

You were a participant, and I'm curious about your thoughts and recollections.

LF: Yes. Well, I'm sure Lin—you portrayed Lin's attitude pretty honestly and correctly—but Lin was not above compromise. While recognizing that some pretty solid people didn't agree with every position he took, he still had disdain for intelligence tests or any of that breed—he never made a secret of that.

But he recognized that somebody like Bob Thorndike had opinions, and he had enough respect for Bob Thorndike to realize that he represented a view that serious people did entertain. And that, if this is what the marketplace believes, and this is what some pretty solid citizens believe, then he wasn't so rigid that he would say, "If you take my products, you have to buy my view, and I won't abide any adulteration of that view."

I don't think I ever saw him adopt that position. He didn't. What he really believed, I think, was that if people subscribed to his views on achievement testing, then every function of an intelligence test could be served by that. So, he regarded intelligence tests to be really kind of a wasteful product as far as school resources were concerned. But if that's what it took to gain acceptance of his product, then you had to be able to market both products.

HTM: It is to the credit of each of you that you all participated and said, "Okay, if this is what the publisher wants, we'll do it." Manuel and I knew through our work in the schools that both achievement and IQ tests were used. Therefore, the comparisons made would be well served if both scores were based on the same normative population. And you did it with great grace. And to this day, I consider that meeting to be one of the most interesting times, actually most memorable, of the many meetings I attended in one setting or another over my years in publishing.

The evening before the triple-norming program meeting, Bob and Lin started to discuss their differences over dinner at the Ox Yoke restaurant in Amana Village, located a few miles from the University. For a while I had visions of the triple-norming program meeting never coming to pass, but the skillful assistance of others present—maybe it was the arrival of the restaurant's exceptionally fine food—anyhow we got off on other topics, and I breathed easily again. Over time, I came to realize there was considerable good-natured needling on the part of both of these icons, put on mainly for the entertainment of all of us, their captive audience.

HTM: Leonard, perhaps you would summarize their positions.

LF: Lin was skeptical about the value of difference between achievement rankings and IQ test rankings. He felt that elementary teachers were well informed though ITBS profiles of a student's strengths and weaknesses, as these related to various areas of instruction. Thorndike, in contrast, thought the differences between achievement and IQ standing could be very useful for a significant number of kids (perhaps ten percent to twenty percent) in each class. They would be helpful to a teacher, especially when the IQ value suggested a child had the brainpower to achieve at a higher level than the child was exhibiting in one or more areas. I really doubt that Thorndike believed Lorge-Thorndike or CogAT scores could make ITBS scores redundant.

The ACT–SAT Controversy

The triple-norming experience serves as an introduction to the ACT–SAT controversy. The Scholastic Aptitude Tests are published by the Educational Testing Services (ETS), publisher of the College Entrance Board Examinations. The American College Tests (ACT) came into being seemingly almost overnight. Let's have Leonard Feldt tell why and how:

LF: As I remember it, the problems of selective admission were not initially felt by the state universities, the non-selective colleges.

But because they, like Iowa, have some commitment within their own states to accept any high school graduate who got a legitimate high school diploma and wanted to attend the University of Iowa or Ohio State, or other similar types of university. We had an open-door policy, and the University had to take them. And as long as we had the facilities and staff to accommodate them, that was not a major problem.

But that commitment became a major problem, when finally universities realized that they couldn't expand their dormitories, their classrooms, to keep pace with everyone who wanted to attend, and those institutions had to become more selective.

So there was a growing problem for college presidents. At first, Lin heard only from one or two other Big Ten presidents. But eventually they all finally came to the point where they felt they could not accept every high school graduate who wanted to attend. At the same time Lin had, for years, battled with the College Board and ETS representatives basically about broadening the nature of what the Scholastic Aptitude Test had become. And there again, it was a case of a statistics-evidence-oriented group versus one man— I can't say it was a group, although I'm sure he had some support—but Lin, who had a philosophical orientation.

Basically, the College Board enjoyed its status of catering to the elite. And the technical group that did the work was very wedded to evidence that this is an efficient predictor—as efficient as we can get—of college grades and, hence, if you're going to use any kind of entrance battery at all, this does the job. And Lin never claimed that any other kind of test was going to be superior to what the College Board had, for decades, been producing.

But Lin had a philosophy that when you start denying students entrance to colleges and universities on the basis of a test, you ought to be able to stand up and say with a good conscience, "The people whom we admit have these well developed skills; they are the critical abilities that qualify them for entrance into the universities. And these are the skills and abilities that the university will try to bring to a higher level."

And the other side of the coin, "The people whom we deny entrance on the basis of test scores don't exhibit in sufficient degree the skills and abilities that they need."

There might be many of those who, by virtue of the weaknesses of their high school education could, if given a chance, develop the necessary skills, but it's a little hard to determine which people have the potential to develop certain skills. If a high school graduate is deficient in certain skills, who can tell why they are deficient? And is it too late for them to start developing and remedying those deficiencies?

And so he said, "Philosophically, if we have to stand before the public and say, 'We are accepting some and not accepting others,' then here are the abilities that the accepted students have and the rejected students don't have to a sufficient degree."

He never argued that when you come down to a composite score on the kind of test he thought philosophically defensible and a composite score on what ETS had been producing for the College Board for years, that there would be any significant difference in the degree of predicted accuracy; he never denied that.

But he said, "If I have to be in a position to explain to parents why their sons and daughters were not accepted, I'd rather do it on a test that I can trot out and show them, 'Here's what we expect our entrants to be able to do, and your child couldn't do it well enough.'"

And it was on a philosophical basis that he proposed a different kind of test. Now he'd tried—I don't know how long—as a member of the College Board's directors to convince them that they ought to pressure ETS to produce that kind of battery. But the College Board always deferred to ETS on technical issues, and so he never could convince them. So, again, it was a case of philosophical position that he couldn't convince others to adopt. This occurred at a time in university history—higher education history—when selectivity was forced upon them, so he brought those two things together.

Now, in retrospect, you have to marvel at Lin's energy and motivation. Think of all the things that were going on at Iowa at that time. Lin had a new textbook that was creating quite a stir; the scoring machines were still in a very flexible state of evolution; the new Iowa Tests of Basic Skills was just beginning to gain a strong foothold, because it was only five or six years that the new battery of Basic Skills was on the market. And here was Lin trying to juggle those balls at the same time, as he took on one of the most sacred cows in the testing scene.

If you thought for some reason that, like right now, there was a place for a third college entrance battery in this country—there probably isn't anyone who would take it on. But suppose there was, how would you go about doing that job? You couldn't get enough money together, and you couldn't do it on a shoestring, but he did it.

HTM: I don't think that there's a leadership group today as powerful in the testing movement.

LF: People like Ralph Tyler (first director of the Center for Advanced Behavioral Sciences at Stanford University) and Lindquist are rare. People who were instrumental, when you look back on leaders in the field of measurement. But at any rate, I don't know how Lin ever summoned the courage or the resources to initiate a project like that. And, again, it was done in a fashion that was almost indistinguishable from the Iowa Testing Program—through which the Iowa Tests of Basic Skills and the Iowa Tests of Educational Development were developed.

We housed the people; we provided my voluntary services as test editor. I didn't have enough awareness to be frightened. But I can remember those organizational meetings for ACT (American College Testing)—and I tagged along, and Lin was volunteering my service left and right, and I didn't have enough sense to be frightened at the whole idea of what he was countenancing.

Attendance at those meetings for me was my opportunity to have some small contact, firsthand, with people who are now regarded as historical giants in both higher education and measurement. I mean, when the people who you would name as leading measurement experts, so far as testing at the higher educational level, there were only one or two names. And I got to see those people in the flesh and to hear them. But eventually the burden became too great.

For me, working alone, to try to keep ITED in the state going; to keep the tests in the constant state of revision and, at the same time, to try to build forms for the National Merit Scholarship Qualifying Test at the time, and ACT batteries, at least three forms a year—it was more than any person could carry.

But Lin was a very persuasive guy, and his energy sort of wore off on me. He challenged people.

I don't regret any of those decisions. Though I look back on those activities, and I sometimes wonder, "How did I do that and keep a family together at the same time?"

HTM: You have a lot of ability in your own right, as I would be the first to attest. You have given a much needed primary source account of how and why the American College Testing program was created. You too, have probably heard differing accounts or interpretations as to how ACT came to be. You have just described Lin's thinking with clarity, and that is much needed. I and many others thank you for doing that.

LF: I think in a very practical way the effect of the existence and acceptance of ACT did what Lin and his words could never do. Lin pushed the SAT in the direction that he wanted them to go and away from reliance solely on the claim it was psychometrically efficient. And it broadened the College Board's content in the SAT. And, in a sense, maybe the two batteries are closer together than they were when Lin started. I don't think ACT has moved so much in SAT's direction as SAT has moved in ACT's.

And certainly, their philosophy changed. If ACT hadn't come into existence, would the College Board ever have deserted its rather elitist commitment to certain kinds of institutions? They really didn't want the riffraff in the club. Well, I think if they had started to let other institutions of second and third rank into the club, they would have lost some of the club members.

HTM: Right. The competition forced their hand.

LF: Yes. Right. And so, in a sense, competition did have some dividends in this area.

You, the reader, must see the element of consistency authors Lindquist, Thorndike, Hieronymus, Feldt, Scannell, and others exercised.

Ensuring Enlightened, Responsible Use of Test Scores

There is another major component, in fact an unforgiving requirement, beyond the development process needed to create and maintain user trust, and this is qualified consultant service. Why? Because the time, expense, and effort necessary to conduct a testing program is a waste if the scores, once obtained, are not analyzed and properly used to improve the educational process.

Directions for administering the test along with manuals discussing the derived scores to be calculated from the tests' raw scores and then used productively, regularly accompany norm-referenced tests. While this information is necessary and helpful, the tailoring of information to each school system's conditions, calling for application to their own requirements or needs to improve their teaching/learning process through insightful analysis and augmentation, often requires the council of a trained and experienced test specialist—a test consultant. Obviously a single score based on the number of right answers, called a "raw score," must be related or correlated to something to give it meaning. Percentile ranks and other kinds of scores—derived scores—do that.

Dr. Edward Drahozal was the company's senior test consultant for many years. I first met Ed in 1963 and on July 15, 1964, he started with the company. A University of Iowa Ph.D., much respected by faculty members, who in fact recommend Ed to me, he was eminently qualified for the position he filled for some thirty-plus years.

At a time when norm-referenced tests and testing, along with most all of public school education, were regarded as valuable assets to our nation's well-being, I was determined to place test consultants with the highest of credentials in the field. The over-arching nature of Ed's career has provided him with an information base and wealth of experience without equal. It is fundamentally the only one of its kind.

Ed's extensive knowledge about educational measurement combined with his pre-doctorate studies' experience in elementary/secondary education soon earned him the full respect of the company's sales representatives, the authors, senior management, and our customers. They soon learned that Ed knew whereof he spoke. He would tell it like it is. He could be trusted. Ed soon became Houghton's senior national test consultant, functioning effectively among customers, authors, editors, and management.

I know of no one, in fact, I'm certain there is no one, involved with testing elsewhere in the nation's educational universe, at any level of textbook and test publishing, who has worked directly with as many test authors, editors, school administrators, governmental agencies, parents, and pupils as Ed—and over as many years. His insightful and dedicated efforts have positively and productively improved the education of literally millions of kids. Ponder on that a bit before you read what follows.

He was engaged in direct consultation with school systems about their test scores throughout the ebb and flow of the ever-changing pedagogical and curricular fads, over almost all of the second half of the twentieth century. He confronted the warts as well as the beauty marks resulting from those various developments, and he tells about them in his interview.

Any reader of this book must have already recognized the wide-ranging, actually singular, inclusiveness of the information feedback system existent within a major textbook/test publishing house. Much of that information flows from the instructional programs, as we learned from reading author Bill Durr's and mathematics author Lee Capps' remarks. Standardized test publishers benefited from yet another information source—namely, test scores obtained from the administration of the test publications.

Beginning in the early 1950s, test publishers provided scoring services for their tests, thanks to new technology that scanned thousands of kids' answer sheets per hour at minimal cost and with great accuracy. Computers then converted the raw scores into many different derived scores for each pupil, including percentiles, item analysis, and averages by classroom, school, and school system. This analysis revealed where pupils needed help or the school system's curriculum needed attention through its comparison with national and regional norms. Norm-referenced tests were the tool that enabled educators to test, analyze, and prescribe.

Millions of individual answer sheets were scored each year. The mass of information feedback was indeed impressive and when combined with the information from the subject matter, or content areas, the publishers enjoyed an overview of the nation's teaching/learning activities unmatched elsewhere. I have never understood why so many educators and people in the news media failed to grasp this strength and, in fact, discounted it. Neither the authors nor the company used our test publications to condemn or to praise. We in the testing arena looked at which textbooks had what market share, but the company did not analyze the test data by textbook program, although realistically trends, at the very least, became obvious. Still, given such a database, it is clear that Ed Drahozal's assessments as voiced in his interview are based on hard data—facts—not groundless opinions.

Ed's interview is not an exercise in measurement terminology—jargon—and statistics. The consultants' charge was to use the test results to help educators and kids involved in the teaching/learning process finish school with a sound education.

Let's turn to Ed and start off with one of the major events that changed U.S. education:

ED: President Johnson's implementation of NDEA (National Defense Education Act, originally passed in 1958) really started money flowing, gushing really, into schools in August 1967, I believe it was. Five of us in Houghton's Geneva, Illinois, Midwest Office—you and I, Fran McElhiney, Chuck Townsend, and Jean Jacklin developed our first NDEA "catalog" for school people.

We sat down and started writing about Thursday night and worked continuously Friday, Saturday, and Sunday, putting together some information we could use to go after the new NDEA business. Then I started going to some of the state meetings. What an eye-opener! The wasted money in that year's federal program went into the millions. Many people were buying garbage because the money had to be spent by December 31. I will bet, in terms of dollars, that there were more useless foreign language labs bought during that period of time than was spent on good, useful labs all the years since then.

Some of this NDEA money went to test scoring beginning in the late 1950s. The schools got better scoring, more accurate test scoring, and more new, good reports to better interpret test scores. That was a useful development. However, instead of using that freed-up teacher time, the time that the teachers would have spent scoring the tests, for good in-service projects to teach the teachers how to use the test, or maybe teach them how to better teach reading, the educators took off in other directions. The tests became kind of a critique of the teachers, especially those teachers who had maybe only two-year or two-year plus degrees. We, the testing people, were the ones that were always the fall guys if there were problems. Many administrators would tell the teachers, "Well, just because you have been teaching for ten years, you still don't really have sufficient educational background; that's why you're not a very good teacher." I think that eventually we are going to see more teacher tests, at least the basic skills test, to make sure that not only the kids, but that the teachers, are well rounded in reading, English language, math, and other subjects.

There are a lot of evaluations of teachers and administrators being done right now. Whether or not you can measure if people can teach or administer using a test is another real question in my mind. But anyway, that kind of activity was going on at that time.

Then about 1968 the other questionable development was the beginning of the push for Criterion-Referenced Tests (CRTs). Every state was going to develop and then administer its own testing program, and they were going to set their own standards. And one of the first meetings that we attended, the first meeting in the Midwest, you went with Harriss Malan, Houghton's Detroit, Michigan, representative, and me to that hearing that was absolutely unbelievable.

When we met the people, I wasn't sure what their jobs were. I had no idea that power could be vested in some people that knew so very little about measurement or research, yet they talked non-stop about developing their CRTs and setting their own standards. There were some ideas being voiced about getting more teachers involved, but they planned to set these standards rather arbitrarily, much more so than is the case now.

HTM: Perhaps I should interrupt you, Ed, to describe CRTs. The idea of CRTs is that an area can be completely defined and covered by a finite number of tasks of items. Recognition of all ten numerals and all twenty-six capital letters might be examples. A realistic expectation often is "correct performance should be close to one hundred percent."

ED: That's what the minimum tests were all about.

HTM: But, Ed, how do you define a performance standard for a goal such as "understands the main idea of a paragraph containing five sentences?" CRTs never were satisfactorily created for higher order or skills that can't be completely and perfectly mastered, such as norm-referenced tests like the Iowa Tests of Educational Development, the Tests of Academic Proficiency, and the Iowa Tests of Basic Skills measured.

ED: The thing that bothered me was, this era with the CRTs started an educational climate with a much more narrow, fact-oriented instruction—facts, facts, facts. And the teachers were not very well trained to understand that good tests should measure the basic goals of education and that good tests should measure far more than just a few simple facts. You have to have items where kids have to put together the pieces of knowledge as part of the higher order thinking skills.

Of course, I know there is the argument that when the kids have to put the pieces together it's really an intelligence test and no longer an achievement test. Well you need to look at some of these items like on the ITED—which has a lot of higher-order thinking skills items. For example, in the ITED science test, after the authors set up a little problem, the kids have to put two or three pieces of information together to solve the problem. The entire ITED requires a lot of thoughtful problem solving.

I don't know how people can call the ITED an abilities test. I think it's an achievement test, pure and simple. It makes the kids put a lot of knowledge together, figure out how the pieces go together, and come up with the right answer, or at least a procedure. Sometimes the right answer is to select a proper procedure.

But in 1968–75, it was really bad; many people in curriculum development just didn't know what they were doing. We had already gone through ten years of so-called modern math where people were starting to realize some of these programs created some real learning problems. Oh, there were some good things in modern math, but the kids couldn't compute as well, and their problem-solving skills were not very good. And then we got into new math and modern science programs and then into reading programs. Then transformational grammar came on board, and later we had Roberts' English series, which teachers just couldn't handle pedagogically. It was as simple as that. A couple of state adoption states dropped Roberts' program after a couple of years.

All that said, and by no means is it exaggerated, the National Defense Education Act, a federal government program, did energize elementary/secondary public school education and those who served it, publishers included. While the post World War II GI Bill, another federal government program, enhanced the quality of instruction in the nation's colleges, unfortunately similar results for the public schools and their pupils were often elusive, as we shall see, but first I digress to describe a dilemma combined textbook/test publishers could and did face periodically.

In Chapter 7, Houghton elementary school mathematics textbook author Lee Capps discusses the virtues of modern mathematics as found in his series. Over the next few pages, test specialist Ed Drahozal cites his findings, which are largely critical of modern math. Yet, both Lee's mathematics textbooks and Ed's tests were published by Houghton Mifflin. The question then is how does the company's corporate management address that dichotomy. This is not to imply that publishers never do and should not publish books that are in contradiction to others on their publication list, for that situation frequently occurs. But here we are concerned with kids' education, and that matters.

By way of resolution, we could have decided to let the chips fall where they may. After all, authors bring forth new ideas; they are on the cutting edge; and it's the publisher's role to get those ideas into the hands of the public. The missing component in that approach is recognition that people, culture, and publications defined the publishing house. The test authors and the math textbook authors were participants in Houghton's culture, as revealed throughout this book. During the years under discussion, modern mathematics, driven by federal funding of the School Mathematics Study Group (SMSG) prevailed throughout the schools. The test authors through their constant monitoring of curriculum trends knew that and gave it full consideration. Our mathematics authors knew it too and were in fact fully informed about the work of the SMSG. It was their objective, with Houghton's backing, to develop mathematics textbooks in the environment of that time that would properly address the teaching/learning process using modern mathematics. The authors and their editors were confident they could fulfill that objective, and management believed them. That confidence was rewarded in due course.

It was imperative, however, that neither the test or textbook publications would influence the other. The integrity of each group had always been sacrosanct and would continue to be. The test and textbook editorial offices were located in the same Boston office building. Their proximity concerned management, for obviously editors do converse about their work, beliefs, and educational trends. Corporate management had become fed up with the hostile Massachusetts business environment and was exploring moving all of the company or at least the textbook divisions into the Chicago area—quite likely to Geneva, Illinois, the location of our Midwest facilities. Additional land had been acquired. In retrospect, it seems that only the force of our long established roots, the culture of Henry Houghton, and the many great contributors who followed him prevailed to keep us in Boston.

While we decided to remain in Boston, the investigation did reveal a solution to our concern about test editorial independence. As early as 1976, parts of the test editorial had been moved to Iowa City, Iowa. In 1979, the Riverside Publishing Company was incorporated as a separate fully-owned Houghton Mifflin company and located in the Chicago, Illinois, area, where it grew and prospered. Its first and primary purpose was to publish norm-referenced tests. Publications, however, were not to be limited just to tests. The separate location, in today's jargon, ensured a firewall between Houghton's test and textbook publishing activities.

One might well inquire how the test authors viewed this decision. I asked Leonard Feldt, author of the Iowa Tests of Educational Development, that question a few years ago.

LF: I hate to think where we would be today if that hadn't occurred. I think it became obvious to you early on—I don't think it would have come to a CEO who didn't have your testing background— it would have become obvious later, but you saved the day by setting up an independent unit for test development and sales.

HTM: One group that was terribly unhappy was the sales group. "You've taken away part of my income," was the complaint.

It is in that context that the following statements by Ed about modern mathematics should be read:

ED: Modern math really killed problem solving forty years ago, because kids kept playing around with games and never really sat down to learn problem solving.

I remember one series, one that a lot of the schools used, and they had been experiencing drops in their math test scores. I would say, "Some math programs have more problem solving than others, and I am not going to tell you which one is number one, but do you use this series, this series, or this series?" And I used to jockey the sequence around. And I still remember the one that I found that had the most serious drops in problem solving. I would sometimes list that publisher first, sometimes second, sometimes third. Anyway, I will never forget that, when people would call, and they would ask me about problem solving—it would often be that same series.

There was a push to measure a lot of crazy stuff in modern math, so we came out with a modern mathematics test, a supplement to the Iowa Tests of Basic Skills math concepts test. A lot of people liked it. Some people didn't like it, because we had items with base two, or base five—I can't remember—at several grades. Some people didn't like it, because they were teaching base nine. And the fact of the matter is, most elementary school kids didn't know and didn't need to know a darn thing about any of them. As soon as they left that classroom that summer, they never again used it in their lives.

There were a lot of things like that, that wasted a lot of important instructional time.

HTM: But Houghton had a real dilemma within the company. You in testing, including author Al Hieronymus, reported what was happening to the math test scores when modern math programs were adopted. At the very same time, within the company, authors Lee Capps and Ernie Duncan developed a math program that, while it wasn't a way-out modern math, it was enough that way to qualify as modern math. The program went like gangbusters.

ED: It was much more moderate, and I know that one of our test authors, H. D. Hoover, offended some people when he spoke to a group of Houghton textbook salespeople in the early '70s as he said, "I think there is too much crap in that program." He used some term like that.

HTM: Well, he was known for using plain English.

ED: And what he didn't like was the fact that in the problem-solving area, they didn't have what he called well-written problems. They would try to minimize the reading load, but not nearly as much as math programs did about '78, '79. In the late '70s there were many books that had questions that read, "Two apples, three oranges—how many all together?" for example. And in that way, they would keep their reading level real low by having all these short, choppy sentences—and all kinds of junk like that. Good math programs require some reading, and although the ITBS reading level was controlled quite well in the math test, good sentences were always used.

As publishers pursued developments such as CRTs, initiated by outsiders, it began to be unclear whether the textbook publishers were the perpetrators of their changing status as leaders in the forging of the nation's curriculum standards or compliant followers. California, Texas, and other adoption states were embracing a movement to set their own standards to be followed by the publishers.

ED: Then someone started the "we've got more stories" marketing gimmick. Schools got enamored with the numbers, not the quality or how well the stories fit the rest of the reading series' instructional program. At the same time, people would be bragging, "We've got more math problems. We've got 4,000 math problems in our fifth grade textbook. The next closest other text has 3,400."

And school people, somehow or another, started believing these marketing gimmicks and voted for some pretty poor textbook series.

HTM: Absolutely. The emphasis changed from the earlier days when they wanted to know the meat and potatoes about textbooks.

ED: Oh, yes. As a matter of fact, because of CRTs and the heavy emphasis on facts in CRTs, everything had to be classified. The local tests were being related directly to textbooks and the emphasis on facts in the textbooks, as well as the guides for the teachers, became so pronounced that a lot of school people didn't have the slightest notion about what became known as "the higher order thinking skills."

HTM: Let's talk a little about the expectations for students.

ED: It's kind of disappointing that we are not doing better. And I think that's what some of the critics of our schools are griping about. But a lot of these people have to keep in mind—the people who are griping about the kid at the store who can't make change, and so on—that kid would have been digging a ditch a few years ago, when we were kids—or when I was a kid, for sure. Instead, they are now in a grocery store, because that is the next level unskilled or semi-skilled job, so they are much more visible. The unskilled twenty-fifth percentile or below high school graduates are much more visible now. And I think we are always going to have this group, some of whom are underachievers. It just kills me to listen to these politicians today saying we are going to get everybody above grade level.

Well, you might get some above grade level, but you are never going to get them all above the third grade level that currently exists. There are some third graders that, even thirty years from now, are not going to be above the third grade level that exists now. But keep in mind, if you raise that level up, now you've got fifty percent of the kids below the new third grade level, even though you have less than fifty percent under the old third grade level.

HTM: The politicians and news pundits tell us they want to get everybody above the average, like Public Radio's Garrison Keillor up in Minnesota, who informs us, that everybody in his town is above the average. The reality is, that's the new political norm.

ED: Yes, but I think it makes some sense to try to improve schools, because we kind of got stuck in no real standards in the first CRT wave, back in the late '60s and early '70s. The state standards were lousy, and local standards were spotty. Simply defined, test standards are a series of cut-points that divide the entire range of possible scores on each test and thereby determine the classifications of categories into which each student's performance is labeled from "very good" to "poor."

I'll say this, I believe the kids that suffered the most during that era were the very able students. Now we're going back to the same thing. Look at the current-day state tests. The tests are built by committee, the noisiest wheel gets the grease, and the standards, the cut points, are set rather arbitrarily.

A couple of years ago, I discussed standards at the Southwest Educational Research Association conference and then at American Educational Research Association (AERA). I said something to the effect that the new standards are part science, part art, and a little magic.

HTM: I bet that went over well.

ED: And this one attendee said, "Well, we have teachers involved, and they work very hard on these standards." And I replied, "Yes, and you've got somebody guiding your teachers saying, 'Here is the middle range of the data from this study that we did. Are you sure you are going to set the standards at this level? Or are you going to shift up or down a raw score or two?'" Take a look at what happened in one state, the great state of Texas. The first time they gave their algebra test, ten percent of the kids passed the standard.

Those standards were set ridiculously high. A state administrator in Colorado three years ago said, "We are going to have standards like you never saw in the ITBS." Then, the first year they stopped using the ITBS and TAP in the state testing program, it turns out that the mid-point on the Colorado standards was at about the fifty-fifth or fifty-sixth percentile on the ITBS. Thus, Colorado's new, tough test was five or six points above the national average, which was almost exactly the mid point of the Colorado levels on the ITBS and TAP one year earlier.

But you've got a situation with some of these tests right now, and this actually happened just during the past year, where one company had to rescore six or seven major state programs. There was a problem with the calibration used to adjust or standardize systematically the gradations of tests. The scoring was done correctly, but because of a problem with the calibration, the score scales had to be redone. It happened because in all the states some common set of items were tied back to each of the state tests, using some mathematical formulas, but the data on the common set of items was faulty. So, all of the states initially released faulty data.

You've got a situation here that a lot of people don't realize is going on. That is, that you are setting standards, very often, with a minimum amount of information.

And you are saying that the standard this year and the standard last year are equivalent, but when school people start screaming, "Oh, no, we're way lower this year than last year," the states change the tests, start a new score scale, or something.

One might reasonably conclude that what you see is not necessarily what you've got. But the problem is more far-reaching than that. As we have learned with the NAEP (the National Assessment of Educational Progress).

That's the big national testing program that dates back to the late 1960s. They are having other problems there too, because with all these separate state programs, they are not getting very good samples. They are having as difficult a time, or a more difficult time, than we are, trying to obtain a good national sample.

But of all of these state programs, Texas is the best example of teaching toward the test. I don't know if these figures are accurate, but I have been told by about half a dozen people now, that in Texas more money is spent on various test preparation materials than for any other part of the instructional program, except reading. It outsells math, science, and social studies, obviously, but not reading/language arts.

HTM: Now that is really special prepping.

ED: Yes, and it's really focused. See, Texas releases their results, some items, and the schools have this list of objectives. So all you do is teach and practice the narrow range of objectives. Now, there are some kids who aren't ever going to get it, and I suspect that they are really lost souls. Then there are these kids up at the top, for whom practice is really a waste of time, because the school administrators want to practice every one of the objectives with two and three workbooks.

Nor does it stop there, for example ...

ED: We keep saying, "Well, we, the United States, can't compete, we can't compete." Thorndike and Dick Wolf were teachers at Teachers College, Columbia University, and schooled me quite a bit on some of these international studies before they got out of it. There are so many sampling problems in this worldwide testing arena that the international comparisons now being made are real questionable. But the worst part of all those comparisons is, that the best kids, really the cream of the crop, can be missed pretty easily, or obtained pretty easily by the type of sampling that you do. And I think that there is biased sampling in some of these countries that want to look good.

HTM: Ed, how do you see ACT and SAT?

ED: Different tests have different ceilings. On the SAT, the highest you can go is 800.

The new SAT is different from the old SAT and is probably better, because it is said to be more closely related to goals of secondary education. And, of course, the score scale has been "recentered," which was long overdue. I didn't understand why they didn't change the test before or at the time they "recentered" the score scale, but so be it. What gets me is that the Blue Ribbon Panel, or whatever the group was called that was commissioned to determine why SAT scores were dropping, came up with a whitewash. I think the panel, or at least some of the people on the panel who were knowledgeable about measurement, knew some or most of the contributing factors.

First, some of the effect was due to the downward trends in test scores in elementary and secondary schools that were published in our manuals and elsewhere. The SAT trends followed the ITBS and ITED trends, period. However, I believe the major effect was due to changes in the populations tested, which I have dubbed *the ACT effect.*

While Lindquist at the University of Iowa and his colleagues were developing the ACT college admissions test in the late 1950s, they also studied the needs of the high school and college people quite carefully. They not only developed a good test, but they offered test results to schools and colleges that people in the institutions wanted, which the College Board would not or did not provide. And, they offered the whole package at a cost that was less than the cost of the SAT.

When Lin, and I believe it was Ted McCarrel, also at the University of Iowa, went out to sell the ACT test to key people throughout the U.S., the College Board people realized their monopoly was over, and they did the same. They signed up a lot of new SAT states, but the high school students in nearly all of these states were quite different from the students in the old College Board states. For example, Georgia and Indiana students then and now do not score as high on SAT, NAEP, etc., as students from Massachusetts and Connecticut. In addition, many more students now began taking SAT, even in the old College Board states.

The effect on SAT scores was negligible at first. One reason was that student achievement in elementary and secondary schools in the U.S. was on the upswing from about 1958 through 1968. These student improvements offset the negative effect of changing populations.

However, once the secondary school students who were infected, and I do mean infected, by modern language programs and some of the poorer modern math and modern science programs, reached grade 11, the SAT scores began to drop. But ETS/College Board was not straightforward about what was happening. I'll give you one example.

We were living in Framingham, Massachusetts, at that time, as you know. The SAT average scores in Framingham dropped two years in a row—about 1973 and 1974, as I recall. Apparently, the Framingham school board or other school officials wanted an explanation, so some College Board person, I think their local rep, came to the board meeting. He said in essence, "Not to worry, the drop in the averages was not even one standard error and hence is not significant." This was nonsense. You don't use the test standard error, which is an index for a student's score, to make statements about changes in scores for a group of several hundred students. The drop in average Framingham scores was very likely significant both years, but I'd bet most of the change was due to Framingham's changing population of students. I'd also bet that the blasé attitude expressed at the Framingham school board meeting by the ETS (Educational Testing Service) person was repeated many times throughout the country! Instead of guiding local school people through a search for possible and plausible explanations for the change, the school peoples' concerns were summarily dismissed.

Friends and acquaintances who know that I was involved in publishing commercial tests often ask if I support the Massachusetts state test. My reply about the test, as with charter schools, is that both are an admirable effort to duplicate what already existed. In the final analysis, to quote test author Dale Scannell, they appear to be "a way of holding the school kids responsible for what the adults have not been doing."

ED: Most people, when you ask, "What are norms for?" reply, "To compare schools." But the whole purpose of norms on an achievement test battery is to be able to look at relative strengths and weaknesses of each student and groups of students. Is he better in math? Is the profile in any way different from last year? Even the lowest scoring kids that might be at the first percentile score on the composite score for the test might have a tenth percentile in reading, a seventh percentile in language, a first percentile in study skills or in math. But they have a profile. There aren't very many kids that have an absolute flat profile. The same is true of groups of kids, classes, and buildings.

The other thing we've always said, "If the kids cannot handle the test under standard conditions, don't give it to them, or give it to them under special conditions, but don't try to apply the norms." What are we doing now in these state-mandated testing programs? We are labeling kids—here is a winner—here is a kid that is borderline—here is a kid that's a loser. And one test for all is the standard. Sure, some accommodations are provided in most states, but neither the less able students nor the very able students are measured very well with this "one test for all" mentality.

That last line about says it all, as I see it. But then, new solutions that work can and do emerge from time to time. Well trained, qualified teachers are a must if we are ever going to improve our efforts to educate our children satisfactorily. A major step in that direction is presented in the monograph titled *Performance-Based Teacher Certification* by Gary M. Ingersoll and Dale Scannell (Fulcrum Publishing, 2002). There is always hope.

Houghton Mifflin invested heavily to ensure proper use of our test publications. Toward that end, test specialists were made available to our customers, at no charge, to assist in ensuring responsible and effective use of the data obtained from administration of our tests.

Remember author Dale Scannell's reference to the sign in the dentist's office, "To see is to know. We X-ray, because to see is to know." Tests do that. They diagnose. No one defines the major purposes of achievement tests more tellingly than author Albert Hieronymus:

Some of the specific purposes which the Iowa Tests of Basic Skills were designed to serve are:

1. To determine the developmental level of the pupil in order to better adapt materials and instructional procedures to individual needs and abilities;
2. To diagnose specific qualitative strengths and weaknesses in a pupil's educational development;
3. To indicate the extent to which individual pupils have the specific readiness skills and abilities needed to begin instruction or to proceed to the next step in a planned instructional sequence;
4. To provide information that is useful in making administrative decisions in grouping or programming to better provide for individual differences;
5. To diagnose strengths and weaknesses in group performance (class, building, or system) which have implications for changes in curriculum, instructional procedures, or emphasis;
6. To determine the relative effectiveness of alternate methods of instruction and the conditions which determine the effectiveness of the various procedures;
7. To assess the effects of experimentation and innovation;
8. To provide a behavioral model to show what is expected of each pupil and to provide feedback which will indicate progress toward suitable individual goals;
9. To report performance in the basic skills to parents and patrons in objective, meaningful terms.

If you apply the information cited in this chapter to evaluate the tests administered to your kids, then the chapter will have served all of us well. If you conclude that the criticism of locally developed and mandated tests in this chapter is severe, be assured it is understood that such programs are essentially self-inflicted. Parents want their kids to play with a full education deck. If the mandated tests emphasize U.S. history at the expense of world culture, they may well reflect the parents' and society's dissatisfaction over our kids' lack of knowledge about the U.S. Constitution and the nation's basic values.

If the kids can't read and count to the satisfaction of the tax-paying population, they will seek corrective measures. The actions taken may not be the best solution, but some kind of action is inevitable.

Norm-reference tests make invaluable contributors to successful elementary/secondary schooling. They tell it like it is. When used properly, they are of great value and assistance to the teaching/learning process. I hope that after reading this chapter, you are persuaded that tests, when properly developed to serve needed objectives, are useful. If so, I will have fulfilled my purpose.

CHAPTER 9

A Growing, Changing Phenomenon

College Publishing

I have been directly involved with colleges and universities—from the 1940s through the remaining half of the 20th century. That involvement began with my student days and included years of service on several boards of trustees and advisory boards for colleges. During this time, the individualistic institutions of higher learning have met and solved the challenges of war, peace, inflation, recession, the technology explosion, demographic changes, and political pressures.

The common denominator functioning in the colleges and universities throughout these challenges was an intelligent and insightful response to change. That remarkable feat was in large measure drawn from their faculties, trustees, alumni, students, and last, but by no means least, the college textbook publishers. The benefits accruing to this country from that constructive strength are immeasurable.

During no period of time have our institutions of higher learning experienced greater changes than in the years covered in this book, when numerous challenges were identified, then addressed successfully. The results directly affected millions of young people, colleges, and college textbook publishing. This singular achievement saved some colleges, created others, and without question did the same for college publishing. A constructive interdependence evolved between the colleges and publishers as this chapter reveals. In turn, their accomplishments created an environment conducive to a boom in the creation of intellectual properties, and all of America profited. Following World War II, obtaining a college education became a way of life that spread throughout all levels of the nation's society previously little influenced by plans to attend college. Rapidly escalating enrollments, encompassing a greater spread of academic aptitude and achievement, markedly changed college course offerings and faculties. These changes spawned a mushrooming college textbook marketplace. More students, more and different courses, and more individuals charged with teaching them brought about a sea of change in the need for textbooks.

What sparked this near miracle of miracles? Much has been written about the GI Bill enacted in 1943 as a major contributor to the beginnings of that growth. Less well known, in fact rarely known, is the major contribution our colleges and universities made to the World War II effort through their numerous programs conducted to train officers and needed specialists for the military services. On many campuses during the war years, it was normal to see more uniforms than civilian attire, as members of such military programs as the Army Specialized Training Program (ASTP), the Navy/Marine Corps V-12 Program, and air cadets of the services went about their assignments. Many of these servicemen had never attended college, nor had they planned ever to do so.

The Navy V-12 program trained more than 60,000 Navy and Marine Corps officers using 131 colleges and universities. Actually, 125,000 men were enrolled, and 60,000 completed the program. That number surpassed the combined output of the Naval Academy, Naval Reserve Officer Training Corps (NROTC), and other pre-V-12 programs. The V-12 program did not turn out the so-called *ninety-day wonders,* given that on average the better part of a year or more of training transpired prior to one's being commissioned as an officer. This significant contribution to the war effort made by institutions of higher learning is little known today, perhaps in part because of the Navy Department's stamping its V-12 summary, "Confidential," in 1945.

In 1987, author James G. Schneider inquired if Houghton Mifflin Company would publish his fine book titled *The Navy V-12 Program: Leadership For A Lifetime.* As a former V-12er at Franklin and Marshall College, I was honored to be asked. Now we both (Schneider, Navy V-12 and Miller, Marine V-12) had an opportunity to participate in making known how the V-12 Program, working through the colleges, had opened the door of educational opportunity to so many of us. On short notice, the colleges adapted their matchless educational know-how to train, and train well, the thousands needed by the military.

Those military programs—combined with the superb performance of the colleges that welcomed us all to their classrooms and their faculty members who taught us so well—did much to impress upon one and all the value of a college education. After the war, many of the veterans using the GI Bill returned to the college where they had taken their military training. Unquestionably, that earlier experience on the part of both the college and the returning servicemen had produced a positive bonding effect on them. For many, the return to campus was like homecoming. Here again, now through the GI Bill, faculty and colleges alike adjusted to meet a new kind of student and in unprecedented numbers. The returning veterans sought out colleges from which they could obtain a degree in the intellectual discipline of their choice. Members of the GI Bill-sponsored student body knew who they were, why they were in college, and, within realistic parameters, where they wanted to go. The maturing burdens of command, of unforgiving responsibilities, and the rewards of discipline no matter how trying, had forged them into a new kind of college student. They wanted an education; they saw the need for it; and they were committed to achieving it.

The colleges, in turn, acted to ensure that the new students' ambitions were fulfilled, as did the college publishers whose authors were almost entirely drawn from the colleges and universities. All of these participants were engaged in launching an era in higher education that would soar to new heights in enrollment, diversity, and course offerings. The nation, in turn, became the beneficiary of the combined efforts as new waves of graduates entered the world of work. Nor were these graduates always disposed to adhere to traditional or customary applications of that college degree once it had been obtained.

In April 2000, it was my good fortune to interview Richard Clowes, an ex-South Pacific Marine, teacher, and superintendent of schools, including the Los Angeles County system, who provides a first-hand account as to how that played out.

RC: When I went to Oxnard as a superintendent in 1950, we were recruiting teachers. We had a young fellow named Ralph Jovanello who applied. He had a scar from his temple clear down to the lower part of his chin. It was obviously a wartime wound. He was a World War II fighter pilot, and he had twice been shot down. We wound up hiring him.

He wanted to teach first grade. So, we put him in there, and he was a marvelous teacher, just marvelous. Subsequently, we had male teachers in all the elementary grades. But that is a move that didn't occur until after World War II.

And the reason it occurred after World War II is that we had, with the GI Bill, hundreds and hundreds of thousands of men who had a college education. They would never have gone to college but for the GI Bill.

The military was a major force in shaping college education and the people of that period. Many of the textbook publishers' authors, editors, managers, sales representatives, and others also reflected that experience. These people had an outward not inward motivation. Try to be helpful—give the other person a chance. These people developed that strength the hard way, and it clearly worked its way into Houghton Mifflin's corporate culture.

No one describes the life and times that forged the members of that early college organization into a close-knit, proud, and dedicated group better than Doug Lowe's widow, Faye. Doug was one of the early post World War II college sales representatives.

FL: Doug grew up in St. Paul. We met at Macalester College in the late '30s. We were married in '41. Doug was in Army Air Corps training to go overseas and served in India for almost two years.

During that time, you learned to live alone, but you weren't alone because the whole country was in the same situation.

At that time, the war ended, and Doug was discharged, he had a degree in economics from Macalester College, but he had no career future in sight. The Guidance Office at Macalester College put him in touch with Houghton Mifflin. He went to Chicago and met the general manager Wheeler Simmons and sales manager Kermit Stolen and had an interview. He eventually was hired and turned over to his mentor Carter Harrison. Carter was a man of great charm and ability. He and Doug traveled together for two-and-a-half to three weeks, and that was Doug's training course as a college sales rep for Houghton Mifflin.

So then he had a company car, an expense account, and five Midwest states to cover. And I discovered that I had married a traveling man. I had thought we were going to settle down in a typical family situation. As it happened, I was pregnant with our first child when Doug started traveling. We lived with my parents until after our baby was born. Doug was at his first college conference when somebody passed a note to him with the news of Barby's birth. He didn't know what to do, because he was so new with the company. Carter stood up in the meeting and said, "We've got to let this man go. His wife just had a baby." So, they sent him home.

I know my doctor was concerned that I didn't have a husband, and if I did, where was he? Why wasn't he there? It was three or four days before Doug could get back to Minnesota in the middle of February in the cold weather.

HTM: And you didn't fly in those days. I bet he had to drive or take the train.

FL: He took the train. In May, we moved to Minneapolis, and Doug really started working for Houghton Mifflin from his home base. We couldn't afford to have his laundry done, and when you were a sales rep for Houghton Mifflin, you wore a shirt, preferably a white shirt. I remember one weekend he came home from the longest trip he had to Michigan. On that trip, he'd been gone about six weeks.

Somewhere along the line, he must have had some shirts done. But he brought me back seventeen shirts, an all-time record, which I laundered on Saturday and ironed Saturday night and Sunday morning. Then we packed them up, and he went back on the road.

HTM: He had been away six weeks on the road, and you were home alone. In those days, he had to stay in hotels. They didn't have motels then. Not all of those hotels were all that great for the traveling people either.

FL: No, some of them were dreadful.

HTM: You couldn't get laundry service in most of them, so if you had a dirty shirt, you brought it home. He got home Friday night or Saturday, and now he left again on Sunday.

FL: Right. Sundays were the hardest, I think, from personal experience, because they are such family days. In a couple of years, our second daughter was born. Doug would always leave on Sunday morning, and I would take the kids to the park near Lake Nokomis. But it was all families. So, we didn't go to the park after a while; we stayed around the neighborhood instead.

In the first days of his traveling, when he left I would dissolve into tears. And then I thought, I can't live my life in a vale of tears. I've got to shape up. After all, I lived while he was overseas. I can certainly do this. So you learn to cope. One of the hardest things, I think, is how much men who travel miss of their families and their children growing up. How much lonelier it is for them, as you mentioned, in miserable hotels or motels. Back in those days, motels had linoleum floors and were pretty sad.

When Doug first started out, the professors were all new to him—he had no contacts. Eventually, somebody would take pity on him and ask him home for dinner, or they would join him for dinner at the hotel.

It always sounds glamorous, "Oh, you're calling on …, you're on college campuses with all these young people around, and how exciting it is." But I know it was hard work promoting a product, if you can call a book a *product*. It was something that he was very proud of, something that he believed in. There was no one to talk it over with when he got back to his room. He would sit down and make out his reports, all the endless lists with comments about various professors and what adoptions had been made or why they had been refused in the past.

Once when he went into the Chicago office, someone broke into his car and stole his suitcase. This was right after the war. He had shirts in it, which were very hard to get at that time. He lost also a couple of suits and all his notes, all his college notes. A particularly devastating loss was for the University of Minnesota, which was one of the largest schools in his territory, with records that went back eight or nine years, at least, and no possible way to ever replace them.

I can remember Doug just scratching down some notes, and then transcribing them when he got home. I used to know all the schools he visited, because I did all his filing. He would bring materials home, and he had a special filing system. That was one thing I felt I could do to help.

HTM: You touch on a point that always impressed me. Many of the wives, in those days, including my wife, Mark, took on a role almost as a secretary. There was the filing, phone calls, and the mail that came in. You were keeping track of the business. You had an involvement with the sales territory that Doug worked.

FL: Yes.

HTM: And in those days, Wheeler Simmons in the Chicago Office and Harold Franz in the New York Office, those managers always stated that each salesman's territory was his business. You ran your territory like you were running your own business. Any commission you got was based against the sales, the expenses. I think that's where part of the feeling of ownership came from.

FL: Right from the beginning, there was a sense of pride in belonging to the staff of Houghton Mifflin, being a very small part of it at that time, and yet a very important part of it. Without the sales reps out there describing the books, calling on the professors, and so on, there wouldn't have been a market.

I know Doug liked the sense of integrity that he felt was evident in Houghton. He was a man of integrity, and he resonated with the way the company was run, the way people were treated—not that there weren't criticisms and complaints. But I remember once, way back, when Doug said, "Nobody ever gets fired at Houghton Mifflin, if you're too old to do your job, they make you the elevator operator." Now, I don't know if that was true, or if it was a myth that someone perpetuated.

When we came to Boston, Steve Grant, at that time, was Doug's boss.

HTM: Well, Steve was then the head of the College Division.

FL: Yes, at that time, and later, president of the company.

HTM: And Doug went to Boston when Steve was head of the division.

FL: Right. Doug was evidently a great one for sending memos to the home office. Steve finally said, "Okay, put up or shut up; come into Boston; and let's see what we can do about some of these things that you're talking about."

HTM: When Doug came into Boston, he became very much a major force in creating the esprit de corps of the College Division.

FL: Yes, very much so. It's interesting. I remember in all the letters and notes I received after he died, how many people wrote about spending time with him, what a mentor he was, and what information he had given them about the College Division, and how it worked, and Houghton Mifflin in general. I knew how devoted he was but didn't know about all the interaction that went on.

HTM: Win Pearson, the Midwest college sales manager, worked for me while I was out in the Midwest, and he often spoke about "Old Dougie."

FL: Oh, yes, Win used to call us quite often, and I think he called you too.

HTM: Yes. You should tell about that, what it's like to have Win call you at one in the morning.

FL: Or two or three. He was a dear friend, a really dear friend. But he would get himself all tied up. The phone would ring in the middle of the night. Usually I was closest to it, so I would answer. There'd be Win, and we'd talk for a little bit about things, and then he'd ask, "Is Dougie there?" And Doug would groan, not because he didn't want to talk to him—well, no, he didn't want to talk to him at three o'clock in the morning. But they did, and it would go on for quite a while.

HTM: Didn't Doug fly the "Hump?"

FL: No, they flew over Burma. Rangoon. They called their group, *The Goon at Noon Club,* because they went up one particular river in Burma trying to bomb bridges. By the time they reached their target it was noon, and the Japanese knew they were coming, and they were sitting there waiting for them. That's why they called themselves *The Goon at Noon Club*. Fortunately, all the crew who went over together came home safely.

Somehow, I just never thought that he wouldn't come home. Never had the feeling that he wouldn't come home. That has nothing to do with Houghton Mifflin. That just has to do with what I remember.

HTM: In a way, it does have to do with Houghton. It's interesting to note how many of the people who clearly put a definite face on the company and had much to do with its culture during the period we are discussing were part of the World War II armed forces: Win with his tanks; Doug with his flying; Ray Miller flying the Hump; Manuel in Okinawa; and the list goes on.

I'm convinced that that training, that experience, taught them a kind of self-discipline, and loyalty to others and to their endeavors—the company—that benefited all of us, and it lasted throughout much of the years under discussion.

FL: I think when people at that point in their careers started with a company, there was a dedication. Well, you talk about loyalty. They weren't looking for another job four or six or ten years down the road. Doug worked for Houghton for forty-two years.

HTM: Yes, total commitment. Faye, you've given me a great firsthand account of just what I was after—a description of what it's like for the wife, and for the children, during those post World War II years when so many of us started our publishing careers in sales. You and the other wives made a major contribution to the success of Houghton Mifflin Company. And you have described how.

The post-war college textbook authors and their editors confronted an ever-evolving, fast-changing curriculum. It is the charge of colleges to create and to analyze state-of-the-art ideas, knowledge, events, and new societal mores and expectations. Texts used by faculty members specialize in each discipline, and it is for those courses that each college text is intended. The formidable challenge for the college publisher is to assemble author/editor teams whose scholarship qualifies them to develop textbook content that is intellectually sound, accurate, and will be respected by the authors' peers. But the task does not cease there, for in addition they must bring to the text if it is to be successful something unique. Houghton senior sales representative, David Levine, describes the dilemma college editors often encounter when endeavoring to include both scholarly content and the teaching/learning features into a college text.

DL: Look at textbooks from thirty years ago and textbooks today, and they're like night and day. Thirty years ago there were no illustrations for the most part, no pedagogy. There was no package for instructors, or even ancillaries for students to work with, nor study guides. Basically, it was the text, and the text was tough going. You had to read a whole chapter, and it wasn't broken up by notes in the margin or by illustrations.

But these days, if you brought out those same books, they would die immediately, because the expectation is that, "You have to bring out a book; it has to be four-color; it has to have lots of illustrations; it has to have learning objectives." You know, basically, it has to have a lot of handholding. This fact has been brought home to me a number of times, because every once in a while I get called into the office to talk with authors when they're revising their books. And usually they have me come in when there are loggerheads.

The authors say, "We don't want to do that." And the editor says, "You have to do it." And they say, "What do you know?" So then, I come in, and because I've been in the field for a long time, they're willing to listen to me. And the biggest issue comes up over pedagogy, and that is basically what I go in to talk about. Authors often feel that if you put pedagogy into a book, it dumbs the book down. It's not the same book.

And my argument is, "Look, it doesn't make any difference. You can have the book, as it is, the same exact content, but with some helping hands for the students, because they don't know how to read anymore. They don't know how to take notes. They don't know what's important. So you have to point out what's important to them. You can do that with the exact same content. And all it's designed to do is to help the student, give them signposts. It's like a road map."

A critical caveat exists here, however, for when editors choose to add pedagogy to enhance the marketability of a college textbook, those editors must first sign up quality manuscripts. Then and only then can the addition of pedagogy matter.

As David says, many college students do not possess adequate college level skills, at least as the authors with whom he engaged view them. Here again, however, we must bear in mind the matter of change—change that the colleges and textbook publishers faced. This particular change centers on the open door policy in the state universities and others.

A much larger universe of students began entering the state colleges under the open door policy. Courses, often labeled as remedial, became standard offerings. Textbooks written for this market opportunity became a standard addition to the publishers' college list. They were written to different specifications.

College textbooks are written by authors from within the same marketplace segments—the disciplines into which their published texts are sold, including their own classes. Market research is helpful, for example, to determine if social, economic, political, or some combination thereof should be emphasized in a publisher's new U.S. history. The resulting textbook is of, for, and by that course in the curriculum.

Publishing college textbooks is largely unlike publishing either school textbooks or trade books. A preceding chapter discussing state textbook adoptions attests to that observation, as does the chapter on children's literature for trade publishing. Editor Harry Foster illustrates my point in the following lines:

HF: The most successful trade books are often done by people who are kind of on the edge of respectable scholarship, or on the cutting edge, or a little unusual or something. I'm thinking of *The Origin of Consciousness in the Breakdown of the Bicameral Mind* by Julian Jaynes, for example. And in the long run, often they turn out to be right.

If you want to publish something that is really interesting, you don't necessarily want to ask the most senior, respected scholars in the field what they think of it. They have their own agendas. And you know, in the history of science in the intellectual life, there are a number of cases where ideas that were later proven to be valid were rejected at first as with plate tectonics in geology, the theory of evolution, and so forth.

College textbooks are sold through bookstores like trade books. The latter are truly retail stores, whereas the college stores, beer mugs and sweat suits aside, are not. The textbooks on the college stores' shelves are adopted publications, resulting from a college traveler sales call on a professor. That professor, upon selecting a text, informs the bookstore as to its title and the course enrollment. The store in turn orders the books from the publisher, with return privileges. The bookstore has also purchased used books for resale from students who have taken the course. Desk copies for the faculty are provided by the publisher.

Both trade and college publishers are dependent on a continuous flow of manuscripts from which they acquire their very existence—new books. Publishers must continually recreate themselves. Trade publishers use literary agents, but with the rarest of exceptions, college publishers have largely been able to stave off the literary agents, using instead a combination of their own travelers and editors to scout out likely authors and acquire their works. Unlike the eclectic freedom enjoyed by trade publishers when acquiring new manuscripts, the college editors' selections are confined to the universe of college courses that require textbooks in the first place, and secondly, by content parameters within those courses. Should, for instance, the next U.S. history text stress economic, social, or political history, or some combination of these to meet current academic trends? No matter which approach is selected, the publication, upon entering the marketplace, will encounter a half dozen or more texts already in use, and one or two of them will be established leaders.

As the years passed following the post World War II boom in college textbook publishing, differing publishing models took shape. McGraw Hill and Prentice Hall, two of the largest and most successful houses, practiced a model that differed sharply from that of Harcourt Brace and Houghton Mifflin.

Marlow Teig, a longtime employee of Harcourt and former vice president of Houghton's School Division, provides an interesting perspective on the origins of these differing approaches.

MT: I've been intrigued by how the principles of the founders of a business and their motivation for going into the business lasts long beyond their lives.

Look at Prentice Hall and Harcourt. How did they get founded? For Prentice Hall, there were two guys who were businessmen, and they had some money to invest. They said, "What kind of business can we go into where we can make some money?" And they chose publishing.

Alfred Harcourt and Donald Brace started Harcourt Brace and Company. They were two publishers, and they said, "We want to publish. Can we make any money at it?" At Harcourt, they wanted to publish, and hoped they could make money. Prentice Hall said we want to make money, let's publish. You get totally different orientations toward the business. And you know what? At least up until the 1980s, those differences were still in the organizations. At Prentice, they looked at it as a business. Can we make money from it? At Harcourt, we want to publish. Can we profit from it?

So the founding principles really drive for a long time.

McGraw-Hill and Prentice Hall in essence subscribed to a publishing model calling for the rapid release of many texts, largely lightly edited. They counted on the acceptance or rejection by the marketplace for editorial revision. This model also enabled them to stay abreast of the fast-changing college market. That approach ran counter to Houghton's prevailing extensive editing model, and it was rejected from within the College Division—actually the entire company.

The College Division's influence and the respect accorded to its continuing publication of such scholarly and superbly written publications as *The Riverside Shakespeare* edited by G. Blakemore Evans, *The Riverside Chaucer* edited by Larry Benson, and the multi-titled Riverside Literature Series, remains significant. These works all warranted publication. We all wanted and endorsed them. But the continuing existence of our college publishing in the new environment demanded more than prestigious works. It demanded sales volume measured in units, revenues, and profits that only market-sensitive publishing could produce. Essentially, the question before the company was how to accomplish that end within our long held corporate culture.

Houghton's college textbook publishing got off to a robust start following World War II. Its future looked promising. Steven W. Grant, chief editor and manager, established a strong list that worked well for that period. However, organizational weaknesses were beginning to emerge. As our college textbook publications list and college enrollments expanded, so did course offerings, faculty makeup, society, and the numbers of competing publishers. As we have seen, our competitors were not all functioning under the Houghton publishing model. Unfortunately, a clearly defined communication link between the division's senior management and its sales and manuscript scouting staff did not exist in practice. The regional office managers hired and directed both the school and college sales forces. That created a semi-matrix management model with unclear lines of authority and communication that resulted in confusion, missed opportunities, misunderstanding, and conflict at middle management levels. The regional managers during those years were under intense pressure to sell school textbooks, with particular emphasis on the elementary school reading series. The college regional sales manager, reporting to a regional general manager, might best be described as a minister without portfolio.

The end result was a regional manager not properly plugged into the college communication pipeline, with the college sales manager not greatly better off. Neither of them was in communication with corporate headquarters at the requisite level to run the business properly.

The organization just described worked very well at its outset in Doug Lowe's initial years, given the limited size of the total textbook operation, but it did not adjust fast enough. By the late 1960s and early 1970s, corporate management was confronted with a troubled college publishing unit and the necessity of deciding whether to divest or stay the course. We chose the latter.

Following the creation of a separate College Division and several turbulent years of testing the Prentice Hall/McGraw model for publishing college texts, under a manager of that persuasion, the challenge was to find new leadership. The division needed a manager who would be fully at home in the Houghton publishing culture and who could apply it, yet could also be competitively responsive to the ever-changing college marketplace.

Within the house, there existed a foreign language editorial group then under the direction of William Berman. In a sense, it was a group without a home, since it edited texts for both the college and school markets. Its function was to publish both college and school texts because over the years both groups were sensitive to the pressure coming from a variety of sources, that foreign language courses be offered. However, said pressure did not convert into hefty revenue figures, given these courses' limited enrollment figures. As a result, Bill's foreign language group was, by and large, left to itself by the divisions, and he thrived in that environment. Now it was decided that Bill had enjoyed his holiday outside the management chain long enough. It was time for Bill to take over leadership of the College Division. And as it turned out, we had found the right person for the job.

Edward Kelly, now president of a successful technology company, worked in Houghton's corporate planning, reporting directly to me for a number of years. Ed's remarks serve well to introduce Bill Berman:

EK: And if you'd like, I could speak some more about the College Division and the explosive growth it experienced in the '80s.

HTM: Yes, please do.

EK: When I was in corporate, I knew the strategy was to get more legs down in the company to reduce our heavy reliance on the School Division and specifically the reading program, and we thought that the best way to do that was to strengthen each of the divisions and to broaden the product line in the School Division. The company was very concerned that if the national trends turned away from our reading program, it would imperil the whole company. Getting the College Division to be a major contributor to the corporation in terms of sales and profits was a major goal. When I started with the company in 1978, Bill Berman had just been named the new head of the College Division. I worked with Bill extensively my first few years when I was in corporate. He was turning around the division and providing great focus and leadership. The strategy was to concentrate on large introductory markets and carefully target the leading competitive books and go right at them. Through extensive market research, very thorough product development and testing, and aggressive marketing, the College Division under Bill Berman was successful at entering one major market after another. We were not publishing that many books, but our rate of success was close to one hundred percent. This turned around the morale of the organization and convinced everyone that we could win against the bigger competitors. We felt like we were David taking on Goliath, and with each success, we became more confident in ourselves. There was an extremely strong esprit de corps developing in the late '70s and early '80s, and I decided that the College Division was where I wanted to go.

The strategy was simple: to concentrate initially on the large introductory text markets and to establish a beachhead and build a foundation in each discipline. Once you had a foundation, then it made sense to publish in the mid and upper levels of each discipline. It doesn't make sense to have the sales force selling upper level books in psychology, if you don't have the introductory books to pay the freight.

I remember well presenting to you, Hal, in the summer of '78 my research on the accounting textbook market in college. I was in your office when you were offering me the six-month marketing assignment, and at that time, you were commenting on my research report, which was recommending that we not enter the principles of accounting market. At that time, three books held a vice grip on the market. The research showed that these books held ninety percent of the market and that professors were very happy with them. It did not look like a promising market to enter from my standpoint. You respectfully said you appreciated my thoughts and observations, but Houghton was developing a new and different book, and we were going to take them on. Sure enough, in 1981, we published the first edition of Needles/Anderson/Caldwell, *Principles of Accounting.* We came at the market with an innovative approach emphasizing learning by objectives and pedagogy, and that was the beginning of a very, very successful assault on the accounting market by this little known business publisher. The big publishers didn't take us seriously until it was too late. We walked in and stole their business. Houghton was now a force to be reckoned with and not because of our size, but because we out-smarted and out-innovated the competition.

Change. Colleges change, as well they should. They changed to meet the demands of World War II, the post-war G.I. Bill, the unsettling years of the '60s, and now change resulting from technology in all its forms, and textbook publishers must keep pace. But Houghton Mifflin was changing too. Mark Mahan, veteran sales representative and longtime Midwest sales manager, was one of the company's stalwart members. When Mark spoke, I listened.

HTM: Now I believe everyone must have sound training. I will always remember the summer we started using television for training. That was early on in the '60s, and you were part of it.

MM: That's the reason Geneva did so well, compared to the others, because you'd spend more money to try and train people.

HTM: Well, we tried. We had some professors from Northern Illinois University in to help us. One of the professors came to me after one teaching session and said, "That Mahan, you know, he really bores in. But you know what, I was not offended. I want someone calling on me to bore in, because then I know what the product is all about." And I said, "Your statement is music to my ears because the entire thrust of what this training is about is to have Houghton representatives come in to your office knowing what books we publish in your discipline so that they can persuade you that they've got a publication that is worthwhile and right for your use."

When Bill Berman took over the College Division, I believe he contributed a great deal to the division and the company.

MM: He did, yes.

HTM: I don't know how long Bill should have gone on with the division, but there were other things we wanted him to do, just as he had done in college, and we moved him onto them. Unfortunately, his departure recreated a leadership problem in the College Division. But back to Bill.

MM: We had that sales meeting up there in Boston, and you came into the room a few minutes before the meeting was about to start and asked me to go with you to your office. There you asked me what you should say to help improve morale and ensure a successful meeting. One thing that I remember about the conversation was my suggestion that you say something to assure the reps that the College Division was going to continue at Houghton and would not be sold off. Whether you knew it or not, many of the college sales reps felt that we were history!

Then when you came into the meeting room and formally announced that Bill Berman was the new division head and that the College Division was to remain an integral part of the company, spirits rose and we had a successful meeting with a group of re-energized salespeople.

I always listened to the Mark Mahans of the company when the chips were down. Give Mark a credible list of college texts, and the professors too listened. Now let's allow Bill to speak for himself:

WHB: I was appointed in January. Mid-January of '78. One of the great strokes of good fortune was the blizzard of '78, because I had just become aware of the magnitude of all that had to be done. I had the college sales managers in for a meeting, and it was at the very beginning of that blizzard. They were here for a number of days.

HTM: You had a captive audience.

WHB: A captive audience. Anyway, after taking over the division, I made a number of organizational and publishing changes in the first four or five months. For example, in 1977, the division published about 105 to 110 books. I reduced the number of titles to between fifty and sixty, thus making the divisional workload more realistic or making it possible to devote the needed editorial time to ensure better quality publications. It also made it possible to have a more focused sales effort.

In contrast, in 1977 the division published three new introductory astronomy books. It was a disaster. If the publications had been published one at a time over three years, the results might have been all right.

HTM: You're talking about the McGraw-Hill model. The manager who preceded you had formally been with McGraw.

WHB: Right.

HTM: Dickinson and various others of the McGraw-Hill people he recruited brought that model up here to Houghton. They signed up a lot of books, got a lot of books out, and then let the marketplace go to work. That model was proving to be very successful in some houses, including McGraw.

WHB: You're right. The philosophy of the division was to use the first edition as a test, or a preliminary edition, so that one could then publish a second edition that would take into account all of the criticism and mistakes in the first edition.

HTM: It was almost a self-editing sort of thing, or at least it seemed so to us at Houghton, given our belief in heavily editing books before their first publication.

WHB: That's right. So, the first edition was really, once again, a preliminary one on which feedback would be gathered. And then the second edition would come out. And it was the McGraw-Hill model, where the sponsoring editors signed up as many books as they could in their respective subject areas. They oversaw the preparation of a manuscript; the manuscript was then handed over to an editorial group that had nothing to do with the sponsoring group.

The person in charge of that group at that time had come up from McGraw-Hill. They just simply got the books out. There was little contact with the sponsoring editors or with the authors, as far as I know.

HTM: Before Dickinson arrived, we had almost the other extreme. I remember one editor who turned out one book in a whole year, and that was only a revision. And when I said, "I don't think that's quite enough," he said, "Well, if you wanted quantity rather than quality, why didn't you let me know?" We had to shake that loose. We tried to shake them up, and we brought Dickinson in. Dickinson did his job in that he stirred things up. He signed up a lot of books. He was a great recruiter, both of people and authors. But we also had to have quality publications.

WHB: Right. And there was no question about that. The McGraw-Hill model, as instituted by Bob Dickinson, was not working productively for Houghton. There was a need to reorganize the group along more traditional Houghton lines. The division was subsequently reorganized along subject matter lines so that each of the sponsoring editors was responsible for both the signing and the development of texts in specific subject areas. Additionally, at that point, further removing ourselves from the McGraw-Hill model, we reduced the number of publications almost in half as noted above. One side effect of that, as you may recall, Hal, is that we cancelled a lot of contracts.

HTM: I sure do, and there were those in-house who were worried about this action.

WHB: We had constant calls from authors. I received calls from all over as a result of the number of contracts we had to cancel. While there were a number of books under contact, we simply couldn't undertake the editorial development needed to publish one hundred-plus books per year. We brought into Boston the college regional sales managers. The sales managers, members of the editorial staff reviewed every contract, title-by-title, list-by-list in order to determine which titles and which programs should be developed. In the '70s, we were publishing in many subject areas. We reduced the number to about twenty.

So, we reorganized the editorial groups, reduced the number of publications, and then established a system of heavy editorial development of those titles that remained. It was also decided that we would concentrate at that point on the first two years of the academic subject areas. So we would only do freshman and sophomore books. We would not attempt to go into any of the higher-level courses, but go after those markets that offered us the best and largest opportunities, which is what we did.

Therefore, the number of publications went way down. And we spent an inordinate amount, as was pointed out to me a number of times, on editorial development. But it worked.

HTM: Yes, and I supported your approach even though it came at the expense of the division's size if measured in terms of its publications list. That decision, however, raised questions in the thinking of others in management about our future competitiveness in college textbook publishing.

WHB: It worked. My sense is that a number of the titles that had been published by Dickinson would have been very successful if they had had greater editorial development. The other factor was we established a market research department within the division, so we could actually go out and survey the markets we intended to publish in and have a pretty good sense of what was wanted by instructors. The department had not existed before.

The introduction of market research, the reduction of the number of titles, the greater editorial input, and the revision of the publishing plan, all of that took place in '78–'79. During that period, we really invested heavily in the development of a few titles. The risk was high in the sense that one was counting on a few books that had to be successful. With the McGraw-Hill model—publishing a large number of titles with the hope that a few would be successful—seemed to work for them. The new divisional strategy really made it imperative that every title be successful. But that was the downside of this approach to publishing. Fortunately, it worked.

HTM: It really did, and fortunately so for the CFO, George Breitkreuz, had been assuring the stockholders and financial analysts that your actions were the correct ones.

WHB: We got higher yield per title, substantially higher. And we were able to focus both the editorial and sales strategy. The sales staff could really spend a lot of time promoting each work because there weren't all that many of them.

HTM: The esprit de corps in the whole division rose sharply.

WHB: It rose, I think, because we were fortunate in having some early initial success. McKay's *Western Civilization* came out in '79 and became the market leader. This was the first book where there was some editorial impact resulting from the new publishing philosophy. And it worked. Then the Marybeth Norton book, *A People and a Nation,* came out.

HTM: The Norton book worried me because I came out of the old school. Here you were coming out with that Norton book, which seemed to me to be so much a departure from the old style political and economic history. I kept asking myself, "Is this thing going to go?" It might be helpful if you described a little bit about how that book was different. And as I look back on the experience, somebody, obviously you and your people, had to have a feeling for the project. Certainly, the authors had a different understanding, if you will, of where today's students and faculty were headed. Why don't you describe that difference?

WHB: Sure. The history market, as represented by Hicks and a whole generation of history books, tended to emphasize political history—the key leaders, the presidents, the ministers, whomever. And in Norton, there was a shift to what was it like for a woman at home, or everyday life in the colonial period? What was the role of women? What was the role of birth control? It was these common, everyday things that made Norton a successful book. On the other hand, in terms of the "social" historical content, it was really the first book to incorporate these elements. And, at the time it was being developed, there was a lot of concern because it was really going to be distinctly different from any other American history book.

HTM: I well remember thinking, "Boy, I hope they're right." It was right about then, or maybe a couple of years later, author Marybeth Norton was one of the scholars-in-residence out at the American Antiquarian Society. We had a dinner for her and some of her friends. During the dinner, I said something about the Indians circling the wagons. And Marybeth said, "You know, the Indians never rode around wagons in circles like that." And I started to say, "Well, all through history." She said again, "There is no recorded incident where the Indians ever rode around the wagons as portrayed in the movies," or something close to that. So she shattered a lot of what had been my image of John Wayne's Wild West. That experience demonstrates why presidents of publishing houses must trust their editors.

WHB: Absolutely. Absolutely. Anyway, Marybeth, Tom Patterson, etc., and the authors of that book really did have a distinctively different voice. Fortunately, it was a voice that was welcomed in the marketplace. And the book did very well and continues to do well to this day. I think somewhere along the line you had mentioned the idea of "unique features."

Well, that certainly is a characteristic that these authors— Marybeth Norton, Bel Needles, John McKay—had in their books. And they weren't just simply things that were peculiar or odd, or off the mark.

HTM: No, they had to be meaningful.

WHB: They were meaningful, and they were able to sort of sense where the market was going, where their colleagues were going. And McKay has the same unique factor component as Marybeth Norton's book in his *Western Civilization*. It takes the same point of view. Needles was distinctively different in its organization from any other accounting book in the market. It was an organization that worked. Yet, the risk involved in publishing it was enormous. But with our editors, they were able to do some very good things and to take into account the fact that the book was different and would have to be sold and marketed in a much different way.

While I was listening to the news about Enron Corporation's difficulties and those of its auditor, Arthur Anderson, I was reminded that, during my CEO years, I regarded the outside auditor's role as of critical importance to my and the corporation's well being. The sense of security existent then, it would seem, might be misplaced today. That said, author Belverd Needles, his coauthors, Hank Anderson and Jim Caldwell, editor Hugh Joyce, who signed up Bel, and editors Frank Burroughs, Ruth Gillies, and David Barton all made a significant contribution to the strengthening of the accounting profession through publication of this highly successful college level accounting textbook—*Principles of Accounting*. Furthermore, their significant contributions to publishing in the classic Houghton Mifflin style constitutes a classic "Case Study."

Again, let's call on Ed Kelly for his insightful thoughts and observations, this time about author Bel Needles.

EK: By spending time with English professors, historians, and psychologists and letting them talk, I learned a great deal about those subjects. It has been my observation that in college publishing, the best authors inevitably are excellent teachers as well; they usually win the teaching awards at their colleges. A good strategy for a college publisher looking to sign new authors would be to focus on the outstanding teachers. If they

can explain difficult concepts well to the class and are motivated, they can probably also write well. Most of Houghton's
best authors are also excellent teachers. And of the outstanding authors that I've worked with, Bel Needles stands alone.
He is absolutely committed and dedicated to improving
accounting instruction in this country and internationally.
He's had a big impact, and I know no one that works harder
or is more committed to what he's doing. I have a great deal
of respect for what Bel has accomplished. Having worked
closely with him for many, many years, he's someone that
stands out in my mind.

So let's go to sections from author Bel Needles' interview, followed by those of his editor David Barton:

BN: I went through my file to find my first contract, which was
dated July 1970, for a book that eventually ended up being
called *Modern Business.* I was very young at the time; in fact, I
had my first teaching appointment in September of 1969, so
this contract was signed only a year after I started teaching. I
think there were several motives and circumstances involved
there. One is that I always wanted to have an impact on a large
number of people, and I felt limited. As a teacher, you have a big
impact on a few; but if you write a textbook, potentially you can
have an impact on millions,

I had two colleagues at Texas Tech University, where I was
an assistant professor, Robert Bonnington and Bernard
Rosenblatt. We used to have lunch together, and we would talk
about how we thought students were coming to college without
knowledge of business fundamentals. It would help them in
their further studies if they had a basic business course, one that
was somewhat more sophisticated than the introduction to business books that were out at that time, which were basically
"vocabulary books." They organized terms, defined them, and
had very little else to go along with them.

So we felt we wanted to show business as a process, and our subtitle was *The Systems Approach*. In addition to going through the processes of business, how they're interconnected and interrelated, we planned a series of six chapters on issues relating to American business, such as the environment, globalization, and other current topics.

We wrote a few sample chapters, developed an outline, and sent the outline to five publishers. I think it was just by accident that we included Houghton Mifflin. I've forgotten if it was a salesperson or somebody else that Bernie Rosenblatt had come in contact with. We sent it to all the major business publishers—Irwin, McGraw-Hill, Prentice Hall. To our amazement, within a couple of weeks we had people flying to Lubbock, Texas, to talk to us about this book, because apparently this was viewed as a big, growing area, and all the publishers were looking for books in the field.

We chose Houghton Mifflin, I think, on the basis that we related very well to Hugh Joyce, who was the business editor at that time.

Hugh was very much of a generalist and humanities person who had gone over into the business area as the editor there, so he was not a typical business editor—that appealed to us. Now I have to say in the short-term we probably made a poor decision, because I don't think Houghton Mifflin was really ready, right at that moment, for doing well in business publishing. We probably could have done better if we had gone with Irwin or McGraw-Hill, who made us very attractive offers.

But all those companies had competing books, and Houghton Mifflin did not have a competing book. That was a factor for us as well.

Our book, *Modern Business,* was just a moderate success. I think it sold around 25,000 to 30,000 copies the first edition, then the second edition, a little less, around 20,000 copies. None of us was happy with that.

I think for me, as an author, it was a critical experience, because it taught me how to be an author. I worked with a terrific

editor named Henry Thoma, who had been with the company
for a long time. He was the developmental editor and was a very
educated person. He taught me a lot about how to write a good
sentence, how to organize a chapter, how to make it readable for
students at a freshman level—all those things that are necessary
to being a successful author.

So going through two editions of that book was a great
learning experience.

HTM: We always gave the author a good deal of help, once the manuscript arrived in-house.

BN: That's right. The developmental editing is extremely important,
because it helps direct the book to make it attractive to the students, which is a critical aspect of having a successful book, as
you know.

When we were in the second edition of *Modern Business,*
Houghton Mifflin was looking to do an accounting book, which
they did not have at that time. Jack McHugh was the accounting editor. He and I hit it off very well, and we began
discussions. The first edition of *Modern Business* came out in
1971. The second edition came out in '74. We signed a contract
to do a principles of accounting text with Houghton Mifflin in
1973, and by then I'd established a relationship with Houghton,
so I didn't really consider any other publisher. It was, I think,
publisher and author working together to develop the idea.

Hank Anderson, who was at Southern Methodist
University, was already a Houghton Mifflin author of a cost
accounting book. I had never met him, but Houghton Mifflin
put him together with me. James Caldwell was on the faculty at
Texas Tech with me. That was the team that was established to
write *Principles of Accounting.*

We began writing and working. It became a much longer
and more involved process than any of us had imagined it would
be. We spent roughly five years developing the initial manuscript

for the book. We went through a couple of editors after Jack McHugh.

And there was reorganization within the College Division of Houghton Mifflin, and Bill Berman became the director of the College Division.

My impression as an author was that there was a major change in philosophy, which was to develop outstanding books that fit the basic course in various disciplines and to work closely with an author team.

HTM: That was the Bill Berman basic philosophy.

BN: Henry Thoma is the person who did the developmental editing of *Modern Business*.

HTM: That's correct. Henry was the outstanding editor and division head, who really was behind McCrimmon's *Writing With a Purpose* and other works that sold in great numbers. There is no editor I can think of who was as skillful as Henry. He was a memorable person.

BN: So after five years, we had the manuscript. The approach we gave the book was very different from the traditional accounting approach. We explained what something was before we would tell you how to do it. Traditionally, accounting had been taught by a rote learning process, in which you would just simply say, "This is how you do it. This is step one. Learn it. Here is step two. Learn it." And you wouldn't get into, "Well, why do you do step one before you do step two?" And so forth.

We began every chapter with a set of concepts that we then applied in the latter part of the chapter. Also, we gradually evolved a system of learning by objectives, which divided the chapters into, in essence, mini-chapters.

This came about because at that time at Texas Tech, I was the coordinator of the beginning accounting course.

We taught it all with graduate assistants. A unique aspect of the course was that we had television sections because part of the responsibility of Texas Tech was to educate people out in the hinterlands of West Texas. The viewers then would watch a course on television, do their assignments, mail them in, get them graded, and we would mail them back. It's original distance learning, I guess you would say.

Houghton brought co-authors Anderson, Caldwell, and me to Boston for a meeting in the conference room. I'll never forget that meeting. To this day, I can see Bill Berman at one end of the table and us at the other end defending our book. We met for a whole morning on this. I remember Bill picking up the Meigs book from McGraw-Hill and asking, "Why does this book sell? Why is it successful? And what can you do to beat it?"

So we made the most convincing argument that we could and discussed it. I think Bill got some faith in what we could do from that meeting. It was the first time we had ever met Bill, and I think he realized that we knew what we were doing.

HTM: Bill agonized over the decision to postpone publication for a year, as he has stated to me in recent years. He was new to the position, but not new to the company. Bill wanted desperately to publish, but still, there was that commitment of not only company resources, but your time and effort too. If this publication didn't work out, it wouldn't be good for you, or for anybody else. But he came down on the right side of that challenge as the passing years have revealed.

BN: Well, in retrospect, it was the right decision. Part and parcel of that delay of publication was so we could class test the book. The class testing was critical. It was class tested at Mesa Community College in Arizona, where we had students fill out questionnaires, detailed questionnaires, after every chapter. We ended up with more than five thousand questionnaires, which I personally spent an entire summer going through, page by page, responding to every student's comment. And that made the book more student-oriented than I think any accounting book had been up to that point.

HTM: As it turned out, the delay in publication put the book "on cycle" with the major competitors' revisions.

BN: Well, I think that a lot of faculty members are wedded to an old way of doing things, but I think one reason we were successful was that we were always very respectful of that. I've always had a great respect for people who have dedicated their lives to teaching accounting. I don't throw what I do in their faces, and say, "This is the only way to do things."

We've always attracted some of those large adoptions that previously used a traditional approach with our book. I've seen so many books fail, even though they have a lot of good ideas in them, because they have a certain arrogance to them, so people just reject them.

HTM: You've got to come up with that edge, that new idea, *the unique factor,* as we often called it at Houghton. That's what you were doing, along with the sound accounting base, obviously.

BN: I think this meeting with Berman really started the notion of the author and company collaboration, which I think has been very unique with Houghton Mifflin.

Well, the book was published the next year, and I remember that Frank Burrows, who was the editor at the time it was published, had an interesting idea. He was only at Houghton for a short time before its publication, but he had a significant influence on it, because he took it through production when we had to make some economic decisions and shorten it.

I was talking with him on the phone one day, and he said, "This book, Pride/Farrell, came out last year on marketing." Then he said, "They were successful. You know, they traveled some with sales representatives, and that got them some sales that I don't think they would have gotten otherwise. Maybe you ought to give some thought to traveling."

So I said, "Okay, I'll do that." The next January, February, and March period, during the peak-selling season, I visited between sixty and sixty-five schools. I went around with sales reps, knocking on doors and talking to people and telling my story about the book and the learning objectives.

HTM: In addition to your discussions with professors, you were achieving something else, and that is you were developing one-to-one rapport with the sales reps, so they started to own you by feeling they knew Bel Needles, and by golly, they were going to get that adoption. There was a sense of family across all of Houghton, and you had become a part of it.

BN: That's right. After two or three years, I personally knew at least ninety percent of the sales representatives, and that was a marvelous thing. They were great people, and they were champions of the book.

I remember when I broke into teaching, the *Cost Accounting* book by Charles Horngren was a revolutionary book at that time. It was a highly technical book. It came with a solutions manual that was copied or typed, I can't remember, but it was just terrible. You couldn't use it, for there were no transparencies or any other useful aides.

The book was very successful because it was in a different era. Today, if that book were published like that, it would never get off the shelf, even though it's a great book.

We also introduced the big package of materials and all the ancillaries that go along with the book. The key to its use was that we integrated all these materials with the learning objectives approach. You always knew what went with what and whether you were working in a study guide, or a test bank, or whatever. It was all tied in together through the learning objectives system.

HTM: It was a total system, and it could be marketed that way. When our people went out, they had the full package before them. One thing was related to the other so that you can talk that philosophy. It became a very fine program, and I can call it a program, for obviously it was more than a book we were marketing.

BN: Yes. We would teach the sales reps how to go through and demonstrate the program. That's another critical step that I don't believe had been taken before. We held a training session in Chicago for sales representatives. The four managers came, and then each manager chose two sales reps. There were, in total, maybe about a dozen people involved. We spent a week teaching them accounting based on our book. We also had all the competing books there.

I remember in Oklahoma, for example, the Larson book had ninety percent of the market. The representative, Felix Frasier, was comparing our book with this Larson book, and we came away from that meeting realizing that our book was far superior to Larson. Felix had sold himself on that book, and within two editions, we had ninety percent of the market in Oklahoma.

It really worked. The sales representatives Mark Mahan, Peter Atwood, Dennis Albrecht, Ron Owens, Mike Goulding were at that meeting. They all came to believe in that book, and they were respected in the sales force, so they passed that belief on.

First, we developed the book with the new system. We class-tested it with students. We trained the sales force in the program that we had, and the lead author went on the road with the book. One other thing we did was, I think, significant. David Barton was the marketing manager for the book at that time, and he kept saying, "Just get me letters, and I'll send them out."

So we wrote letters on our philosophy. They weren't typical sales letters. They were going for two or three pages, singled-spaced, but they were explaining the philosophy of the book. David would send those out. He had a mailing list of faculty members, key faculty members, and we just kept bombarding him with letters.

We revised the second edition. We had more success on the second edition. We had a great editor in David Barton. He was the best editor we ever had.

HTM: David made an effort to understand the market and to understand the authors.

BN: He was a very author-centered person. He believed strongly that the ideas come from the authors, and you need to back the authors up and support their ideas.

David encouraged us to develop a proposal. We met at Marco Island in Florida; we always call it *our Marco Island meeting*. We spent four days there to develop a strategic plan. It was in 1985 that we developed a history of what we had done up to that point, and we came up with four basic ideas between strategic objectives. One was top management support, starting with Hal Miller and Bill Berman.

HTM: This I saw. It was brought to me. But go ahead, I didn't mean to interrupt.

BN: That's okay. I'd be interested in your reaction. But some people have said, well, that's presumptuous of us to do that. But our first objective was to get the company to make a public goal. We had one thing in mind: we wanted the company to be committed to making this series the number one book in accounting. We also wanted an integrated plan where the production and marketing worked together with the authors to develop the plan.

Our second objective was our project plan. Our third objective was a marketing plan. We had developed what we thought were good marketing strategies based on market research, retention of our current users, and analysis of competitors, focusing on large and urban schools. We felt that schools that used a lot of part-time people would be the best candidates for our learning system. On the other hand, they were also the ones that were usually the most entrenched, because it's hard to move away from something they've been doing—customer service and communication.

Then, finally, we expressed our commitment to the company, the authors' commitment to this plan. We all agreed as authors that we would take a stock ownership in Houghton Mifflin and that we would align ourselves with the future of the company.

We went to Boston, and we presented it to Bill Berman and his staff. We were nervous about how it would be received, but I think it was well received, and many of the things that were in it were implemented in the third edition. We did indeed make a very significant increase to the level that we wanted to get to.

If you take all of our books together, we became the number one book in that field.

HTM: And you were doing something else then that was extremely important. You held the accounting conferences, and I recall going to them.

BN: That's right, and you spoke at each one. We are now in our fourteenth annual conference, this summer, so we must have started that right about the time we are talking about. I guess it would have been probably 1985. Our idea was, and is, that we needed to teach faculty members how to use our system. If we could do that, they would be dedicated to what we'd done.

HTM: Those were good meetings. I enjoyed those meetings and still would. I sensed in talking with the attendees that they were thrilled to be there, and they felt that they were getting something worthwhile. A number of people expressed their appreciation for what was being done.

BN: They've been very positive over the years. We've had approximately two thousand people who have gone through these conferences. The authors wanted to do these for two reasons.

One is that we wanted a means of being in contact with our users in a meaningful way. This would enable us to find out what is on people's minds: where are they going, and what are they doing? Over the years, it's been invaluable in helping us keep our books up-to-date and being the pulse of what's going on in the marketplace.

The other side of that, of course, is that these people came and learned what we're doing. We've had a rule that we would never take a copy of our textbook to these conferences. We have materials, and the conference is organized around the approach that we take, but it's not a hard sell situation. We've kept it at the level of a professional meeting. It has continuing education credit that goes along with it, and we've just tried to keep it at that professional level.

Throughout Bel's interview, reference is made to his editor, David Barton. I've repeatedly made clear the important role editors hold in a publishing house. From David Barton's interview, it's obvious that the writing of a college textbook and its accessories is a demanding process.

DB: Bel, in his interview, mentions that the authors had been looking for a publisher and they had looked at the traditional hard side publishers, and the main reason why they came to Houghton was because the company did not have an accounting book. It had a business list, but it did not have an accounting book. The other companies already had at least one accounting text, and some of them had more than one.

So he thought that the company would do a good job with his book from a promotional leverage standpoint. And it struck me when I read that remark that he made in his talk that the benefit, the true benefit to him in coming to Houghton Mifflin, probably was not so much that Houghton Mifflin did not have an accounting book, but rather that we had a pedagogical background and a teaching and learning knowledge-base, which he would benefit from no end. And I'm not sure that when he signed up with Houghton Mifflin that he was necessarily highly aware of the teaching/learning resources that were going to come his way.

HTM: I'm pleased you're making that point, because if there was one place where the company excelled all across the board, it was in that teaching and learning area. You're sighting in on a core value of our publishing philosophy.

DB: If he had gone to McGraw-Hill, they would have taken his manuscript, and they would have published it and sure, it may have done well, but the chances of that happening in an area like accounting at the time—at that particular moment in the early 1980s—the chances were not good, because the major books were very strong. Southwestern had a book that sold as many as 300,000 copies a year, and Richard Irwin had a book that was selling more than 150,000 copies a year. McGraw-Hill's own book—the Meigs book—was doing about 85,000 copies a year as well. So Bel was coming into a marketplace that was dominated by three or four highly successful books, and they were published by business publishers.

   In coming to Houghton Mifflin, which had a strong background in pedagogical skills, he was engaging with a house that knew how to bring to his book key differentiating values. From a value-added standpoint, Bel was getting something that he could never have gotten from Irwin, McGraw-Hill, or Southwestern, because they simply didn't have the editorial background in pedagogy that Houghton had.

HTM: As you said earlier, you weren't editing paragraphs and sentences. You were bringing to the editing process—to Bel's book—this element of the teaching/learning facet of the editorial activity, which did not exist to the same marked degree at other business publishers.

There was a very thorough editorial understanding and application of the teaching/learning process from grade one right on up through college. It distinguished the house.

DB: That's right. Well, Bel's book, when I started looking at it and getting to know it—this was before it was published—I found out that his book in particular had been under development within the company for a period of five years, and the person who did most of the editorial development on it was Ruth Gillies, a very experienced developmental editor. I spent quite a bit of time with her trying to find out what she had done to work with the authors to give the book the distinction that it had. It turned out that what she did was sit in her office for five years, and she had the competing books on her desk, and she went through Bel's manuscript and compared it on a line-by-line, paragraph-by-paragraph basis with the materials that were in the competing books. And she would send Bel letters every day with all these questions, and I've seen the file—I had the file of her letters in my office at one point—just letter after letter after letter with detailed, paragraph by paragraph, line by line analysis. She asked questions about what makes a good accounting book, what makes a good chapter, which chapters do you need and which chapters do you not need, and which learning objectives within the chapter do you need and which do you not need.

So Ruth had a lot to do with the successful structuring of that book. She was the one who convinced me of its superiority over the other books. I would get together with her, and I would ask, "Now, Ruth, what makes this book better than these other books that you've been working with?" And she could show you, and it was convincing.

I think that by making a single person accountable for the success of a book's development and promotion, by pinning it onto one individual, the sponsoring editor, and tying it to that person's salary and financial world was a good motivator to make sure that the book was taken care of throughout the whole process and the whole time it was in the house.

So the outcome of Needles coming to Houghton was, I think, the relatively unforeseen outcome that in a discipline, such as accounting, which had never previously concerned itself with anything but debits and credits really—suddenly a book appeared that was concerned with the *teaching and learning* of accounting as well as the booking of transactions. And that, to a great extent, was a product of the coming together of this great author with this great house, Houghton Mifflin.

And when the book eventually came to market, its pedagogy was the key differentiator, the key value-added piece, over and above the accounting that was in the book. The teaching and learning value-added pieces were the key differentiators that sold the book. The sales staff had something new to talk about in accounting. They could clearly articulate the pedagogical values, because they already had the vocabulary from selling Houghton Mifflin's other books with that same pedagogical orientation.

With Bel's book and with the orientation that Houghton Mifflin was able to bring to it working with him as the author, we truly had something that was unique. There is no question that Needles is a highly talented author, but there is also no question that the values added were well over and above what competing publishing houses supplied. There were resources that only Houghton Mifflin could and did bring to the development of that book to differentiate it and make it into the clearly value-added product in its market. And I think that that's what made the book so successful—both here and around the world.

HTM: Yes. I've known of few successful textbooks that did not qualify for the use of the word "unique" you just used in describing them.

DB: Accounting texts also require formatting skills that we, who were not accountants, were not familiar with. We were essentially softside people, and we did not know the formal niceties of the accounting profession. We didn't always know when something had to have a single line under it, or a double line, for example. We weren't totally sure about that. And accounting professors are often casual about that kind of thing. They do these T accounts on the blackboard and they don't really care about—especially the Ph.D. types—they don't want to be bothered with the formal requirements of accounting documents. So, when the book was published, we had quite a bit of trouble with those issues.

I remember one woman, Sharon Robinson, a professor at Edinburgh State University in Pennsylvania. She ran into me at a meeting one time, and she was furious with us, because she said that she had a Needles solutions manual that had all these errors in it.

So our way of dealing with that was to ask her to review the book for us and to let us see what she thought were all the errors. So she sent this package into the office and it was a marked up solutions manual, and she had determined that there were 563 errors in the solutions manual. And we looked it over, and there were some errors, but mostly what she was drawing our attention to were these format requirements, and she had a very rigid idea of what an accounting document had to look like.

Well not all professors agreed with Sharon, but we found that we had to have—we had to inculcate standards, some kind of criteria that we could say that here's the way that we're doing formats. And the way that we came at that was by going to an accounting firm. I remember this thought came up when we were discussing what to do about our problem. The thought came up that we just had to find somebody who knew all the answers. And I remember one night, it was around six o'clock in the evening, and I was in the office working, and this guy—this big, genial bloke—showed up, and we started chatting, and it was Tom McDermott of Arthur Young & Company.

We started chatting, and he sat down with me for maybe two hours that night, I think, and we went over some of these issues. And I was a bit bashful to bring this up to him, but in the end I said, "Well, the thing that occurred to me is that it would be really nice if we could get somebody with the kinds of skills that you and your firm, Arthur Young & Company, possess to look the text and solutions manual over and then sign-off on them, just as if you had done an audit."

And sign-off on it and say, "Arthur Young looked at this text and its solutions manual, and as far as we are concerned, it is up to standard, up to GAAP standards." Well, that was a cost unique to Houghton Mifflin that went onto the book.

HTM: It paid off, though.

DB: It did pay off, because the next edition of the Needles book that came out did quite a lot better than the first one.

The next book that we did after the *Principles* was *Financial Accounting* by Needles. This is a book for accounting majors and for business majors. And the conversation with Tom took place in time for Arthur Young & Company to look that book over. And then we came out with the book and inside it, we bound the page with their opinion.

Publishing house presidents, through the lessons learned from the success or failure of their publications, easily subscribe to the Latin proverb: *De gustibus non disputandum* (there is no accounting for taste). They also learn early on the economic realities of earnings, for which there is an accounting. Accordingly, they preside over what some characterize as a simultaneous function of mutually exclusive penchants. Michael Winship, in his carefully documented *American Literary Publishing in the Mid-Nineteenth Century: The Business of Ticknor and Fields,* beautifully states this dichotomy in one line, "Like his mentor, Fields, Osgood clearly possessed a flair for attracting literary talent, but his enthusiasm for literary publishing unfortunately often remained unchecked by economic realities."

Ultimately, the marketplace exercises accountability on the editors' tastes in manuscript selection sometimes every bit, if not more, binding than the publisher's financial accounting systems. Still it's what the editors do that creates the financial numbers in a business dependent on constantly recreating itself through new publications. Franklin K. Hoyt and George W. Breitkreuz, the two Houghton Mifflin chief financial officers I was privileged to work with, each possessed an uncanny psyche that enabled them to bring productive publishing mutuality to expected exclusivity. Because they knew and understood both the culture of book publishing and financial accounting, they saw to the melding of the two diverse forces.

The publishing balance resulting from their insightful leadership was basic to Houghton Mifflin's success. Therefore, it seems appropriate to conclude this chapter on college publishing with excepts drawn from an interview with Thomas McDermott, who, as a partner of Arthur Young & Company, now Ernst & Young, headed up the New England region. Tom was in charge of our account and, through that relationship, became directly involved with author Belverd Needles' *Principles of Accounting* text. Editor David Barton described that involvement above.

I asked Tom to give me his assessment of the relative importance of the textbook in the process of learning about accounting and becoming an accountant. Now to Tom:

TM: It plays an extraordinarily important role. The number of people studying accounting at the college level is as many as a million people a year. There is a market out there—a demand.

Accounting is where a lot of knowledge has to get transferred in the process of learning a little bit about accounting. It's not a small injection. There are a lot of things that one gets to learn, but they are all in the nature of the business. I've always felt that accounting is a language. It's got the complexities of any language. Simply the vocabulary, by itself, just being able to get your mind to recognize words that have larger meaning and, secondly, then being able to manipulate that knowledge and use it skillfully takes a great amount of learning and experience. I just couldn't imagine students acquiring this knowledge without the help of a textbook.

In the days that preceded mine, people told about faculty notes that were basically books. By the time a person completed a course in fundamentals of accounting, or the basics of accounting, the faculty notes that a teacher would have provided in mimeograph form were bound and, in fact, were a book. And, of course, the textbook, as it came along, filled that need, but it brought a much higher level of skills to the process because of the added value that publishers were able to bring to it.

You asked me why did I think that Arthur Young's role in the process of the development of the Needles text was important. Well, just to mention for a minute what our role was. We basically were asked to take *Principles of Accounting* in its, I believe, second edition. We were to think about that book within the context of causing it to be a completely error-free text. I could see that it is very hard to compose an accounting textbook that is error free the first time. And I think that, in general, in the marketplace that had been the experience. But we talked about the idea that if we could somehow develop a mechanism by which we screened his book to its finest point and then gave it also not only a meticulous look, but a strategic look, that we could also bring some extra value to it.

I can tell you that the book had met ninety-eight percent of its goals by the time we got there, so that it was already a really fine piece of work. The place where we were coming in was to give it a last screen. And not only a last screen in order to pick up a few things that needed to be fixed before it could finally go out, and we did have our share of those, but also to be able to let the marketing people convey with a great sense of honesty and integrity that the book did go through this final process. And in fact, the Arthur Young letter or opinion introduced the textbook that we reviewed, so that the name recognition of the company, I think, was useful.

I was impressed from the beginning with the Needles text. It had an abundance of coverage, and in a smart, shorthand way, the no-frills with words, got right to the point quickly. It divided these nuggets of knowledge into easily consumable, you might say packages, and in a building block sort of way so that pieces of knowledge that preceded were gained and became essential to the next transfer. I could see from the beginning that a great deal of thought had gone into this process of design, and that quality also was going to have a material effect on the speed and completeness of a student's learning process.

I volunteer a reasonable amount of my time at Babson College working with young people who are there for their MBAs. Babson is a business college. It's entirely focused on business, and accounting is a key ingredient in that process, and the textbook is the thing that people carry around and go back and forth to dorms and home with. I believe the textbook will be around for a long time and that I could not imagine a person acquiring the level of knowledge that is needed at the entry level in accounting or even in the early stages of life, using your background in accounting, how that could be accomplished without the efficiency that comes with textbook-accompanied learning.

HTM: I like your analysis of what is in the book, the expertise that's brought to the book, and the value of that presentation for the students as they go through the accounting training program.

An added dimension came about when editor David Barton and independent auditor Tom McDermott decided to bring an accounting firm into the editorial process. Normally, auditors never get involved with authors and editors. Here we had an independent accounting firm, working with an author and an editor team, which is basically the editorial function.

Through that process, I am sure you developed a better sense
for what the company was about.

So what were your observations? What about the role that
the author played, Bel Needles in this case, and the editor David
Barton?

TM: I came to see and know David Barton first. And I could see him
as a person who was skilled in academia and skilled in the ability to transfer knowledge. He had been a college professor. But
I also saw that he had a knack for the business side. He would
not have been a very useful person if he wouldn't have been able
to see opportunities for improving the textbook, and you might
say anticipating what the uses of the text were and seeing opportunities to improve it.

It was clear when they were together that he and Bel
Needles enjoyed each other's company. I think a key ingredient in all joint undertakings is that people really have a great
deal of respect for one another. And I could see that that was
the case. Bel Needles was also a classroom professor. He had
seen the delivery of accounting from one angle, his angle, for
years and years. And he had dreamed about the improvement
of that process through the excellence of a good book. But he
was not a publisher. David was able to bridge this gap, you
might say the teaching of accounting, which he had never
done, and also to the whole accounting and business world in
which he had no first-hand experience. He had a sort of a
human instinctive desire for entrepreneurship and how to
make things better, and how to make more money by developing a product that would sell.

And, yes, it was, in fact, one of my few experiences in seeing that editor and publisher role very up close and to see it
work well.

HTM: There's another problem, namely used textbooks. The authors
and publishers receive no return once the initial sale occurs. The

tendency therefore is to revise a text more and more frequently. It used to be every three years. Now it's almost every year.

Authors and publishers can understand students wanting to buy used books for less money. However, the process increases the price of new books, and the rush to revision weakens the work. I'm curious if you had any reaction to it.

TM: Today, at the university level, I sit in on lectures in classrooms at Babson College about new issues that crop up all the time. The controversy over the issue of stock options alone—accounting for stock options—is discussed intelligently. Students, and certainly faculty, are expected to be able to convey their best feelings and thinking about this issue. If that's the constancy of change, if that's the rapidity of change, then the textbook has to stay in tune with it.

It would seem to me, in some respects, that a textbook does have to go through revision frequently. Whether it's one year or two years, I don't know. But I would imagine it's closer to one year. And I think the author and the publisher have to devise a mechanism by which they make that happen. The world is complex. It's complex for all of us. And we still can't give up.

This chapter started out stressing the ability—the capacity—of colleges and textbook publishers to capitalize on change. As Tom so clearly documents, we continue to live in a changing world—so the colleges and the textbook publishers must continue to change—just as they did during the years under discussion. College textbook publishing is a fast moving, challenging business.

CHAPTER 10

Independence

How We Protected It and Why

Part A:
How We Went About Continuing Independence

As the corporate world's merger mania activity escalated throughout the 1970s, it became clear that Houghton qualified as a prime takeover target. My membership on the board of directors of a company embroiled in a takeover battle brought home to me the importance of Houghton having a professionally developed plan in place immediately for our defense, which thereafter would be managed as a work in progress. It would be strengthened through the crafting of additional strategies, as those engaged in the takeover business dreamed up a succession of new attack modes.

We would, of course, maintain our all-out effort to publish well—that was a given. Yet, realistically, considering the inanity of those years, outstanding performance was tantamount to an invitation to be taken over. The prevailing mindset reminds me of the old saw— "if you can't teach, then teach others to teach." It was obvious to old hands, particularly in school textbook publishing, that the publishers most actively acquiring other publishers were not themselves publishing top-of-the-line texts. Harkening back to my standardized test publishing days, the unfortunate result of the activity was a regression to the mean; publishing standards fell victim to the consolidation measures of cost cutting, high powered marketing programs, outsourcing of editorial work, touting product give-aways, and in the process, less and less about what was between the covers of the textbooks.

Synergy was the silver bullet of those days. It persists to this day, although now *platforms* seems to be the buzzword. Let's explore the concept and how it sometimes can play out at Silver Burdett, for example, as told by Jack Williamson, its former president:

HTM: When Time purchased Silver they really hadn't thought through what they were going to do with it, or at least I guess that's the case, judging from what you have said at other times.

JW: They really hadn't. They thought the key word at the time was *synergy.* We have to have synergy here, and they thought that Time could bring all this reference material that they had and the talent of their type of editing. I don't know how much money and how much time was spent trying to get a fix on how all those vast resources available in Time could be applied to the publisher.

HTM: So Time was really of the opinion that they were going to give Silver a lot more than Silver could give them, under the blanket of synergy, because they had this great storehouse of information.

JW: Yes. And they sent people over to work with the Silver editors and so on, and they came up with nothing. The one product that they suggested, and we did it because we felt we should, was a monthly wall chart of current events. The poor salespeople were told, "Get subscribers to this."

HTM: No matter what, sell it.

JW: Yes, even if they had to pay for it out of their own pockets. I think some of them did.

HTM: This was one of the great assets from the synergy basket they brought to you.

JW: And the salespeople worked it, and they worked it, and they worked it. But they weren't working as hard on their other products as they were on this chart. And it was an artistic success, but for the most part it was too expensive for one thing, and schools didn't need it.

HTM: That experience documents one of the great misconceptions about textbook publishing. People who are not in education and textbook publishing are always trying to supply the classroom with materials about which they have fixed ideas and which they believe should be used in the schools and press to have them published. The problem is the schools often as not will not buy them, for they probably do not comply with the state curriculum. There's no money for another thing. They couldn't buy them even if they wanted to buy them.

JW: It's all they can do to buy approved textbooks.

What is not immediately obvious to outsiders when applying the synergy concept to publishing textbooks is that the resulting publications must correlate to the continuously revised standards established by the nation's educational community, especially in the state adoption states. There is a certain arrogance existent among many individuals within the business, media, and political communities, who put down educators, textbook authors, and their publishers.

The following story would border on the ridiculous, if it didn't concern kids.

JW: When Time tired of owning Silver Burdett, the story is that Jen Lennan, who was the head of Time at the time, and the head of

General Electric were playing golf. As they went around, the subject of educational publishing came up, and they began to talk about what wonderful things they could do jointly with the vast resources of GE and Time. It ended up with a handshake that GE would buy half of Time's ownership of Silver Burdett.

Then the fun began. More experts coming down from GE, bringing their little phonograph records with them and things that were totally useless in terms of doing anything in education. And before long it got so crazy that I thought, "I can't work at this place anymore."

I was in charge of putting together this massive project which would involve a specially designed motor vehicle with little classroom seats in it for the electronic material that was going to be developed. The salespeople would drive from school district to school district to demonstrate the material, and they'd have the teachers sitting in these little seats. That was the least of it. The whole thing was just blue sky with no notion of what the schools would spend, so I left.

I was offered a job down in Washington in the educational division of an institute for writing educational materials that told kids all about the mind. It was a good experience.

When the Time-GE fling collapsed, Silver asked me if I would come back, and I did go back. But by that time, it was still General Learning, and it had its president. I was president of Silver. But it was an incredible thing what non-publishing industries did to educational publishing in those years, and Houghton Mifflin was one of the ones, in fact one of the few, that escaped disaster.

HTM: We had firsthand knowledge of the tragedy that was being fostered on education, and we fought hard to remain independent.

Development of a plan for our defense to remain independent obviously required outside professional help. The question was who?

Our investment banker was Paine Webber. We knew the management there. Nelson Darlin, George Gardner, and Donald Stacy were all well known to us. Paine Webber had taken Houghton public in 1967 and was always helpful. Even so, George Breitkreuz, the chief financial officer, Marge Dyer, vice president of corporate planning, and I traveled to New York City and interviewed other investment bankers who were much involved in merger and acquisition activity. Little seen or heard during their high-powered presentations instilled our confidence in them. We would stick with Paine Webber.

Then came the question of a law firm. Two New York firms, Watchel, Lipton, Rosen, and Katz and Skadden Arps were purported to be leaders in the mergers and acquisitions business. The decision to use another law firm flew in the face of Houghton's long standing relationship with Goodwin, Proctor and Hoar, whose senior partner, Richard Nichols, was our first outside director and a loyal personal and business friend. We were not persuaded, however, that the takeover game was their forte, so again we three traveled to New York. The first stop was at Skadden Arps where we met with Joe Flom, the firm's senior partner.

Flom informed us that he had just the partner to assign to Houghton—namely, Robert Pirie. So down the hall we went to meet Bob Pirie, who although the partner in charge of Skadden's Boston office located at One Beacon Street, as was Houghton, spent most of his time in New York, while Louis Goodman held forth in Boston. Connecting with those two lawyers was a most fortuitous event for us. They are both outstanding in their work and always a pleasure to be with. I've often been asked how I could trust our lawyers and our investment bankers. The basis for the question being, neither were to be trusted in the takeover business. My answer has remained constant—I trusted ours, and they never let us down.

The meeting with Bob Pirie that day, and I say it without qualification, made the difference between Houghton Mifflin retaining or losing its independence. We had in Bob an individual deeply interested in publishing, who understood it and the Houghton culture as well. He had empathy for our values, our publishing culture, and he also knew the company's history of which we were so proud. He has been described as "an iconoclast who loves a fight." A colleague once stated in *Skadden: Power, Money, and the Rise of Legal Empire* by Lincoln Caplan, "He affects a kind of entitlement when operating in his 'larger than life way' and a flair that enables him to pull it off." In later years, following some incident, he and I half kiddingly would comment to one another that these takeover fights would be fun if there wasn't so much at stake.

We shared the view that the standard legal firm, investment banker, anti-takeover defenses were not all that successful. Often the defenders ended up going through the uninspiring traditional defensive maneuvers, generating major expenditures and then were bought anyway. We had the good fortune of assembling an outstanding defense team, and I trusted each one of them. Their counsel and guidance was unbeatable, as the future proved.

The first test of our defensive strategy came in 1978. I was attending a meeting of the Educational Division's regional office managers in New Orleans, Louisiana, when the news arrived that Western Pacific Industries had made a hostile move on Houghton. By Sunday afternoon, our defense team had assembled to discuss our course of action, and on Monday morning, we were meeting in my office. Author Ken Galbraith was present by his own choice.

Ken Galbraith was and remained a long-term author of over thirty books published by Houghton Mifflin. Unbeknown to me over the weekend, authors Ken Galbraith, Archibald McLeish, and Arthur Schlesinger had conferred about the Western Pacific action and decided they did not like it. There was at that time major concern within the authors' ranks about the consolidation of the book publishing industry.

Now we began to realize the value of the company's established reputation as an author-centered house. Bob Pirie, given his penchant for operating with a flair, immediately saw the value in Ken's offer of our authors' assistance in warding off Western Pacific and gave his support to them. He also made sure that lawyer Lou Goodman provided his insightful legal analysis. Paine Webber's support for this unorthodox action fell under the leadership of Don Stacey, head of corporate finance at Paine Webber, and was supported by Bill Lester, Bob Baldrich, and Lynn Long. Lynn was both a lawyer and investment banker, and she had plenty of aptitude for flair—à la Pirie's brand—herself.

Early novels written about America's frontier days often described the fierce fights between the fur trappers and Native Americans, as of a nature wherein "no quarter was given, and none was asked for." That kind of mind set existed within our group as the following comments by Lynn Long Hoffman demonstrate:

HTM: Lynn, you were a key player in seeing to the survival of the company when Western Pacific Industries decided it would add us to their gas pumps. You understood the basic philosophy and values that long-termers in Houghton Mifflin Company possessed about the company and publishing. It would be great if you would tell any and all the things that come to your mind about those years. But especially talk about the days when we first became acquainted, and Houghton was under a corporate takeover attack. You played a very crucial role then—a very important one—a role that is little understood by those who read the press about takeover fights.

LLH: There was some common philosophy from the beginning ... a passion about the preservation of a venerable institution like Houghton Mifflin, which had created and sustained a culture for publishing—for art—over hundreds of years, and which deserved to be preserved in perpetuity.

Opportunities are very rare to make any kind of contribution to something of that kind of scope and value. That's why it made it all the more egregious to contemplate, as we did, after Mickey Newman, the chairman and CEO of Western Pacific Industries, bought that stock—I think we called it a *toe hold*. In a situation like that, it's uncharted water. An event occurs from left field that's extraordinary. It's destabilizing; it's disruptive; it's frankly scary. And I remember the first instinct was to know our enemy.

HTM: Right.

LLH: And the process of gathering research; background material; learning as much as was publicly available at the time about Western Pacific Industries; discovering that its genesis, unlike that of Houghton, had been a defunct railroad.

That his biggest asset was a net operating loss carry-forward. That his operating subsidiary, Vider Root, unlike the claims of Emerson, Hawthorne, and Thoreau, had the ability to calibrate over $1 per gallon for gasoline during the Arab oil crisis. And, horror of all horrors, his view of Houghton was that of a cash cow to be raided on his string of bankrupt railroads and calibrating gasoline pumps.

It was easy to see why Houghton Mifflin did not belong in the string of tin cans that Mickey Newman had in his conglomerate at that time. So I remember the intensity with which we undertook that research. And I think I said to you earlier, "We wanted to know him in full measure. Not just what his company balance sheet looked like and what his subsidiaries looked like, but also, who was the individual?" That meant doing a great deal of legwork and investigatory work out of New York and determining just exactly what kind of a person were we contending with. I think that information gave us all some measure of comfort—really right from the beginning.

HTM: You were the chief architect and instigator of that activity, were you not?

LLH: I was. It was my firm instinct to know everything about him that we could possibly know. And I remember coming to the first board meeting that you convened after the acquisition of the minority interest. I had put together a little Paine Webber blue binder, and it contained the public data that was available. And it was, essentially, this discussion—know your enemy.

Who is he? What are we up against? What do we think his motives are? And with that knowledge, we had a better sense of what we had to do.

All too often the acquisition of a publishing house is viewed as the manifest destiny for a highly egocentric conglomerator who's made his wealth and his mark in the commercial world and now feels this right to metamorphose into a publisher. And the credentials were not overwhelming.

HTM: But in bringing that research material to the forefront, and we had to have it and know who we were dealing with, there were other things that also had to be done.

The board of directors at that time counted a number of outstanding members. Abe Collier, chairman of New England Life Insurance, was absolutely fearless, and Mary Lindsay, through her many New York City contacts, was extremely helpful. I had made it clear where I stood, knowing from my days in the military service, if you're the leader, you have to lead.

The loyalty and commitment of the board was outstanding. On one occasion, a special board meeting was called for 7 P.M. It was snowing. Bob Cushman, chairman and CEO of Norton Company, was on the phone from Germany, Mary Lindsay on the phone from New York. At least two members, John McGee, chairman and CEO of Arthur D. Little, being one of them, came from a black-tie awards dinner still in that attire, and Lou Goodman was patiently helping me manipulate the phones—I used a wrong button, thereby disconnecting Germany, much to Bob Cushman's annoyance. The point is, every one of the directors was participating in the special meeting. That's when boards were boards, and the CEOs were very glad of it.

But it still was important that the CEO not let the board down through making some ill advised, or at its worst, self-interested decision by taking unilateral action that would place the board in jeopardy. At that time there was too a continuing strong loyalty and a concern for the employees—a long held tradition within the company. A key consideration for the CEO and the board of directors in corporate takeover battles centers on a valuation of the defending company, and on this occasion, Houghton Mifflin was the defender. Don Stacey was insistent that Paine Webber conduct a valuation. I asked Lynn about this undertaking, for Don had assigned her to getting on with that job.

LLH: It's a very interesting process. And you're right to say it's obtuse. And it's not visible, unless you've been involved in something similar and have had some experience, because you might assume that valuing a company is straightforward, particularly a publicly traded company, which has a freely traded stock.

You know the number of shares outstanding; you know the current market price of the stock; you multiply one against the other, and you have valuation. Well, fair enough, you have a market valuation, but that's a far cry from the value of the company in an acquisition scenario.

So there are many factors that are classically looked at in that kind of a process. Starting with some sense of context of what the company's worth is within its peer group in the industry; looking at all of the other publishing companies with a business and buildings somewhat similar. Each company is obviously unique. But there is still a range of similarity within which you try to place an individual company to start the process of valuation.

And we did that—looked at publishing companies, generally; tried to make adjustments for size and profitability; and looked at all of the financial markers and performance characteristics that you would traditionally look at in that kind of a situation.

But even that doesn't begin to tell the story. Because even if you can make judgments about relative valuation, add it in to market valuation, which is the starting point, there's still this further intangible: what is the value of a company as a going concern? Strategically—taking into account the likely future.

And that's where the whole process becomes truly esoteric and highly judgmental. Judgmental, but on the other hand, it has to be, in the final analysis, entirely well reasoned and defensible. Because, in this whole process, as you might well remember, it's the directors of the company who are ultimately charged with protecting the interest of the stockholders—the owners of the company. And, have that fiduciary requirement to be able to know what is fair, and what is in the best interest of the shareholders.

So selling at, or valuing the company at, too low a price is obviously unfair. And valuing it at too high a price, which puts too great a premium on the likeliness of attaining certain results in the future, is also not in the best interests of shareholders.

So the ultimate analysis, while very esoteric and judgmental, has got to be defensible on the basis of hard and reasoned data and analysis. Which makes it, I think, a particularly challenging process. And, in the final analysis, it' s about valuing intangibles.

HTM: The chairman and chief executive officer really has the responsibility of making certain that the people selected to perform these defensive tasks will provide the board with, as you point out, sound information, which will enable them to feel confident that they can back management and put their neck on the line in a defensive stance. Will we defend ourselves or will we not?

But fundamentally, the CEO at that point is charged with having a conviction—one, that he is headed in the right direction; and two, that he has people who will see to it that all of this body of information that you have collected will withstand challenge at some later date if a lawsuit is brought or charges that we really sold too cheap, or whatever. So there is a crucial point in such events where faith has to take over—the board must have faith in the CEO that you're not letting them down; that you're giving them proper information; that you're not leading them down a road that will create a liability problem for them.

At the same time, the CEO must have absolute faith in the individuals chosen to provide the necessary information to act. The team we had of you and Stacey and Lou Goodman, and Bob Pirie at Skadden, Arps—these were all people whom I trusted, as did the board, and had absolute faith in.

In February 1999, I interviewed Bob Pirie in his New York City office. We reminisced about our years of working together on Houghton matters—years over which we became personal friends, and I sought out his counsel beyond any other source on many matters, obtaining inspiration and confidence in the process. Bob Pirie must go down in the chronicles of Houghton Mifflin as a key contributor to its success and survival.

Let's see how the Pirie flair and the Houghton unique factor functioned when working together in harness. We enjoyed it. You, the reader, are invited to join:

BP: Well, I remember the first meeting down in your office after Mickey Newman's bid was launched. And I remember, we sat there, and Ken Galbraith came into the office…
But I don't think Arthur Schlesinger did. Did he?

HTM: It was only Ken.

BP: But Arthur got on the phone to Archie MacLeish. And that lady, who was the math author, came later, I guess.

HTM: Mary Dolciani came later on in the battle.

BP: Dolciani, that's it.
And there   was created the famous "disappearing author" defense. Which was a pretty far-out thing.
I remember Mickey called me up and said, "Come on, Bob. That's all a lot of nonsense. You know God damned well it doesn't mean anything. It's ridiculous. And, you know, we're going to take over."

And I said, "Mickey, you're not going to like what happens."

And then Mickey wrote Mary Dolciani a very stupid, very arrogant, long letter. And she let him have it back in spades! I remember that letter was just unbelievable.

HTM: You know she went to see him in person.

BP: She went to see him in person? I didn't know that. But she really let him have it.

HTM: Oh, she made it very clear what would happen.

BP: And she made a believer out of him. And then he called, and we had lunch at the Four Seasons. The three of us had lunch.

HTM: He didn't have a case—any good reason why he should own Houghton. He really got, you might say, "blind sided," because no one really thought the authors would be that loyal to us. But the authors meant it.

BP: You bet they did. You bet they meant it.

HTM: And he got hundreds of letters from authors that made that point. And authors can express themselves well. And many of those letters left no doubt as to where the authors stood.

BP: Yes. But the other thing, of course, was that you couldn't tell from the proxy statement how much Houghton stock the families owned at that point. And I think, in fact, it was more like thirty-six percent, although it looked like it was a lot less than that, as I remember.

HTM: Yes. I've heard various people make statements about the amount of stock owned by family. What they didn't realize or know, was that there were other names on that proxy list that, while they meant nothing to outsiders, were known to a few of us who had been around the company a long time. There were a number of what might be called "old Yankee" types that weren't about to budge, and they were very loyal. We also had the help of the "old guard" employees, who had retired from the company, in calling on these people (stockholders) and explaining the situation.

Now when you added all of that group in, the percentage got to be rather significant. Yet we had this uninformed outsider count come up over and over again, even into future years. We knew who these key stockholders were. You know, in the final analysis, there was still a sense of family there—the Houghton Mifflin family—and it counted for something in those days.

BP: Yes.

HTM: And we had ways of getting to them. And they got mixed up in the fight, and they were not going to let this takeover happen either.

BP: Yes.

HTM: I don't know what would have happened if a different relationship had existed.

BP: Well, I think in those days, there was a lot more concept of loyalty to a company. And you had a group of old investors who had been there a long time. You had a group of officers who felt very loyal. I'm not sure that either of those emotions prevails today. At least if it does, it's not in very many companies.

HTM: Also, it's well to keep in mind that the authors, through the Authors' Guild, were fighting consolidation in publishing. They were afraid that it would reduce publishing opportunities for new authors, as well as many of the old hands.

BP: Sure.

HTM: So, fortunately, we had that powerful group backing us, our authors. Houghton's tradition of being an author-centered house was a key factor in marshalling them to our defense.

But I'm curious how you assess our actions in retrospect. My belief is that the key to our success was our use of unorthodox procedures. We could well have lost the fight, if we had used usual or prevailing defense tactics then or during the later battles—legal battles and financial-based negotiation between investment bankers.

BP: Oh, absolutely. Yes. A standard battle in the law courts—it was just going to be one more takeover battle. Judges were pretty cynical about takeover matters. And on the whole, they were pretty disenchanted with the kinds of tactics the defenses were using to tie up the court system.

So you really created a fear in Mickey's mind that he was going to get stuck with this company, and it wasn't going to be worth anything after he bought it, if half or more of the company's revenues were lost due to the authors walking out on him.

That's what really did it. It wasn't that we beat him in the courts; it was that we changed the economics on him.

HTM: We never went to court.

BP: Never. Never. And it's one of the few battles I can think of where we never went to court.

But it was a remarkable event. There were only three companies I knew of who had survived hostile takeovers without making any change in their business; Houghton Mifflin was one.

In fact, all three of you guys, who were the heads of those companies, were at the house for dinner one night at the same time. It was Unitrode, Houghton Mifflin, and Woolworth's.

HTM: I remember that evening. I was proud and pleased to be part of it, and it was most enjoyable.

I believe the authors enjoyed that fight. I remember one time when departing the *Auld Lang Syne* cocktail party Ken Galbraith holds following the Harvard graduation, Galbraith leaned over and he—tall as he is—put his arm around me and he said, "You know, I figured that if the fight went any further, there were a couple more little things I would have unleashed on Newman through forces down there in Washington."

BP: But that was so great. And I think there was a strong feeling on everybody's part that the role that Houghton played as an independent publisher was a role worth preserving.

There was, of course, concern about the course of action put into place as the following extracts from attorney Louis Goodman of our law firm, Scadden Arps, reveals:

LG: On the authors—actually just to back up maybe before we get there—the whole goal of the defense was trying to defeat Western Pacific's ability to go into the market and buy stock and then buy more, forcing more and more stock into loose hands. Is that forty percent "Family and Friends" really solid, or can you start losing a bit of it so that Newman can control the company? In this case, you had to create the impression in Mickey Newman's mind that he shouldn't be buying stock, because he could end up owning a company where the most important asset, which is the author base, would walk out the door. This is a strategy people talk about with technology companies, or have in the past.

It's a strategy, Houghton Mifflin aside, that is considered really never to have worked, that it sort of lacks credibility, that people are economic animals and that one way or another they'll accommodate themselves to a new situation and maybe gain a bit somewhere else. But the whole idea that all the computer scientists, or all the authors, will walk out the door is not credible.

Obviously, that wasn't the case with Houghton Mifflin. On the one hand, my role at that time was in the trenches helping to implement this process with the authors. There was a certain, I suppose, discipline to the process in that people had to act together. The company's professional advisers—PR and legal advisers, and investment bankers—who understood the process we were in, wanted to make some specific points through the authors. These were people, God knows, who had the advantage of being their own bosses. I worried that these independent people—that would be like herding cats—that we couldn't get them to function as a cohesive group. And it really struck me that they all were willing to sublimate that and be part of a group. I haven't looked at those letters in whatever, twenty-five years, twenty years, and I suppose I should do so. But I'm sure some things were said the way a bunch of them wouldn't precisely say it. But there was never a complaint about that.

Also, on the trade author side, the leader of this was Ken Galbraith. His lawyer at the time, and I suspect his lawyer still, is Bill Truslow of Hill & Barlow, and Bill was clearly sympathetic to this, but also cautioning his client about liability issues and getting too involved, and so on and so forth. Basically, Galbraith was certainly undeterred by that. I worried that Bill would prevail. And that he was being—I mean, he was doing what a lawyer should do—but I guess at the time I wished he would keep his mouth shut.

As I discovered then about Houghton Mifflin, you had trade publishing, which was not the great contributor to revenues or earnings but for which particularly you would get attention in the news magazines and so on, with these authors—Paul Theroux, Arthur Schlesinger, Ken Galbraith, Archibald MacLeish. To my knowledge, of all the people who were approached on this, the only Houghton author who said, "No," and maybe not coincidentally, he's a lawyer also, was Louis Auchincloss. He worried about the liability, and this is something I don't want to get involved in, and so and so forth.

HTM: Auchincloss told me some years later, he didn't think it would work anyhow.

LG: But he was, to my knowledge, the only one.

HTM: I think that's right. Actually, I'm sure that was the case.

LG: On the educational side, that's obviously where the revenues and earnings are, but names like Mary Dolciani and Bill Durr are not household names. They probably had a lot more to lose in that—and you can explain this better than I can—they were, I don't want to say "quasi employees," they were tied to a particular house anyway. They would certainly antagonize their new boss, if he were to win.

Now, back to Bob Pirie:

BP: What was the next takeover bid?

HTM: Well, the next one, of course, was *Time* magazine.

BP: Some guy started approaching you.

HTM: Yes. He was someone on Time's legal staff. He was the representative to the Association of American Publishers. That was about the time I was either vice chairman or chairman of the AAP. So suddenly, I had this guy who was right on my elbow every minute. And I called you about it.

BP: I know. I called Dick Monroe. It was between Christmas and New Year's. And Dick Monroe was down in Barbados or somewhere. And I remember—"Dick," I said, "You know, you've got this young kid on your staff." Now this guy was in his sixties or something.

HTM: He was not a kid.

BP: But I purposely wanted to paint it as being a youthful indiscretion. I said, "You've got this young kid on your staff, and I know exactly what he's telling you, Dick. What he's telling you is that 'Houghton Mifflin says, no, they don't want to be taken over, but the reality is that's just talk. They wouldn't mind being taken over at all.' Because that's the way these guys think, because he wants to stir something up."

I said, "Dick, it's none of my business what you do. And I'm certainly not telling you you shouldn't do anything. But I just want to make something absolutely clear to you: Houghton means it when they say, 'We don't want to be taken over. And if you try, there's going to be blood in the streets. And it isn't going to be ours.'"

And Dick started stammering and stuttering. And he said, "Forget about it. Don't worry." And, "Yes, you're right. But no, we're never going to do it. I hear you. And I understand that message. And we'd never do anything out of sorts."

And that, I think, was the last we heard of *Time* magazine.

HTM: No. Sometime later, we had one more incident. They approached you, in a friendly way, suggesting maybe we would like to buy Little, Brown's trade division, or something of that nature. George Breitkreuz and I met with their financial officer and others. You didn't come along. Frankly, I liked the idea of a Houghton Mifflin/Little, Brown trade book publishing division. It could have made for a great trade publisher.

BP: That's right, I was not there.

HTM: And we started talking. And we said, "Well, we buy for cash." And they said, "No, no. Stock!"

BP: That's right. That's right.

HTM: And we started laughing at them.

BP: Yes.

HTM: We said, "Look, we came here, because you said you wanted to sell the Little, Brown trade division. That stock arrangement doesn't sound like you're talking about selling anything."

BP: Yes. I'd forgotten about that one. Well, I don't think being part of Time would have been a good place for Houghton.

HTM: It would have been a disaster as the ensuing years have revealed.

BP: Yes.

HTM: Well, another experience we had, of course, was with our friend Bass, a Texas venture capitalist.

BP: Well, I remember Bob Bass—I guess we woke up discovering he had, what? About 400,000 shares?

HTM: A large block. Suddenly he had it.

BP: Yes. Boom. We all knew he'd owned Bell & Howell. And he liked the publishing business. And we had a board meeting about what to do.

HTM: Hadn't he also been after Macmillan, or somebody down here in New York, before that?

BP: Yes. He had. He had made a hostile bid for Macmillan. That's how I'd gotten to know Bob Bass, because I was representing the other Bob—Bob Maxwell, the international media entrepreneur.

HTM: Right. I knew you'd had prior contact. In fact, you speculated even before Bass made his move on Houghton, that he could come at us. Toward that possibility, you may recall, Lynn Long collected a large folder about Bass. I think we even knew his shoe size. Once again, we did our homework.

BP: Houghton had a board meeting. And by then, I'd ceased being a lawyer. I'd become a Rothschild investment banker, and Houghton Mifflin retained us to deal with takeover threats. And I remember I took the position that one thing we could be absolutely sure of was that, if we sued Bob Bass, (a) he was going to get really mad; and (b) we were going to lose. Because this was a check he could write out of his spare cash.

And so, we didn't have any of the conventional pressures that you could bring on a guy like that. There wasn't any antitrust law. He was just going to do it, or force us into doing something else we didn't want to do.

But I thought—from my viewing of it—that this is really, actually, a very honorable guy—and a very sensitive guy too. I think he was chairman of the National Trust in this country at the time.

HTM: He was and remains a civilized person.

BP: Yes, he is a gentleman and a civilized person.

HTM: He had culture, a virtue seemingly rare among corporate takeover types.

BP: Well, he was, you know, a culturally interested and an active person.

So, I suggested that we just sit down and talk to him, and try to explain to him what Houghton Mifflin was all about. And why we thought it was really important that it stay independent.

And so, I called him up. And we decided we didn't want to do it where anybody could see us. So it happened there was an airstrip near my farm in Hamilton, Massachusetts, where he could land his jet. So, you and I had lunch with him and David Bonderman, who was his right-hand man, at my farm in Hamilton.

HTM: Right.

BP: And while the four of us had lunch, you laid out to him what we believed in; what Houghton was all about and why; and then you did something that was very, very wise. You said, "You come into the office, and you can meet anybody you want; we'll show you everything you want, and if you believe in what we are doing, we hope you'll support us. And if you don't, well then, do whatever you want to do."

And then he came by. I think it was about a month later or something.

HTM: About that.

BP: So then, he called me up afterwards, and he said, "I give you my word that if I sell the block, I will sell it in such a way that it doesn't disturb things."

Because my concern was that if he decided to get out, and anybody else bought that block, we'd have a new problem. And it probably wouldn't be with anybody as nice as Bob Bass.

HTM: All the way through. Well, there are two other parts to the story well worth telling. One, Deirdre, your wife, had a wonderful meal for us that day in Hamilton.

BP: Yes, yes. She put on a very grand gourmet lunch.

HTM: That was wonderful; she was part of the team.

BP: I remember we sat out in the conservatory, with all the flowers around the piano.

HTM: This refined hospitality far exceeded a business lunch at a faddish "in" place, like the Four Seasons. But the second thing—of course, I wouldn't have invited him into the company like that if you and I had not discussed our strategy. And, once again, your talent for seeking out the unique, the unorthodox, made the difference in enabling us to achieve our objective. What you and I were really looking for was a way to resolve our problem, other than by using the usual defensive methods employed by traditional investment bankers and law firms, neither of which, you excluded, could necessarily be trusted.

BP: Yes. Yes.

HTM: Lou Goodman—wasn't that sure we ought to be taking such action.

BP: Lou was very, very opposed to it. In his mind, it was a totally off-the-wall idea.

HTM: I had some inkling at the time that he did not fully support the plan, but I was committed.

BP: But you had the hurdle to leap for a lot of people, including the Houghton board.

    I thought it was a great tribute to you that the board went along with this kind of thing, because it was totally unconventional, and it was a high-risk scenario.

    But to me it wasn't as high risk as a fight, because I didn't see how we could win a fight.

HTM: No, I didn't either. And I liked the unique aspect.

    If you think about publishing, it's always seeking out for the unique factor. I always maintained in the house that "anything we publish ought to have a unique factor. Something that's different and worthwhile."

Many people don't know how to or want to deal with something that's unique—different. And that was the case in our takeover fights. You had a gift for devising responses to our challenges that upset the standard takeover practices. That was a major part of what brought the working relationship between the two of us to the forefront. I thoroughly subscribed to your practice—philosophy—of going into an attack mode and deciding, "Well, we aren't going to just do all the legal 1-2-3. We're going to look to a better and a different way to do it."

BP: Nobody had ever done anything like that before. You sit down and basically say to the guy, "You know, if you want to take us over, you probably can do it. But here's why you shouldn't." It's a discussion that involves two rational people and relatively mild egos.

HTM: You stayed away from that meeting with the three authors that came in. They were, as you recall, Chris Van Allsburg, Belverd Needles, and William Durr.

BP: Yes.

HTM: As I told you earlier, I've since talked with the authors who met with Bob Bass, and they were in the fight to win.

About twenty minutes before the meeting was to start, Bass's financial officer arrived. At the same time, Chris Van Allsburg, who had written *Polar Express, Jumanji,* and other best-selling books, arrived. When I introduced the two, the financial officer asked Chris if he was really the author of those books he read to his kids. Chris said, "Yes." Well, you would have thought the financial officer had just been introduced to the divine creator himself, and so I figured maybe we've got this guy on our side pretty early on.

BP: Yes, right.

HTM: When the meeting started, the Bass lawyer, as I recall, slumped down in his chair like, "Oh, God! I've got to listen to this!"

I intentionally started off the discussion with author Chris Van Allsburg and editor Walter Lorraine. Walter's authors have won more awards for children's books than any contemporary children's book editor I know of. If there was ever an editor's editor for children's books, it was and is Walter. When Walter and Chris started off discussing how they create an idea for a book, the lawyer sat up straighter and asked, "You mean you don't start off with a pre-determined topic?"

And they looked at him like, "Nobody, no real author/editor team would start off with a topic! You have to explore, delve, conceptualize, and then you go from there. That's the way we create these books."

And all the time they were talking, the lawyer kept sitting up straighter and straighter and paying more attention. In fact, he became hooked. And why not? The Bass group was being given a lesson in publishing by three of the best authors and their editors in book publishing, and they had just heard from the first team.

As I walked down the hall at the end of the meeting with Bob Bass he said, "I wouldn't break this up for anything. It's the first time I ever found out what really goes on in a publishing house between the editors and the authors." And I knew then we had it—that our instinct—the search for and use of the unique factor had once again proven to be the way to go.

BP: Yup, it was really terrific. It was a great tribute to Bob Bass, because most of the guys who make their money doing what Bob Bass does are ego-driven, insensitive, and purely financial. There's no emotional or intellectual understanding whatsoever.

And, you know, we took the gamble that he was different. And it tuned out, he was.

When talking to Chris Van Allsburg, Bill Durr, Bel Needles, and Walter, I've inquired about their recollection of the meeting with Bob Bass. I've extracted a substantial portion of Bel Needles' comments, with follow-up from Bill, Chris, and Walter.

HTM: That day with you there, Bel, along with Bill Durr and Chris Van Allsburg, that was a high point in my seventeen years as the company's CEO. I have often wondered what your thoughts were about that experience.

BN: I was very proud of it, for one thing, and I really valued the relationship with Houghton. I have published books with some of the major publishers, the more conglomerate type publishers, and there's just no comparison between what you feel with Houghton and what you feel with the other publishers.

The idea that Houghton is an independent company was something that was very near and dear to my heart. So, I was very concerned about the possibility of Houghton losing that status. I've seen so many big companies buy publishers with the idea that they're going to be tremendously successful. But the fact is, they own them for two or three or five years, and then they sell them to somebody else.

I've seen publishers that end up with, in the worst case, eight introductory economics books. I know of one author team that has nipped at our heels over the years that has been with five or six different publishers. You know, after a while they just couldn't compete with us any more. I mean they lost all credibility in the marketplace, although they're a decent author team. Stability is of major importance in maintaining the market.

Before that particular meeting with Bass, I was giving a paper at the European Accounting Meeting in Stuttgart, Germany. The only way that I could get to the meeting in Boston was to take the Concorde from Paris. I didn't sleep at all the night before, because I was so wrapped up in this whole thing. It's silly to think I could sleep. Anyway, I had to catch a

5 A.M. flight from Stuttgart to Paris, and then take the Concorde from Paris to New York. It was quite an experience. I was glad to have that experience once in my lifetime. But I was groggy. In New York, I had to catch the Pan Am shuttle into Boston. My wife had sent by express a clean suit and a shirt to the Parker House in Boston, where I arrived about 12:30 P.M., for the meeting that was to start at 1:30 P.M.

And now, Bill Durr's comments:

WD: Probably my biggest feeling was plain, blind fear. I'm sitting here with all these billionaires, you know, and what I do, not for myself, but I have an important job to do. The fear left after a while, but I was scared to death, because I thought, what I do here is probably as important as anything I'm ever going to do with Houghton.

HTM: Well, it was an important day.

WD: And, how do I sell this rich man, help him understand what I'm supposed to help him understand. But they were pretty nice guys. They sat there, and asked questions, and they listened.

And, now, Chris Van Allsburg:

CVA: The thing that I remember, was trying to explain to them the difference between just the recording of an event and the story. And I used as an example the artist who might sit down, having remembered fondly the experiences he had with his granddad when he was eight or nine years old, sits down and actually writes about granddad and me, and, "Granddad and I, we went out and we caught a big fish, and on the way home we bought some corn on the cob," and all these little kinds of local color details. "And then they get home and they have the fish, and then they curl up and they go to sleep," and that's the end of the story.

And having used that as an example of what is not a story, I said to the group, "That is not really a story, that's just an event." And one of these fellows raises his hand, and he says, "Well, it's a story for the fish." And I don't know if that immediately made me change my opinion of all the suits that were sitting there, but I thought, "Well, at least one guy is really on the ball. One guy is really on the ball here."

Walter Lorraine comments, "I always figured that those guys became so frightened of those crazy unpredictable characters, Lorraine and Van Allsburg, that they would not touch Houghton Mifflin with a ten-foot pole."

Now let's pick back up on the interview with Bob Pirie:

BP: And that leads us to Mr. Maxwell?

HTM: Yes, our friend, Mr. Maxwell. You must tell how that relationship came about, because nobody believed me when I said, "Maxwell was not a takeover concern." In fact, at the time, I couldn't even get the Houghton Trade Division to believe that they didn't have anything to worry about from Maxwell.

BP: I remember there were a lot of people in publishing in this case, including Simon & Schuster and Bob Maxwell. With both of them, I told them a condition of my representing them was that they could never make a hostile bid for Houghton. And they both agreed to it.

And after, with Bob Maxwell, we took over Macmillan. Maxwell had a guy who was advising him—some Ed Ney. What happened was Bob wanted his authorized biography published in the United States, and not by Macmillan for obvious reasons. And nobody would even touch it with a long pole.

And I was talking to Ed Ney and I said, "Well, I'll get Houghton Mifflin to do it." And he replied, "Houghton Mifflin? They'll never do it in a million years! They're terrified, because we're working on making a bid for them." And I told him, "Well, Ed, you'd better check a few things out, because Bob Maxwell and I have a deal that he can't make a bid for Houghton." And he asked, "What do you mean? What do you mean?" And I said, "That's the deal I made when I agreed to represent Bob—that he can't make a bid for Houghton Mifflin. And Bob will keep his word. So don't waste any more time planning a takeover of Houghton Mifflin."

And I called you and said, "Listen, Bob Maxwell has kept his word. How about publishing his biography?" So, you said, "Sure." You were happy to publish his book. You knew it was going to cause an uproar.

HTM: Yes, but I liked the prospect, given the situation.

BP: But you were happy to.

So I called Bob, and I said—you have to play to Bob's ego—so I said, "Bob, you know Hal really appreciates the fact that you've been an absolute man of your word, and you haven't made a bid. And he knows you've been under a lot of pressure to make a bid for them because everybody looks at them. And Hal said the least he could do to pay you back is publish your biography, which he'd be happy to do."

And that's how that came about.

HTM: Well, that's what I tell people. They say, "But you published his book," and I respond by saying, "I respected the guy. We had an agreement. He kept his word. That's what counts with me." And they think I'm kidding or not telling it all.

BP: In all my dealing with him, he was absolutely straight. He never asked us to do anything even remotely improper. He was a brilliant businessman. He had an intuitive judgment for ideals and stuff that was extraordinary. He was certainly the only person I ever met who would do the business equivalent of playing twenty chess games at the same time.

There's another story—you might not remember—but Lord Victor Rothschild was very anxious to get his essays published.

HTM: Oh yes! I recall the incident.

BP: He was very anxious to get his essays published in the United States, and he was having no luck at all. So I said, "Look, Victor, let me see what I can do."

And I sent them to you, and I also sent them to a friend of mine at Knopf. And you were very nice. You called me up and said, "Bob, look, it really doesn't cost very much to publish a book like this. And if it will be helpful to you, we'll be happy to do it."

And I said, "The one thing that I'm sure would finish my career is if Victor found out that his book was published as a favor to me. So I think we'll just scrub that idea. Forget it."

The Knopf people were less polite than you were. The Knopf reader's report came back saying, "This is a book written by a man who's gone to great lengths to be judged as an amateur."

HTM: There's one defensive move we did execute, which caused a lot of raised eyebrows. I still remember selling the board on this idea. They even considered giving me an Admiral's hat, when we decided to buy a seagoing barge.

BP: Oh yes, that's right, because of The Maritime Act.

HTM: Yes. You had mentioned its restrictive provisions.

BP: You wanted a U.S. documented vessel—that's right

HTM: No one could believe "Houghton is buying a barge!"

BP: Did we buy a tugboat or a barge?

HTM: It was a large barge—a seagoing barge.

BP: It was a whole barge. Yeah, there you go. That's it.

HTM: Which, when we finally sold it, we made money on the deal. But the day I walked into the board, and I said, "Well the proposal here, as you see, is that we buy a barge."

BP: God! I had forgotten about that.

HTM: "A barge?" And they looked at me like, you know, "What's happening to this guy?"

So, we went through the whole scenario about buying a barge and how our ownership of the barge made for a strong anti-takeover defense. And they said, "Okay." Well, they called me "Admiral" for a while. And a few people asked, "Why do you own a barge?" I didn't try very hard to explain it. But there was a darned good reason for it.

BP: Yes. Years before, we had nailed an English company that had made a bid for—I think it was General Host. They had a paddle wheel steamer in some lake out in Colorado and another one in the Okefenokee Swamp.

And we claimed that these were U.S. documented vessels, and it was a violation of The Maritime Act to have foreign ownership for U.S. documented vessels. And it caused enough turmoil to tie things up enough so that we got away.

HTM: That was another of those unorthodox acts. And so suddenly, Houghton owned a barge. Probably the only time in the company's history.

BP: You were probably the only publishing company to ever own a barge.

HTM: During the period when we were in the Bass fight, some of your investment banking competitors were bound and determined that we would get rid of Rothschild and switch to them. I sent you some of the correspondence.

BP: Yes.

HTM: I wasn't about to do that. One day, one of the Houghton directors called up and tried to persuade me to switch from Rothschild to Merrill Lynch.

BP: I know which one too.

HTM: I told him, "There's no way I'll do that. I know what we're doing, and we're getting through this okay. If I go with another banker, we're gone, so Bob Pirie and Rothschild will handle this." And he finally said, "I will take the matter to the board. You've got an obligation to do this—to change, etc., etc." and I responded, "Well, if you do, I'll go public with it. That it was you that forced the change." Had I switched, it's doubtful we would have survived as an independent publisher.

BP: We always said to everybody, "When somebody hires us, I want to do their next deal. I'm not worried about this deal. I want to do the next deal. And I want to have a relationship with them."

I said, "We're not pushing the usual boilerplate at them. And we're not just trying to get a fee and get on to the next thing." I'm sure—had you ever been taken over, we would have gotten a much larger fee than we ever got on any of the defenses.

But that wasn't the object of the game. And we built a very nice business. But interestingly, we built a business around people who were fundamentally entrepreneurial in their companies. Whether it was you, or whoever.

HTM: The Houghton trips to Europe, I've gathered over time that some people didn't understand that there was a purpose for going over there and making presentations.

BP: And they weren't vacations.

HTM: They were hard working trips.

BP: The theory was that those investors—the kind of Swiss Bank investors that we were talking about—were people who, when they bought your stock, they'd stay with the stock.

We were, in effect, creating another block of stock that would not respond instantly to a hostile takeover.

Your big fear in a hostile takeover is that you lose control on day one, because the institutional investors sell; the arbitrageur is selling it; and you've now got an inherently very unstable situation. And you can't put it back together, even if you win, and that's a reality frequently overlooked.

You're in deep, deep trouble, because you've got a whole new group of shareholders whose horizons are measured in minutes, not in hours, and we felt that the foreign shareholders would be much less likely to do that.

We also used to encourage people to go out and talk to savings banks in towns like in Iowa, and get them to put money into stock.

HTM: George Breitkreus and I made many trips out into Iowa, Colorado, Kansas, Minnesota, and Illinois.

BP: Exactly. And it was the same thing: that these were investors who would take their time. And so, you'd have a chance to get your case across, before you've lost control of your company.

HTM: I think we benefited another way, in that the European trips gave us better international visibility.

BP: Sure. Sure.

HTM: In due course, the people in Geneva and Zurich and other places seemed glad to welcome us back. In fact, in certain respects I came to feel more at ease in Geneva, Switzerland, than in New York City.

BP: Those people are fed up with people who come once and leave. It was the fact that you went back regularly and saw them. And, as I say, "It takes time to build credibility and for them to get to know you." And that happened.

And, yes, I think it was good. And I don't know what percent of the stock ended up overseas, but we got a decent percentage. What was it? Ten, twelve percent?

HTM: I can't recall the exact number—but it was up toward that level. And it was in firm hands with people who did seem to value us for what we were.

BP: Yes. And Houghton Mifflin was not a name that would normally have come up on anybody's radar screen in Europe as a stock to buy. You had to go and expose it to them. And it was a good policy. We did that for a bunch of companies, and it worked out very well.

HTM: And I still recall the day when the head of Rothschild's Geneva bank stood up after the luncheon and announced, "I really think you all ought to buy Houghton stock; we do!"

And here were thirty-five or forty people representing heavy finance.

BP: Yes.

HTM: And what better recommendation could one ask for?

BP: That's not bad.

HTM: Bob, you certainly display a great interest in and aptitude for publishing and books, and you know a great deal about the business.

BP: Well I love the publishing business. I love the book business; I always have. As I say, "I guess I've always sort of had a passion for the book world, even when I was a law student at Harvard."

Bill Jackson was the great, legendary rare book librarian of Harvard. And he took me aside one day, and he said, "I want you to be my successor as the rare book librarian at Harvard." And I asked, "Good heavens, why?" And he replied, "You're the only person I've ever met who's as greedy as I am."

I really felt that Houghton Mifflin should stay independent.

But you know, I don't think even in the industry most people really understood—had a lot of sympathy for it. It was a way of making a living, and that's part of the problem with the consolidation that's taken place. It's really wrecked the trade book business. Everybody says, "Trade, trade, who the hell wants trade?"

And you always told me those people who bought trade publishers because they thought they could get movie films out of it, were totally fooling themselves. And that's certainly been proved to be true.

But I remember you always said you felt there was an obligation to publish even—I remember we talked about a poet called Galway. And you said you probably never made a dime on any of his books, but you thought there was sort of an obligation to publish some poetry books.

And I don't think a lot of people in the industry feel that way. I believe Bob Bernstein at Random House did. I think he was a guy who had that sort of sentiment.

The following insightful observation by Lynn Long Hoffman, sums up not just the key to Houghton Mifflin Company's success in retaining its independence, but also its basic author-centered value system—its authors "who go up and down the elevator."

LLH: So, while I think our defense has come to be known as the "disappearing author" defense, I think that that is too superficial a characterization. Because I think there really was an appreciation, by virtue of the comments the authors made and the stance they took, that your assets do go up and down the elevator. And if you acquire a firm of the composition and history of Houghton Mifflin aggressively and adversely, and challenge that culture of collaboration that a publishing firm really is, you maybe are left with nothing. No matter what you paid for it.

Part B:
What Was at Stake

The maple trees were in full color as my wife, Mark, and I drove into Sutton, Vermont. The township, with a present-day population of 1,000 residents, is located about thirty-five miles south of the Canadian border. Sutton itself consists of some dozen houses and a school situated on one of the many hills forming the topography of the region from which the visitor is able to see several of the surrounding working dairy farms and Burke Mountain, well known to skiers, off in the distance. Having "escaped" (the word used by the historically knowledgeable town clerk—she was most helpful and engaging) the hordes of incoming flatlanders, Sutton still possesses a quiet charm and serenity reminiscent of the past.

Henry Oscar Houghton was born in Sutton on the April 30, 1823, the son of Captain William Houghton, a native of Bolton, Massachusetts. His mother was the daughter of Captain James Clay of Putney, Vermont. The conjoining of the two participating founders of America through their service in the Revolutionary War in Henry Oscar Houghton appeals to anyone with a sense of history. The two Captains helped set in motion our great democracy, and Henry

Houghton's legacy was the founding of an influential printing and publishing company. The contributions of that company through literary works and textbooks meaningfully contributed to the democracy brought into being by his forefathers.

Off to Burlington, Vermont, in 1836 at the age of thirteen, with the sketchy education of the time and place, according to Horace Scudder in his *Biographical Outline,* Henry Houghton described the purpose of the trip: "…to be initiated into a knowledge of printing, an occupation which I have followed chiefly since that time until the present, and am still in my humble way engaged in it."

Continuing with Scudder: "(Houghton) brought … a native gift—the gift of good taste, that quality of selection and reserve which lie at the bottom of genuine success in any mechanic art that appeals in the last analysis to the cultivated eye and mind."

From those austere beginnings, Henry Houghton, by dint of hard work, farsightedness, and strength of character, brought into being The Riverside Press and in turn Houghton Mifflin Company. In doing so, he started a publishing culture that endured for a century and a half. Established criteria for assessing corporate cultures and the traits of those who create them elude identification. Different businesses confront their founders and their successor with disparate opportunities and challenges. Still, the decisions made, the actions taken, and management's style in executing them over time are the components of corporate culture. So it was at Houghton Mifflin Company, as we have seen, where a Yankee independent-minded culture existed that was centered on a commitment to publishing books that mattered. We, who followed were the beneficiaries of the culture, traditions, and, truth to be told, the personalities, of Henry Houghton and his successors. It was our charge to keep Boston publishing moving forward. It was understood that change must always be part of that effort. Effecting change, however, does not entail publishing books as others believe they should be. Rather it was what we believed they should be. We were not therefore dependent on focus groups or a commodity-oriented publishing culture. As wonderfully expressed earlier by editor Walter Lorraine, your liking all of our books was not our objective. That culture, once understood, goes far in helping outsiders grasp and appreciate our unyielding, never-ending effort to retain Houghton's independence.

Peter Rollins, president of Boston College's Carroll School of Management's Chief Executive Club, who has met and dealt with hundreds of corporate leaders, observes that over time what evolves as a corporation's culture is largely of a CEO's doing. Jack Welch, in his recent book, *Straight from the Gut,* states, "Great people, not great strategies, are what made it all (General Electric) work."

Robert Baron, founder of Prime Computer, in his book, *What Was It like, Orville?* observes, "… as with all leaders, they are eventually measured by what they do with these resources. The creation of jobs has largely been the effect of good leadership. The decline and destruction of established companies has largely been the effort of poor leadership. Growth or decline is largely in the long shadow of management."

Media's Hollywoodization of the CEO moniker over recent years has tarnished the title's luster. Egocentric proclivity among leaders of start-up businesses, a vanishing sense of corporate memory within established firms, and unconscionable financial shenanigans were all contributors to this unfortunate development. Is it possible that the time has arrived for giving corporate leaders the traditional title of corporate president, with the implied element of class and refinement?

Edward Land, founder of Polaroid Corporation, is remembered for his camera technology. Ponder on the following story that goes to the point I am making.

David Godine founded his own one-of-a-kind Boston-based publishing company in 1969. As with many start-up companies, the beginning years were a major challenge. According to David, "The best design job we had was for Edward Land. Land hated to go through conventional routes and heard about us. He decided that we would be the perfect people to design his annual reports. This meant the entire month of April working with Dr. Land. I mean, you were on call twenty-four hours a day, seven days a week, because Land never stopped working.

"And that was a great experience for me. We did three annual reports. And we never discussed money, ever. But on the twenty-third of December, Dr. Land would call and ask, 'Well, how much money do you owe?' I would tell him how much money we owed, which was usually in the twenties, and he would send over a check the next day, the day before Christmas, for everything we owed, and that's how we stayed out of debt for many years, by virtue of Dr. Land."

The human element in such creative and entrepreneurial leadership fostered an enduring corporate culture to be believed in and supported. It was part of the spirit that fosters the creation and growth of the United States' successful free enterprise system. I was always cognizant of Henry Houghton's "long shadow" before and while at the helm of the company he founded. I kept a sign in my office, given to me by a Detroit Public Schools official. It read, "The world does not want to hear about the storms you encountered at sea, but did you bring in the ship." Failure to do less than that would have compromised the charge handed to me.

But why that loyalty? Was it really right for the times? We all know that with the progression of time, change happens. Corporations that never see a need to change, therefore, never change, rarely last. During the years under discussion, a move to conglomerization was afoot. Hostile and friendly takeovers, bear hugs, and leveraged buyouts were the order of the day.

Book publishers were caught up like a badminton shuttlecock in the movement. Early on, publishers were acquiring other publishers, then both were gobbled up by non-publishers. U.S. based conglomerates that were infatuated with the prospect of using the publishers' intellectual properties electronically. Finally, along came the foreign-based conglomerates seeking access to the large U.S. marketplace and, of course, the synergies to be derived from merging backlists. Independent U.S. publishers soon became a rarity. To those skeptical of my claim, examine the following list showing original U.S. companies, their year of founding, the current owner, as I write this, and the owner's nationality.

Yet, as of this writing the once proud house of Houghton has joined the list, but not of my doing. Now on the financial auction block, its future, whether in whole or in part, is uncertain.

Company	Founded	Owner	Nationality
Abrams	1950	La Martiniere	French
Addison Wesley	1948	Pearson	English
Allyn & Bacon	1868	Pearson	English
Aspen Publishing	1959	Wolters Kluwer	Dutch
Ballantine Books	1952	Bertelsmann	German
Bantam Books	1945	Bertelsmann	German
Berkley Books	1954	Pearson	English
RR Bowker	1872	Reed Elsevier	Dutch
Delacorte Press	1963	Bertelsmann	German
Dell Publishing	1921	Bertelsmann	German
Doubleday	1897	Bertelsmann	German
Dutton	1852	Pearson	English
Farrar, Straus, Giroux	1946	Von Holtzbrink	German
Franklin Watts	1942	Lagarde Group	French
Funk and Wagnalls	1872	Harper Collins	Australian
Gale Research	1954	Thomson Corp	Canadian
Ginn	1867	Pearson	English
Greenwood	1967	Reed Elsevier	Dutch
Grosset & Dunlap	1898	Pearson	English
Harcourt, Brace	1919	Reed Elsevier	Dutch
Harper and Row	1817	Harper Collins	Australian
D. C. Heath	1885	Vivendi	French
Hill and Wang	1956	Von Holtzbrink	German
Henry Holt	1866	Von Holtzbrink	German
Houghton Mifflin	1864	Vivendi	French
Alfred A. Knopf	1915	Bertelsmann	German
Lippincott	1792	Wolters Kluwer	Dutch
Pantheon	1942	Bertelsmann	German
Prentice Hall	1913	Pearson	English
Putnam	1838	Pearson	English
Random House	1926	Bertelsmann	German
St. Martins	1952	Von Holtzbrink	German

continued next page

Company	Founded	Owner	Nationality
W. B. Saunders	1888	Reed Elsevier	Dutch
Scott Foresman	1896	Pearson	English
Silver Burdett	1867	Pearson	English
South Western Publishing	1903	Thomson Corp	Canadian
Steck-Vaughan	1936	Reed Elsevier	Dutch
Van Nostrand Reinhold	1848	Thomson Corp	Canadian
Viking	1975	Pearson	English
Wadsworth	1956	Thomson Corp	Canadian
Franklin Watts	1942	Lagarde Group	French
West Publishing	1804	Thomson Corp	Canadian
John Wiley	1807	Thomson Corp	Canadian

European conglomerate, Bertelsmann of Germany, is far more than a publisher and claims its need to access the large American markets for its survival. Other reasons include finances, taxes, and aggrandizement for synergistic expansion of existing publication lists. These boiler-plate explanations soon submerge discussion into the deep green swamp of confusion and self-justification.

From Henry Houghton's company has come works providing a vision for America. Do the owners of foreign-based conglomerates share that vision? Is there a dedication to reworking a reading or mathematics textbook series until its right? Can the spirit and the commitment to an ever stronger and better U.S. culture through literature and textbooks prevail—at all times? We are seeing limited disposition of that nature among foreign nations today, including some of the ones listed above.

Alexander Solzhenitsyn has written, "Literature transmits incontrovertible condensed experiences ... from generation to generation. In this way literature becomes the living memory of a nation." Do we dare leave this important role to others? In this age of globalization, no one claims that only publishers native to a nation should publish in that nation. Still, the history of publishing in the United States is one of close relationships between authors, their editors, and the culture of America—a relationship that from our beginnings was often uniquely American.

The telling concern is textbooks. As demonstrated throughout this book, our public schools are called upon to educate millions of kids to be productive participants in our society, who arrive on our shores from around the world. No other nation's educational system has faced a task of this proportion. Throughout our existence, our textbook-based system has worked. Few of the nations in which the conglomerates just listed permit more than limited use of foreign textbooks. Yet we as a nation have shown a marked lack of concern over the off shore ownership of our textbook publishing entities. As one observer quipped, "We have had our collective heads in a bucket as one after another of our country's textbook and trade book publishing houses were sold to foreign conglomerates."

Wouldn't it be in the nation's best interest to be sure that more than just financial interest be evaluated, by way of due diligence, by corporate boards of directors selling U.S. publishing companies, to U.S. based as well as foreign entities? Isn't there good reason to take responsibility for ensuring the nation's educational well being when publishers with a proven successful record for publishing texts are sold? Can we be sure of the continuing financial investment and commitment of author, editorial, and other publishing services necessary to preserve and grow our textbooks to meet the demand of educating our kids, if only dollars count?

Chapter 4 on state adoptions discusses the increasing fragmentation of the textbook market as large states establish their individual curriculum standards and mandated tests, then purchase just the texts meeting those standards. This development represents a marked change from earlier years, when the same edition of textbooks created by outstanding authors and publishers could be sold across all fifty states.

Still, in the face of the ownership changes discussed here, the state adoption states may turn out to be our protectors. The fragmentation development is opening an expanding door of opportunity for small and niche publishers.

Some of these new entities will prosper, others fail. Their leaders, however, are the beneficiaries of the opportunities for meaningful innovation that often accompany start-ups. Do we see in them more Henry Houghtons? One can hope for that. I've endeavored to communicate the Houghton environment in which those with ideas that mattered could publish. A culture dedicated to that accomplishment attracted many dedicated individuals whose contributions significantly influenced the well being of millions of people. One can only wonder when Henry Houghton traveled down to Massachusetts from Sutton, Vermont, and stated up a printing press if he had even a glimmer of what he was creating.

Acknowledgments

In a letter to college textbook author, Bel Needles, I commented that in some after life, should I once again head a publishing house, I would never inform an author that a deadline had been missed. Every publishing house president should encounter firsthand the time-consuming demands authors face when writing a book. The things authors do are not the same things publishing house presidents do and vice versa. Yet, books resulting from the combination benefit people, often millions of people, sometimes over future centuries.

It is my great good fortune to have spent most of my adult life, while working and in retirement, with authors who created books, editors and their co-workers who saw to the finished work—the book being published—and people who read them. My fairest and most accurate acknowledgement must be all-inclusive. It must encompass all the individuals from Henry Houghton's day to my retirement whose contributions, large and small, created the totality—Houghton Mifflin Company—on which the interviews and this book are based. The friendliness, cooperation, and support so freely and conscientiously given by those I sought out to interview and the many others whose assistance was requested, created the deep feeling of gratitude I extend to each and every one of you. I'm over-awed that it all could happen.

Once launched, the interviewee roster expanded at an exponential rate. Its sheer extensiveness necessitated the separate listing appearing on pages 309–314. Interviews from which I took excerpts are starred. Often it was like a homecoming, as I traveled across the country for the interviews. The hospitality and the good meals enjoyed were indeed appreciated. I realize that your business, writing, and family schedules were often adjusted for my visit. Again, I thank you.

Special recognition must be given to the people who provided substantial amounts of time and help over many of the years during which this project was in process. Now a few words about them.

At the very outset, there arose the question of transcribing the tapes on which the interviews are recorded. Anne Guerrette, my administrative assistant for years at Houghton, did a number of them, but she had undertaken to raise a family and a steady flow of tapes—often two for an interview—created a scheduling conflict.

Then the Yellow Pages brought to light Arlington Typing and Mailing, Inc. (ATM). Norma Natale Panico, the founder and a former teacher, became interested in the project, as did several of her transcribers, and that was the start of an association that continues. I marvel at the ability of those ATM transcribers to decipher conversations recorded in restaurants with their background noise and often with individuals prone to speak softly and drop their voices at the end of sentences. Norma's awareness of the need for accuracy resulted in repeat transcription, if need be. Norma and her transcribers become a part of the team.

Upon their return from ATM, each transcription was carefully checked by me, corrected, and edited. Then they went to Arbee Beck, who had retired from Houghton Mifflin's College Division where she worked for a number of years as an administrative associate. Arbee knew the company, its people, and is possessed of a strict code demanding that all things be correct. She was my drill sergeant as along with numerous phone calls questioning various details, she typed up each transcription for me to send to the interviewee.

Carol Case, the former director of Houghton's School Division advertising department, worked for many hours day-in and day-out—weekends included—carrying out the following tasks. Entering each interview returned by interviewees or Arbee's copy as the interviewees approved them, into the computer and onto a computer disk. As the book progressed, Carol edited all of my copy and, increasingly as we got into the project, provided valuable help with the shaping of the book. We kind of fought our way through a number of knotty challenges.

Ruth Hapgood, whose extensive experience and thorough knowledge of the Houghton Mifflin publishing culture, brought into being the subtitle of this book—*A Leap from Mind to Mind.* That is what this book is about.

Anita Silvey was publisher of children's books at Houghton and editor-in-chief of *The Horn Book Magazine.* Anita is now actively at work writing her own books. Using copy provided by Carol Case—computer-to-computer—Anita brought her professional editorial skills to the project. Actually, she was both teacher and editor—and was also very patient as she read and reread my numerous drafts, chapter by chapter.

Then there were those long timers—old hands—upon whom I relied for conformation, a sense of the people, and encouragement.

- Harry Rowe, editor and manager, read many of the interviews, discussed them with me and helped place them into the proper historical context.
- Franklin Hoyt (Jim), the financial officer, whose participation in the company's inner workings provided me with a sense of history and answers to questions.
- Kathy Rideout, a legal secretary at Houghton Mifflin, who tracked down facts where Jim Hoyt, Manuel Fenollosa, and I could not rely on our own recall.
- Jean Muller, retired consultant for the company's language arts programs. We worked in adjacent sales territories when I was in sales. Jean arranged for and participated in the interviews conducted with various California educators. She also read a number of interviews and the draft of certain chapters in the book. Jean never hesitated to point out the error of my ways. Why not? We started on the same rung of the corporate ladder.
- R. Sidney Cooper, retired sales representative, regional manger, and national sales manager at Houghton, who reviewed much of my material and personally arranged the important interview with Craig Phillips, North Carolina's superintendent of schools.

- Gary Smith, retired from Houghton Mifflin. He was a member of the legal staff, an administrator, and above all an unequaled advisor about many things including matters related to my project.
- Edward Drahozal, the national test consultant, whose interview is much used in the book. Ed also read and reread drafts of the test chapter and provided me with resource materials.
- Sidney Beshkin, head of the Xerox Copy Center at Staples in Waltham, Massachusetts. Sid is a former book manufacturer's representative, and not only saw to my getting good service for the many copies of the interviews that I needed, but who also took great interest in the project and often discussed with me issues relating to it.

Then there was that helpful triumvirate of William Berman, former head of Houghton's College Division, David McElwain and David Levine, both longtime Houghton Mifflin College Division people, who patiently heard me out about my project. They had ample and repeated opportunity to do so, for the four of us have met for dinner one night each month for some years.

Robert Baron, president of Fulcrum Publishing, played a major role through most all of my project. He read many of the interviews and was instrumental in arranging for the entire collection being placed in the library of the American Antiquarian Society in Worcester, Massachusetts. It was his persuasiveness and diplomatic persistence that prevailed in convincing me to write this book. The personal attention he has given to the full undertaking all along the long journey begs measurement.

In conclusion, I state without hesitation that I've been blessed with the valued and essential assistance of a great team of people. More to the point, it was their efforts that made possible their contribution to that publishing entity by the name of Houghton Mifflin Company.

By way of a postscript, it is only fitting that Arcadia in Waltham, Mel's in Wayland, and Café Diva in Westwood—all in Massachusetts— be acknowledged. It was their tables on which Anita, Carol, Gary, and I, in varying numbers, piled our papers as we drank their coffee and worked through the book's pages.

A Note of Clarification

The nominal date of origin for the publishing house of Houghton Mifflin is 1864, when the firm of Hurd & Houghton, its precursor, was originated. However, the founder's connection with the Boston trade began in 1849, when as printer, not publisher, he purchased John D. Freeman's interest in Freeman & Bolles, a Boston "book-office" founded in 1828. If the right to ancestors inheres in purchase, Houghton Mifflin may claim an even earlier date of origin, for in 1876 Hurd & Houghton acquired the stereotypes and publishing rights of Crocker, Brewster & Company, organized in 1818. Indeed, on occasion Houghton facetiously claimed for his house descent from the first printing establishment in colonial America, pointing out that his great-grandfather Jacob Houghton had married Mary Willard, a descendant of Harvard's first president, Henry Dunster. In 1640, Dunster had married the wealthy widow Glover, thereby acquiring the printing equipment which Jose Glover, Elizabeth's first husband, who had died on the crossing from England, had destined for Cambridge and the service of the recently funded college there. In Houghton's view, the owner of the press, rather the artisan who sets type, is the printer. Claims to antiquity have small merit.

(Note: Taken from Ellen B. Ballou's *The Building of the House: Houghton Mifflin's Formative Years.*)

List of Interviewees

(*=quoted or cited in book)

Name	Role
Anderson, Albert (Al)	Corporate services
*Anderson, Henry (Hank)	Author, college textbook, accounting
Bachand, Albert	Trade book production
*Baker, Morton H. (Terry) [deceased]	Adult and children's trade book manufacturing, The Riverside Press
*Baron, Robert (Bob)	Founder and President, Fulcrum Publishing
*Barton, David	Editor, college, accounting
*Barrett, Anne	Editor, trade
*Beck, Rosamond (Arbee)	Administrative Associate, college
*Beggs, Donald (Don)	President, Wichita State University
*Berman, William (Bill)	Head of College Division

Name	Role
Blessing, Marlene	Editor-in-Chief, Fulcrum Publishing
Bowman, Joan	Head of Human Resources, Houghton Mifflin Co.
*Breitkreuz, George	Chief Financial Officer, Houghton Mifflin Co.
Brown, Christina	Publicity, trade
Bueschel, Richard T. (Dick)	President, Time Share Corp. Software
Butts, Charles (Charlie)	Marketing and corporate services
*Capps, Lee	Author, elementary mathematics
*Case, Carol	Head of school advertising department
Chaney, Bev, Jr. [deceased]	Sales, trade
*Chute, Carolyn	Author, trade books
*Clowes, Richard (Dick)	Superintendent of Schools, California
Conway, James (Jim)	Chief Executive Officer, Courier Corporation, printer
*Cooper, R. Sidney (Sid)	School, sales and marketing
Darehshori, Nader	Chairman and President, Houghton Mifflin Co.
*Davol, George	Vice President, Educational Division
Doll, Helen	Secretary, administration
*Donelson, Harold W. (Hal)	Sales, elementary/secondary
*Drahozal, Edward (Ed)	Consultant, norm-referenced tests
*Durr, William (Bill)	Author, elementary reading

Name	Role
*Essex, Cyntha	Supervisor, secondary programs, Perkins School
*Feldt, Leonard (Len)	Author, norm-referenced tests
*Fenollosa, Manuel [deceased]	Senior Vice President, Educational Division
*Foster, Harry	Editor, trade books
*Galbraith, John Kenneth (Ken)	Author, trade books
*Gladstone, Richard (Dick) [deceased]	Editor, elementary/secondary
*Glass, Richard (Dick)	Sales management
*Godine, David	Publisher, David R. Godine Publisher
*Goodman, Louis (Lou)	Lawyer
Goroff, Sandra	Publicist, trade books
*Grant, Stephen [deceased]	President, Houghton Mifflin Co.
Green, RuthAnn	Consultant, marketing, elementary
*Hansen, Betty	Assistant Superintendent, California public schools
*Hapgood, Ruth	Editor, trade
*Hieronymus, Albert (Al)	Author, norm-reference tests
*Hoffman, Lynn Long	Administration
*Hoyt, Franklin K. (Jim)	Chief Financial Officer
*Hoyt, Norris (Norrie) [deceased]	Senior Editor, Educational Division
Johnson, Harold (Harry)	Sales
Johnson, Timothy (Tim)	Author, elementary
*Kelly, Edward N. (Ed)	Sales, management, college

Name	Role
*Laufenberg, Francis (Lauf)	Superintendent of schools, California; President, California State Board of Education
*Laughlin, Henry [deceased]	Chairman and president, Houghton Mifflin Co.
Lee, Winford (Winnie) [deceased]	Human resources, The Riverside Press
Legru, Marica	Subrights, trade
*Levine, David	Sales, college
*Lister, Wanda	Supervisor, public schools, California
*Lorraine, Walter	Children's Editor
*Lowe Faye [widow of Doug Lowe]	Sales, college
*Macaulay, David	Author, children's books
*Mahan, Mark	Sales management, college
Malan, Harriss	Sales, elementary/secondary
McAoo, Richard (Dick)	Senior management, trade
*McDermott, Thomas (Tom)	Professional accountant, college accounting
McElhiney, Frances (Fran)	Regional office management
*McElwain, David	Sales, college
McKee, Thomas (Tom)	Vice president, Association of American Publishers
Meskis, Joyce	Owner, Tattered Cover Book Store, Denver, Colorado
*Miller, Harold T. (Hal)	Chairman and President, Houghton Mifflin Co.
*Miller, Raymond (Ray)	Sales, elementary/secondary

Name	Role
*Muller, Eugenia (Jean)	Consultant, elementary
*Needles, Belverd E. (Bel)	Author, college accounting
*Nichols, Richard (Dick) [deceased]	Corporate Director
Olney, Austin	Editor, Head of Trade Division
Osburn, Hubert A. (Ozzie)	Administration, inventory
*Osgood, Stanley (Stan)	Editor, norm-referenced tests
Otto, Calvin (Cal)	Publisher, book collector
Palmer, Dennis K.	Editor, norm-referenced tests and Time Share Corp.
Pekich, Steve	Administration, production
*Phillips, Craig Andrew	State Superintendent of Schools, North Carolina
Pikulski, Jack	Author, elementary reading
*Pirie, Robert (Bob)	Lawyer and investment banker
Powers, Marian	Author, college accounting
Price, Edith	Consultant and sales, elementary/secondary
Price, James A. (Jim)	Sales, elementary/secondary
*Ridley, John	Marketing and editorial, elementary/secondary
Rheault, Charles (Charlie)	Manufacturing, The Riverside Press
Rowe, Delores [deceased]	Consultant, elementary/secondary
*Rowe, Harry P. [deceased]	Editorial and management, elementary/secondary

Name	Role
*Sargent, Nancy	Editor, head of Reading Department
*Scannell, Dale	Author, norm-referenced tests
*Shaw, Michael (Mike)	Regional sales management
*Silvey, Anita	Editor, children's books
*Smith, Gary	Corporate lawyer
*Spaulding, William (Bill) [deceased]	Chairman and President, Houghton Mifflin Co.
*Stinehour, Roderick (Rocky)	Chief Executive Officer, Stinehour Press
*Stokes, Howard	Sales, elementary/secondary
Stokes, Mary Ann	Consultant, elementary/secondary
*Teig, Marlow	Head of School Division
Talese, Nan	Editor, trade
*Theise, Jerry	Sales management
Theise, Judy Diamond	Author, children's books
*Thompson, Lovell [deceased]	Head of Trade Division
Thornhill, Arthur, Jr.	Chief Executive Officer, Little, Brown
Timmerman, Clarice (Tim) [deceased]	Regional office management
*Van Allsburg, Chris	Author, children's books
*Williamson, Jack	Senior management

Bibliography

The American Textbooks Institute. *Textbooks in Education*. New York, 1949.

Ballou, Ellen B. *The Building of the House: Houghton Mifflin's Formative Years*. Boston: Houghton Mifflin, 1970.

Baron, Robert C. *What Was It Like, Orville?: Some Observations on the Early Space Program*. Golden, Colo.: Fulcrum Publishing, 2002.

Bloomers, Paul, and Robert A. Forsythe. *Elementary Statistical Methods in Psychology and Education*. Boston: Houghton Mifflin, 1977.

Brooks, Paul. *Two Park Street*. Boston: Houghton Mifflin, 1986.

Burkett, Nancy H., and John B. Hench. *Under Its Generous Dome: The Collections and Programs of the American Antiquarian Society*. Worcester, Mass.: American Antiquarian Society, 1992.

Buros, Oscar. *Mental Measurement Yearbook*. Washington, D.C.: The Buros Institute of Mental Measurement. Published annually since 1938.

Caplan, Lincoln. *Skadden*. New York: Farrar, Straus & Giroux, 1993.

Clement, Richard W. *The Book in America*. Golden, Colo.: Fulcrum Publishing, 1996.

Ebel, Robert. *Essentials of Educational Measurement*. New York: Prentice Hall, 1986.

Fields, James T. *Yesterday with Authors.* Boston: Houghton Mifflin, 1882. Printed by The Riverside Press.

Gehres, Eleanor. *The Best American Novels of the Twentieth Century Still Readable Today.* Golden, Colo.: Fulcrum Publishing, 2002.

Harrison, M. Lucile. *Reading Readiness.* Boston: Houghton Mifflin, 1936. Printed by The Riverside Press.

Ingersoll, Gary M., and Dale Scannell. *Performance-Based Teacher Certification.* Golden, Colo.: Fulcrum Publishing, 2002.

Madison, Charles. *Book Publishing in America.* New York: McGraw-Hill, 1966.

McKee, Paul. *The Teaching of Reading.* Boston: Houghton Mifflin, 1948. Printed by The Riverside Press.

Schneider, James G. *The Navy V-12 Program: Leadership for a Lifetime.* Boston: Houghton Mifflin, 1987.

Scudder, Horace E. *Henry Oscar Houghton: A Biographical Outline.* Boston: Houghton Mifflin, 1897. Printed by The Riverside Press.

Silvey, Anita. *The Essential Guide to Children's Books and Their Creators.* Boston: Houghton Mifflin, 2002.

Terman, Lewis. *Measurement of Intelligence.* Boston: Houghton Mifflin, 1916. Part of the Riverside Textbooks in Education; printed by The Riverside Press.

Thomas, Isaiah. *The History of Printing in America.* Worcester, Mass.: 1810. Reprint, New York: Weathervane Books, 1970.

Thorndike, Robert L., and Elizabeth Hagen. *Measurement and Evaluation in Psychology and Education.* New York: John Wiley, 1955.

Tryon, W. S. *Parnassus Corner.* Boston: Houghton Mifflin, 1963. Printed by The Riverside Press.

Winship, Michael. *American Literary Publishing in the Mid-Nineteenth Century: The Business of Ticknor and Fields.* New York: Cambridge University Press, 1995.